IMAGES
of America

BERLIN CENTER

OHIO

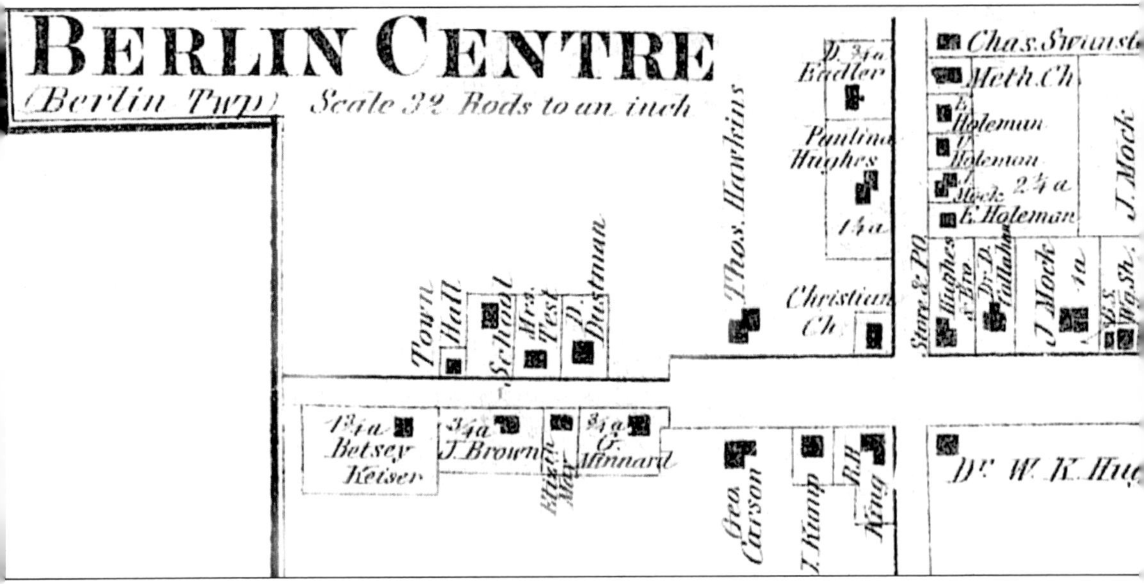

The above map shows the Berlin Centre (note the early spelling of Centre) business district in 1874. The area business directory featured the following operations, some of which appear on the map: Chester Bedell, manufacturer of and dealer in stoneware, also farmer; A. Dustman, manufacturer of and dealer in stoneware and drain tile; W.K. Hughes, physician and surgeon; Daniel Callahan, physician and surgeon; John Folk, proprietor of steam sawmill; H. Kline, proprietor of cider mill and lime kiln; Simon Hartzell, farmer, stock raiser, and lime burner; S.W. Christy & Co., manufacturers of stoneware, drain tile, and washboards; David King, farmer and stock raiser; George Shilling, proprietor of saw mills and dealer in flour, feed, lumber, and shingles; and Joseph King, farmer, stock raiser, and proprietor of threshing machine.

IMAGES
of America

BERLIN CENTER
OHIO

Berlin Center Historical Society

ARCADIA
PUBLISHING

ISBN 978-0-7385-0709-5

Published by Arcadia Publishing
Charleston, South Carolina

Printed in the United States of America

Library of Congress Catalog Card Number: 99-069410

For all general information contact Arcadia Publishing at:
Telephone 843-853-2070
Fax 843-853-0044
E-mail sales@arcadiapublishing.com
For customer service and orders:
Toll-Free 1-888-313-2665

Visit us on the Internet at www.arcadiapublishing.com

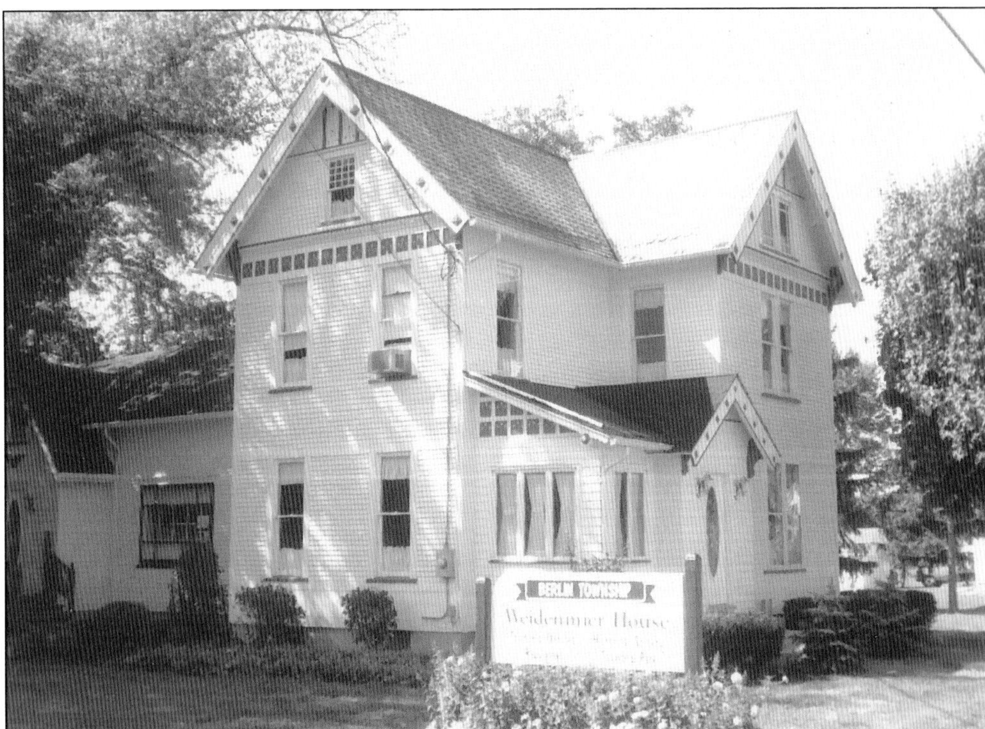

The Berlin Center Historical Society was founded March 31, 1987, and chartered by the State of Ohio October 15, 1987. It is located at 15823 Akron-Canfield Road, Berlin Center, Ohio, 44401. The house name pays tribute to the memory of Dr. and Mrs. Carl Weidenmier. This house was their long-time residence and doctor's office combined. On display are hundreds of interesting artifacts.

Contents

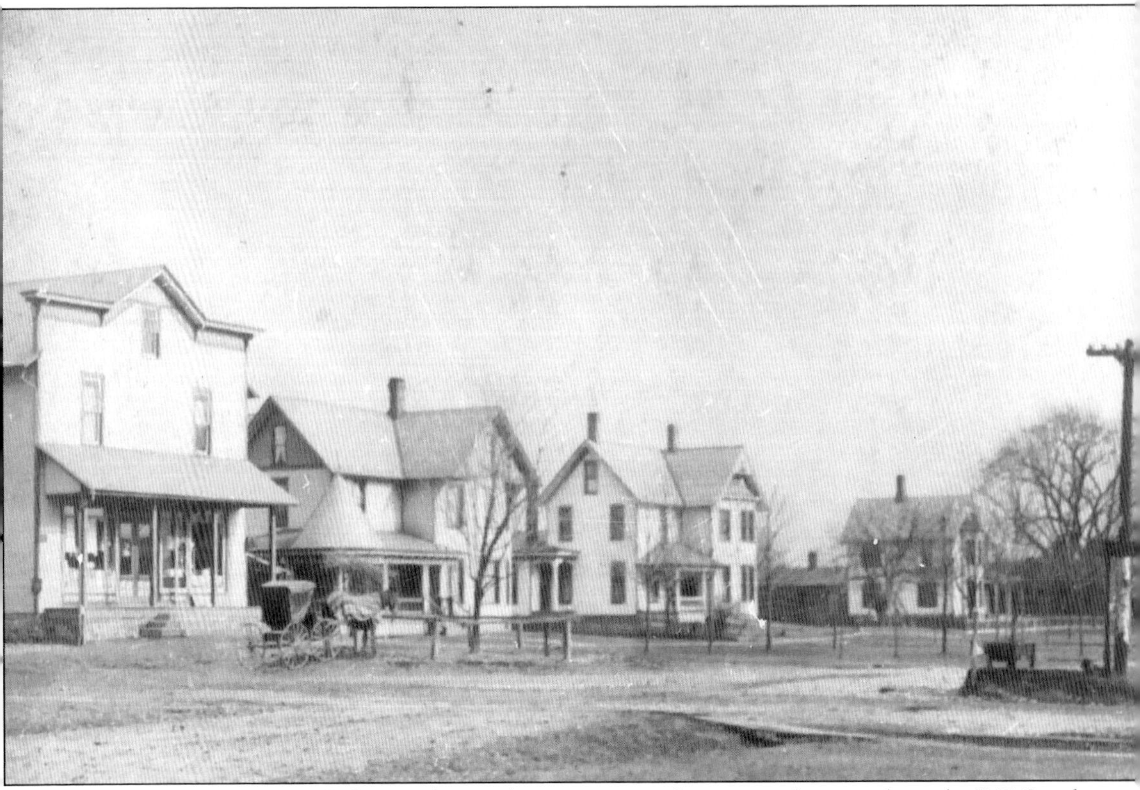

This 1909 photograph depicts the northeast corner at the center of town, where the B.T. Stanley store was situated. A hitching rail surrounded the tree, and a watering trough is visible on the right side of the image. Pictured from left to right are the B.T. Stanley Store, B.T. Stanley home, Dr. Callahan's home (later known as the Robert Weasner home), and the Jacob Mock home (later owned by Lewis Mock).

Acknowledgments

The book committee for the Berlin Center Historical Society, which consists of Ivan and Barbara Hoyle, Sandie Engle, and John and Mary Hawkins, wish to thank those who contributed pictures and information for this book. The names, dates, and events are accurate to the best of our knowledge and resources.

Introduction

The 239 pictures contained in this book are not intended to give a detailed history, but rather a glimpse of a largely self-sufficient farming community and its inhabitants situated at the crossroads of State Routes 224 and 534 in a quiet country town called Berlin Center. Many changes have occurred in Berlin Center over a period of approximately 100 years, and this book attempts to capture some of these events so that we can better understand the past. The contained photographs reveal old businesses and homes, as well as the way people looked, worked, and played in days gone by. The spoken word is soon forgotten, but photographs provide visual images that endure.

Berlin Township was originally a part of the 1798 land grant of the state of Connecticut, and the Trumbull County Commissioners deemed the area a township in 1828. Because the early German settlers wished to be reminded of their homeland, they recommended Berlin as the township name.

This township abounded in natural beauty. American Indians reportedly used it as a hunting ground because it was heavily wooded, and many breeds of wild animals roamed in great number. Shallow caves along the Mahoning River were used by Native Americans as they passed through the area. Many smaller streams also cross the township, the most interesting of which is called "Turkey Broth." Local lore gives Garrett Packard, the first settler in Berlin in 1809, credit for its name. While encamped along its bank one winter night, he shot a wild turkey and cooked it in water from the stream, hence the name "Turkey Broth."

Colonial settlement began around 1824, and in the next ten years Berlin Township gained many residents. Five small villages sprang up in the township: Amity, later known as Shiltown (also as Shelltown); Belvidere (which means beautiful view in Italian), later known as Shilling's Mill; Christytown; Lumberton; and Berlin Center.

Amity was located in the northeast corner on the old diagonal stagecoach route. It boasted a post office, tavern, and "ashery" where wood ashes were sold at ten cents a bushel for making soap. Belvidere appeared on the Mahoning River in the northwest section. A grist mill, sawmill, and store operated there. Christytown, in the southwest section, supported two thriving potteries, a sawmill, a creamery, and one of the earliest tanneries in the township. Lumberton, with its grist mill, photography shop, and blacksmith shop, was located on the Berlin Damascus Road at the edge of Goshen and Berlin Townships.

Around 1833, as more families settled near the center of the township, several businesses were initiated. These grew to include a hotel and livery stable, general store, shoemaker, tannery, blacksmith, carriage shop, mill, cabinet shop, cooper shop, and several saloons. A post office was established in 1833. The mail carrier arrived once a week from Atwater, continued on to Canfield, and returned the following week.

Stagecoaches ran east and west from Cleveland to Pittsburgh, and ox teams with as many as 20 yokes of oxen hitched to a covered wagon were not an uncommon sight. The animals journeyed with a family and their possessions from Connecticut to what was then the far western state of Indiana.

In 1882, the Ashtabula and Alliance Railroad (which later became the Pennsylvania Railroad) traveled through the township. It provided passenger and freight service twice daily, which added to the area's prosperity. Featured there were a freight office, passenger ticket office, weight scales, cattle holding pens, a load chute, and a telegraph office. Water for the steam engines was provided by Hawkins Lake, which used piping and gravity to fill the water tower located beside the railroad station. By 1900, many roads had been improved, and Route 224 was hard surfaced sometime around 1915.

One of Berlin's most coveted features was a commons shaded by a huge elm tree. President McKinley spoke here, as did James Garfield when running for the presidency. People thronged the streets to hear their speeches. At one time, this multipurpose area was also used for butchering hogs on days set aside for this purpose. Women and children also attended, as hog butchering was considered a gala day.

At first, the churches in Berlin Township failed to flourish because the buildings outnumbered the population. In 1839, the first Methodist Church was erected, ultimately replaced by the present church in 1890. In 1828, the Lutherans constructed a log church, but built a new frame structure across the road in 1836. Both churches remain in operation today.

In 1933, a fire in Berlin caused $100,000 in damage (by 1933 estimates). Four buildings on the southeast side of the village square were destroyed and two homes damaged. Because Berlin had no fire department, firefighters from Sebring, Alliance, Salem, and Youngstown answered the call for help.

The Flood Control Act of 1938 authorized the Berlin Project for flood control in the Ohio River basin. The reservoir stores flood waters originating in the 249 square mile tributary drainage area, and releases the stored water during the period of low flow in those same streams. Construction started in 1941, and the dam has been in operation since 1943. Many area farmers were devastated to learn that their prized farm land was to be flooded and tried to fight the government possession, but to no avail. It would have been difficult for them to believe that their then worthless farms would become valuable lakefront property in fifty years. Berlin Lake is presently one of the more popular recreation centers in northeastern Ohio.

The landscape of Berlin Township has changed again in recent years. The predominance of family farms has given way to new houses on two to five acre tracts of land. The flavor of country living has remained, however, and the tranquillity and beauty of the area is a reflection of the civic pride of the community. It is our hope that this book will give the readers insight to the Berlin Township of the past, and serve as a reference source for future generations.

One

Shillings Mill and Berlin Dam

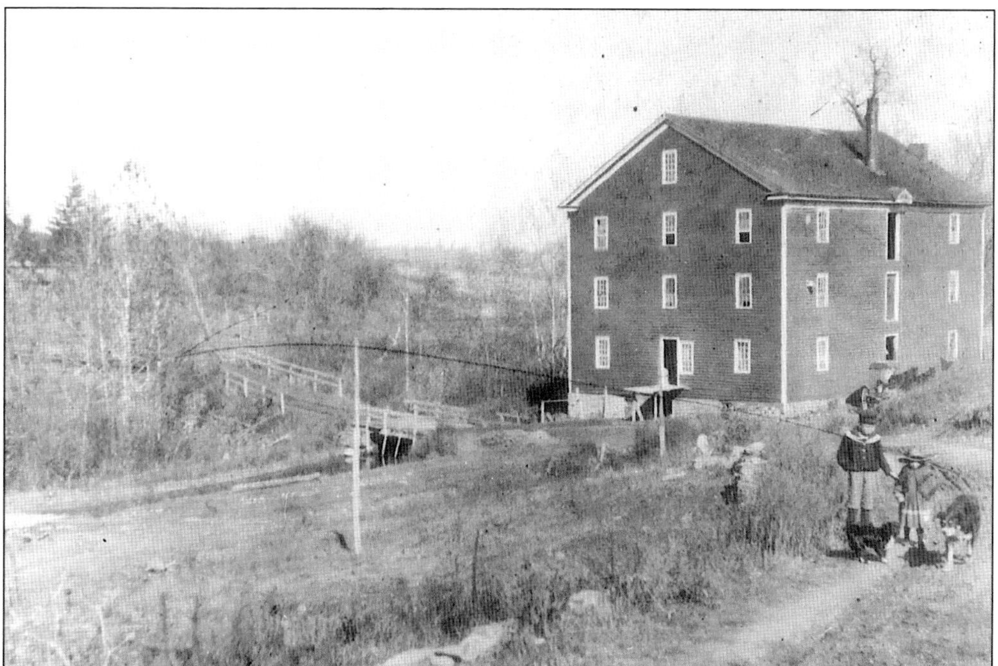

In 1825, Matthias Glass built the first grist mill on the Mahoning River, up river from Fredricksburg. Mr. Glass, a native of Berlin, Germany, is given credit for suggesting the township name as a reminder of his fatherland. The area pictured here was called Belvidere, which translates to "beautiful view" in Italian. Belvidere is known today as Shillings Mill.

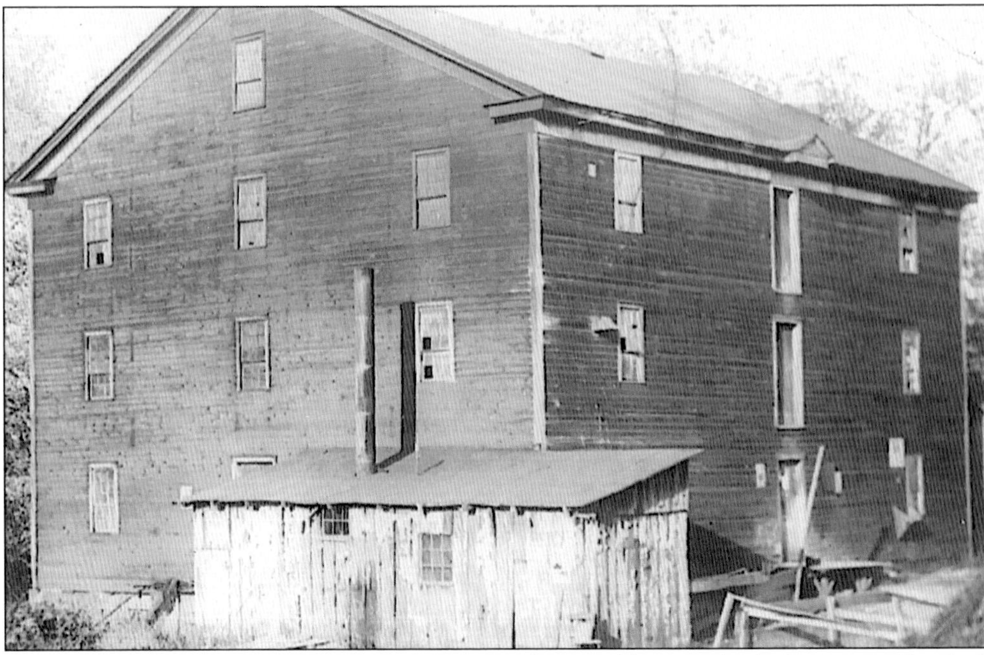

After the first mill was destroyed by fire, Isaac Wilson and his sons built this new mill, which they operated until 1856 when George Shilling purchased it. George had traveled through the area 16 years earlier at the age of 18. He told his companions that someday he would own the mill. When finally securing the purchase, he presented half the money in the form of gold and silver in a gallon crock covered with cloth.

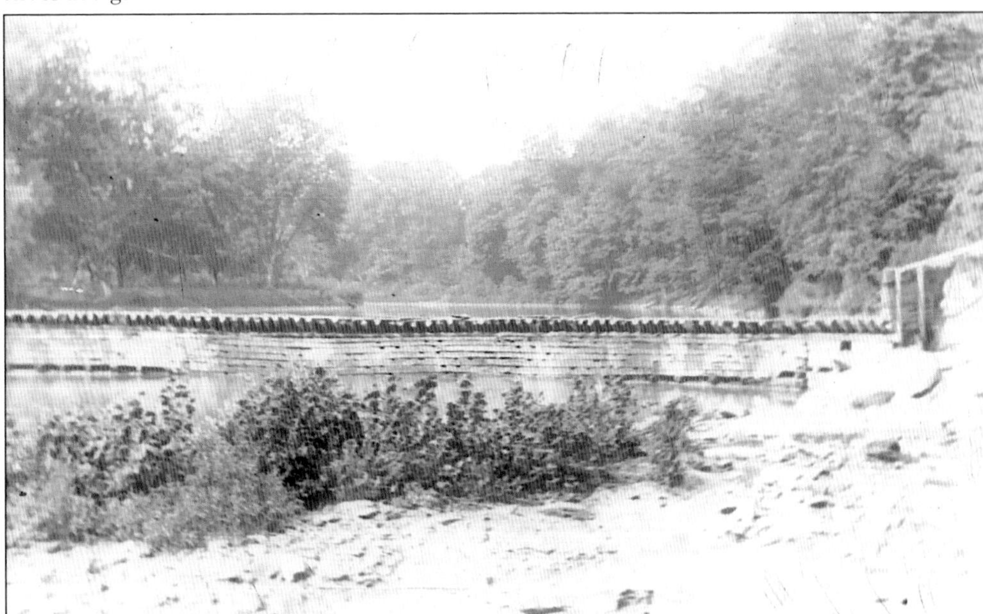

This dam constructed across the Mahoning River provided water to power the mill wheel. The mill had an overshot water wheel that was replaced in the late 1880s by a turbine powered by a steam engine. In the absence of a bridge across the river, teams of horses crossed the water to reach the mill.

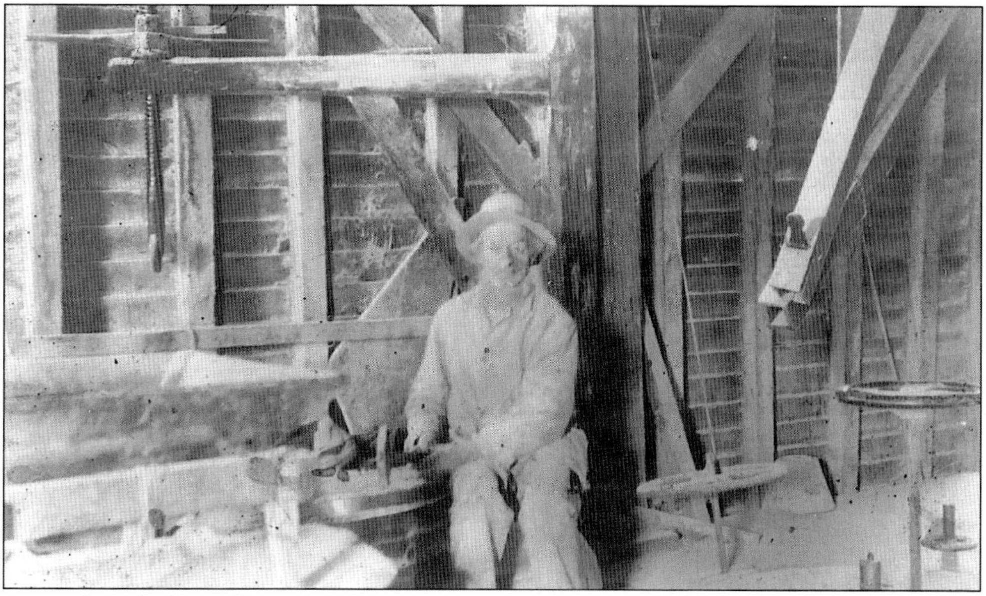

Pictured inside the mill in 1895 is George Shilling. The mill was noted for grinding buckwheat flour from locally grown grain. One year, 23 tons of buckwheat flour were shipped to the area markets.

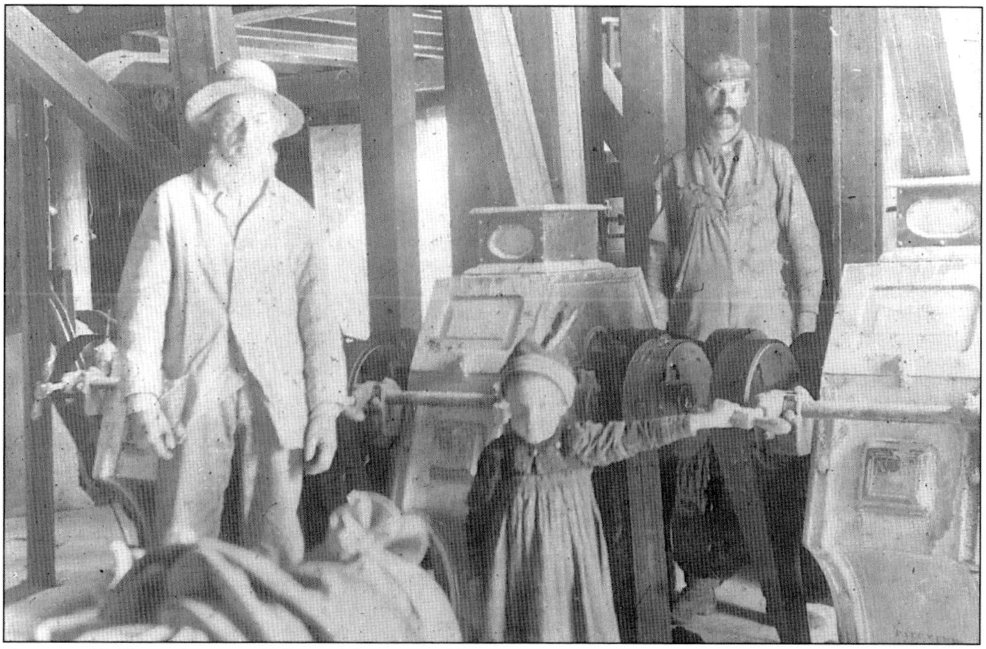

George Shilling, his son Ed, and his granddaughter Lucile are shown inside Shillings Mill in 1895. Patronage for the mill extended from Newton Falls, Salem, and Youngstown. Lease Brothers of Salem are said to have placed a single order for as much as 200 barrels of flour. Orders for ten to 20 barrels of flour were common for city grocers. The mill continued to operate with other owners until Milton Dam was built in 1915. After the damming of the river flooded the area, the mill was demolished and its timbers floated down river to build boat docks at Canyon Park.

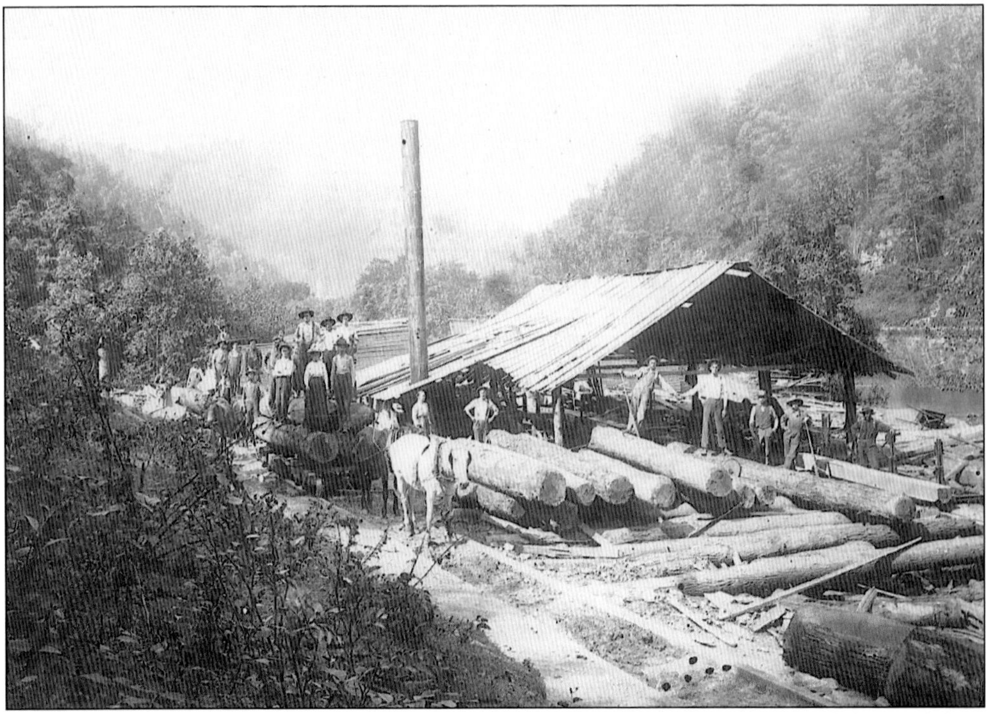

George Shilling also operated a water powered saw mill on the opposite side of the road from the grist mill that sold lumber and shingles. In 1879, a fatal accident occurred, and George's son, Willie Shilling, tragically lost his life. The boy was struck by a piece of falling timber and fell into the revolving saw.

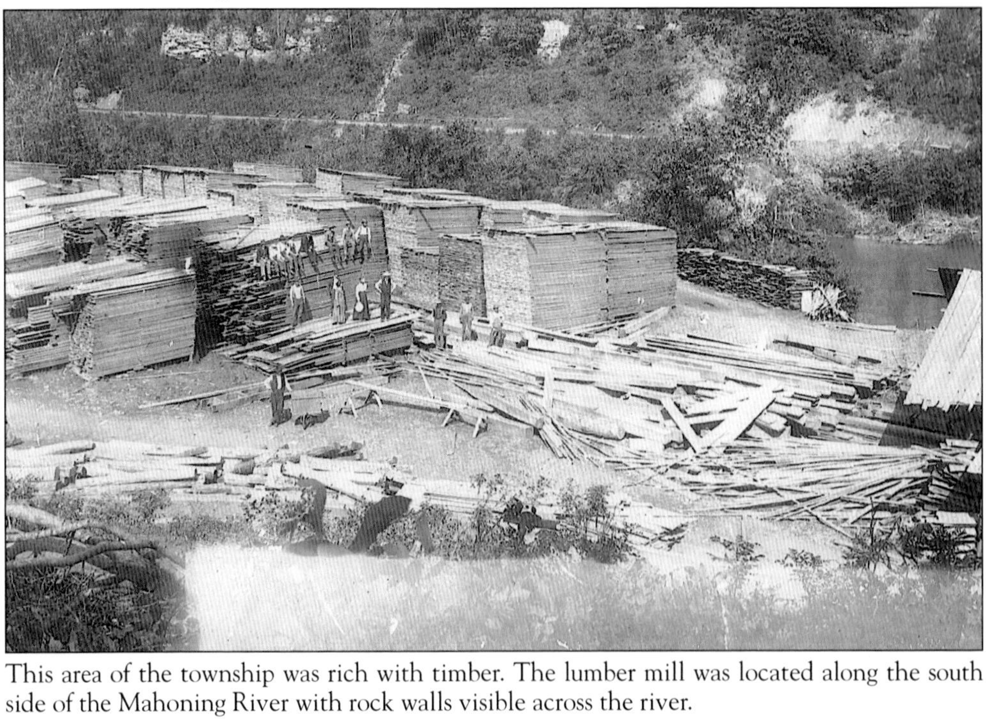

This area of the township was rich with timber. The lumber mill was located along the south side of the Mahoning River with rock walls visible across the river.

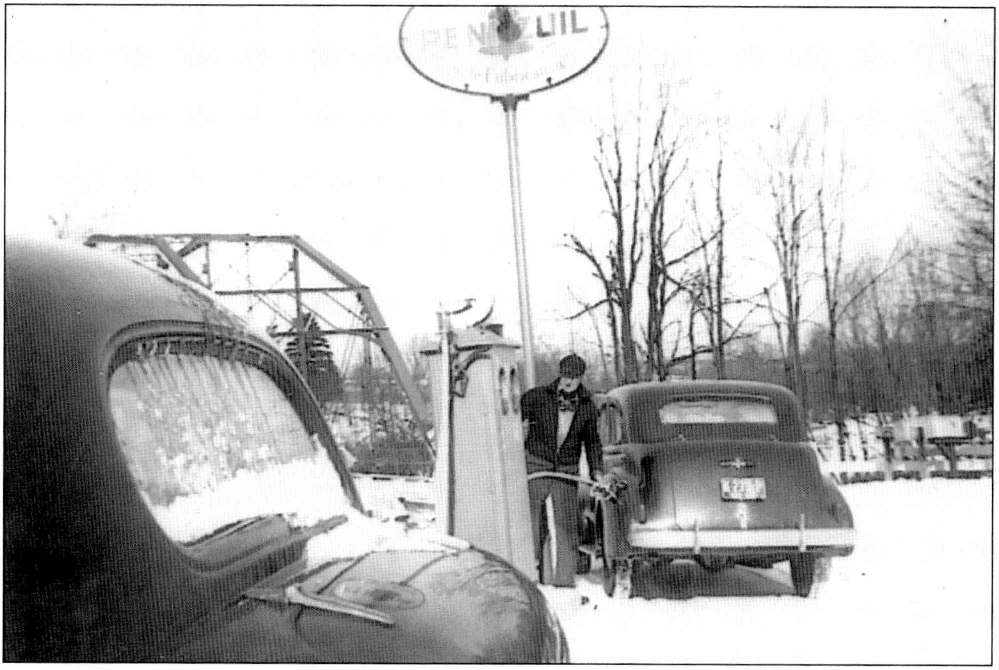

Earl Shilling pumps gas in the 1940s against a backdrop of Shillings Mill Bridge and a Pennzoil sign.

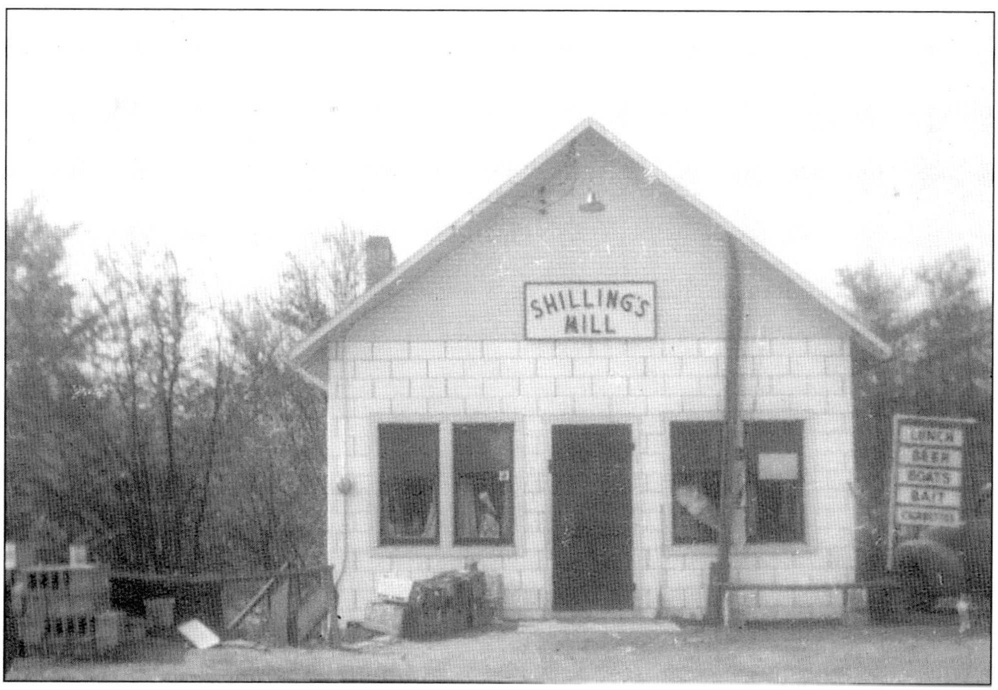

Located at Shillings Mill, this store was owned by Earl and Verda Shilling, who sold gasoline, groceries, bait, and light lunches.

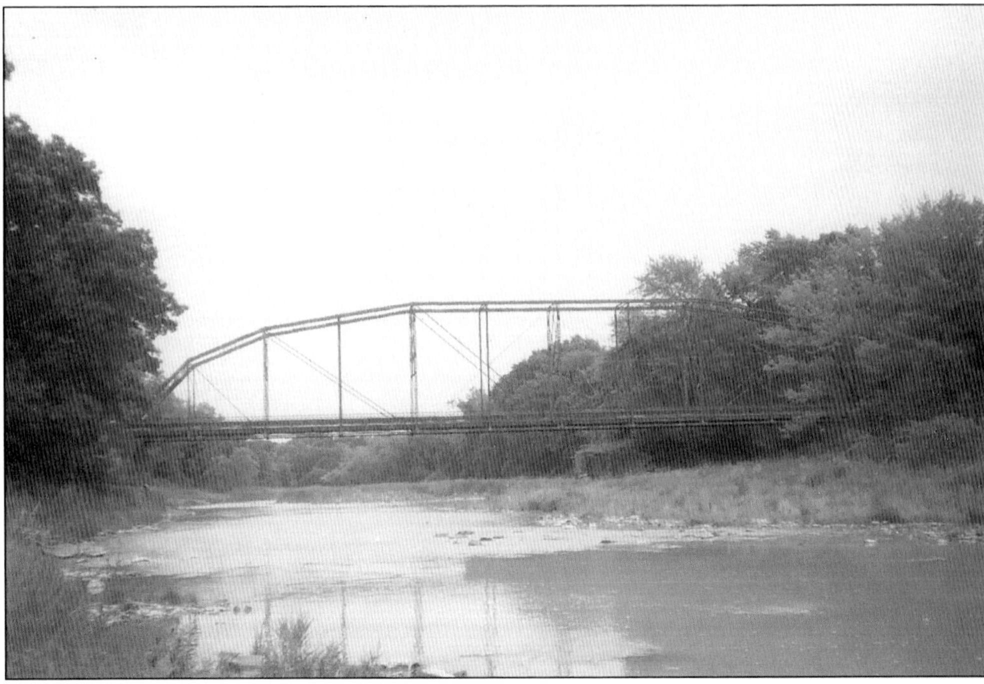

The Shillings Mill Bridge across the Mahoning River was originally located on Route 18 at Lake Milton. It was floated upriver and rebuilt here in Shillings Mill. After many years of service, the bridge was declared unsafe and closed to traffic.

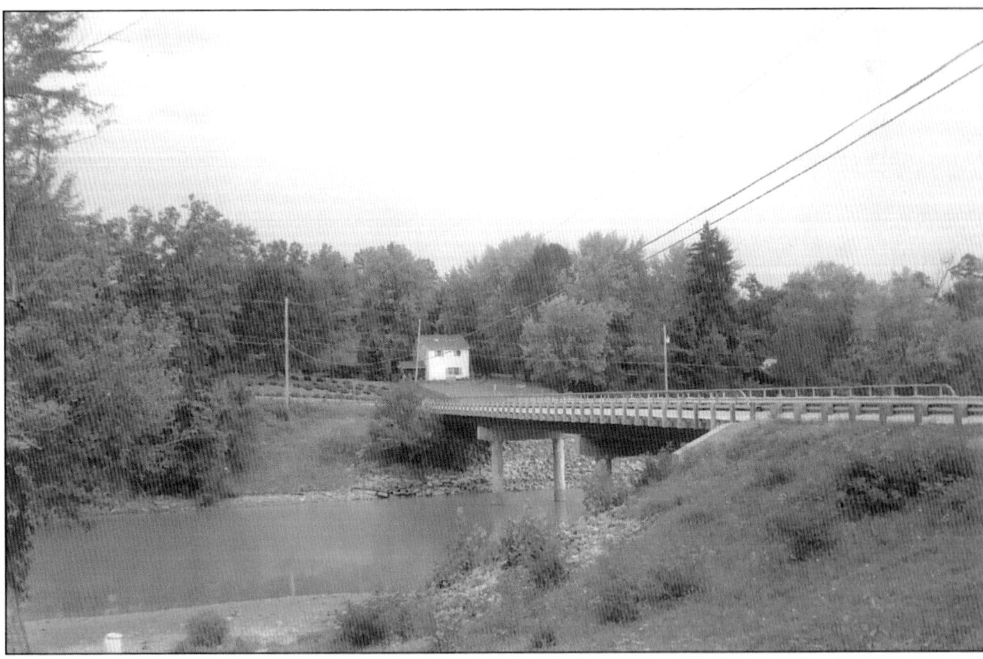

This new Shillings Mill Bridge was built and dedicated in 1989, replacing the bridge pictured above. Mill Road, located across the bridge, was later rebuilt by the township.

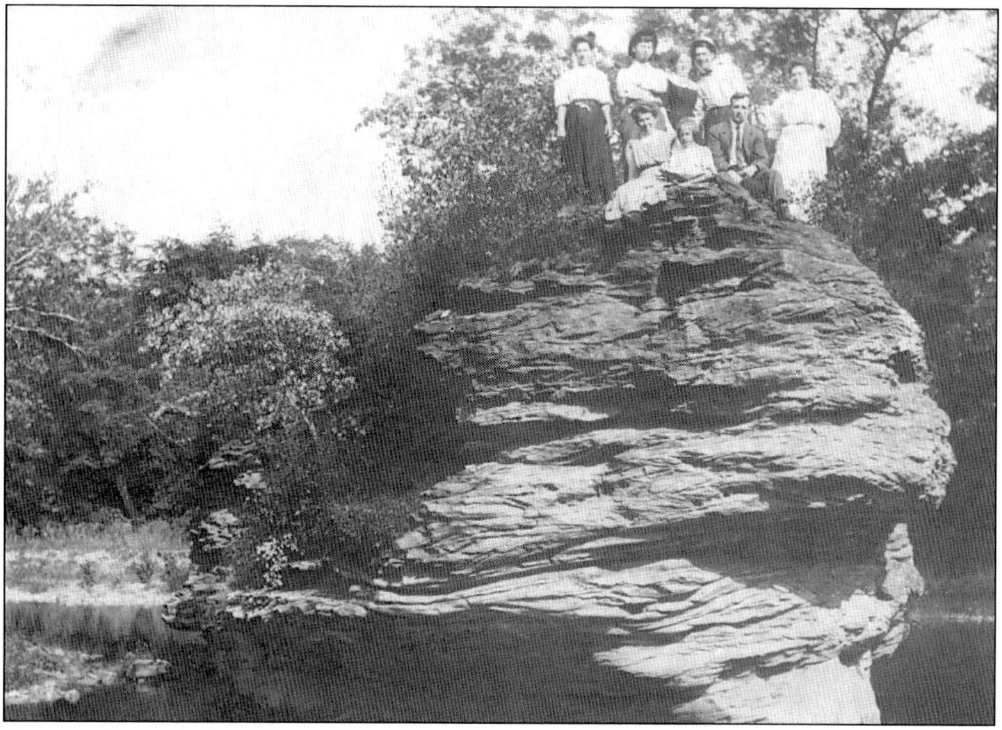

Up river from Shillings Mill about one-half mile is a popular photo-opportunity: Standing Rock, a large boulder at the river's edge that was left by a glacial deposit. This 1910 photograph features from left to right: (bottom row) Della Detcheon, Ione Renkenberger, and Emory Detcheon; (top row, standing) Austia Renkenberger, Roy Renkenberger, Opel Klingeman, Carl Klingeman, and Pearl Stitle.

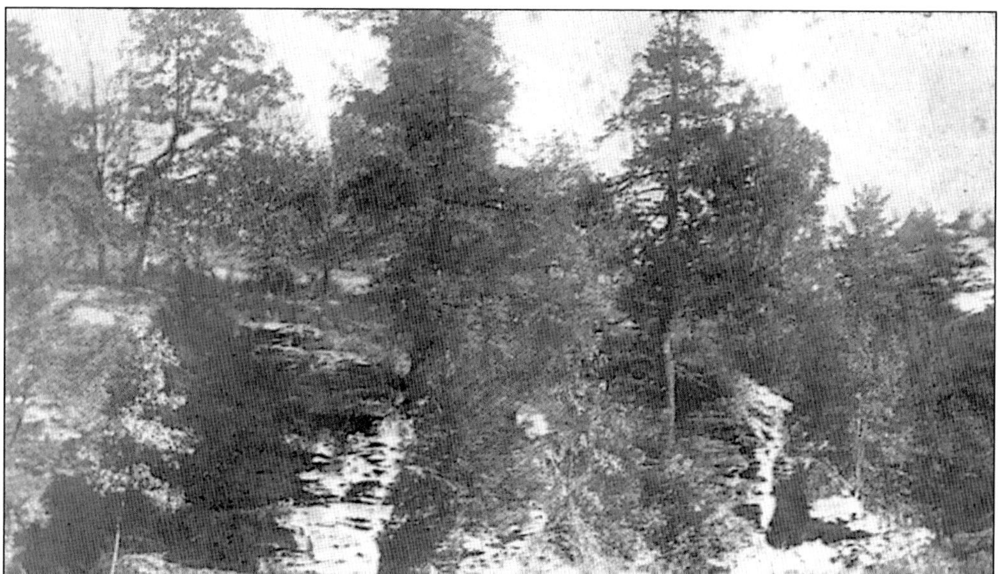

American Indians hunting in the Mahoning River area used shallow caves along the rocky banks of the river for protection. These are located in the same general area as Standing Rock.

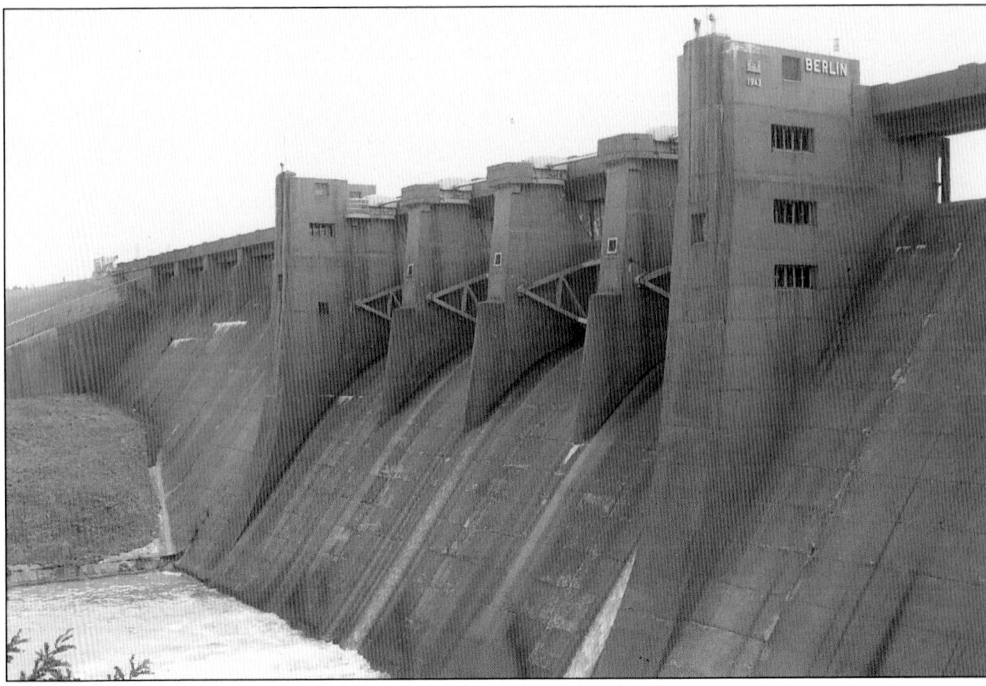

Berlin Dam construction started in November of 1941. The dam was dedicated and put into operation in July of 1943, but not completed until 1951. The Flood Control Act of 1938 authorized the Berlin Reservoir for flood control in the Ohio River Basin. The lake, because of its clean water and scenic setting, is a popular recreation area for boating, camping, fishing, and picnicking.

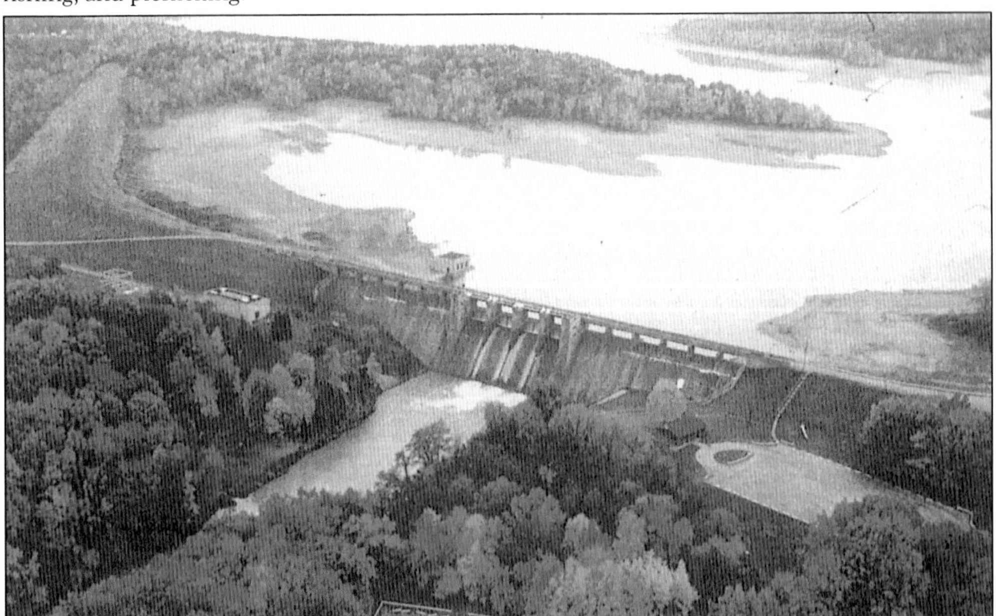

This is an aerial view of Berlin Dam and Lake looking south. The reservoir-full pool covers 5,500 acres, and contains 91,200 acre-feet of water when full. The area near the dam features picnic and fishing areas. In the winter, the grassy hill is used for sledding and tubing.

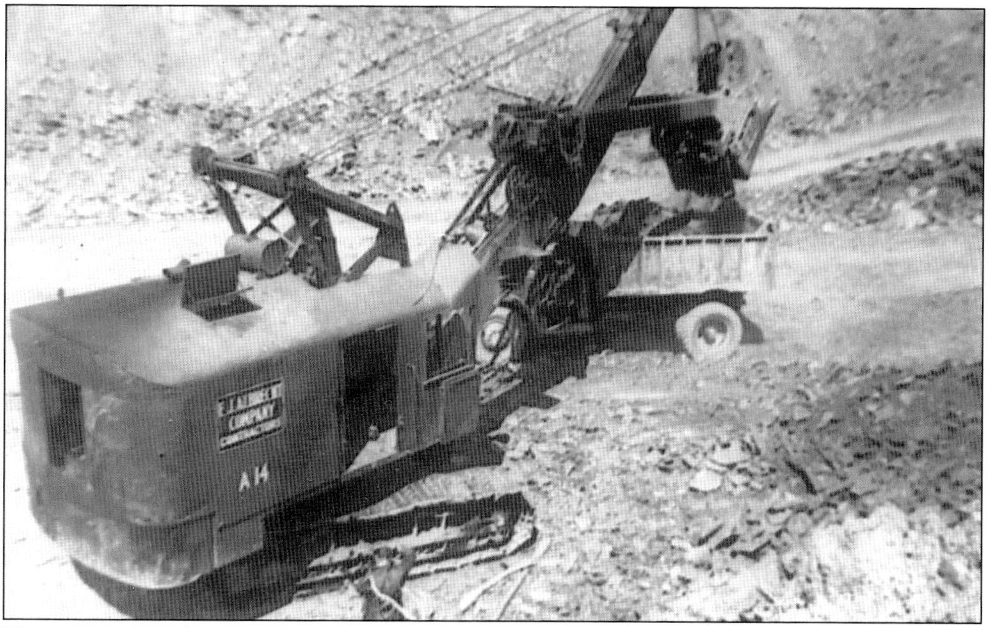

This power shovel and truck were part of the equipment used in the dam's construction. When finished, the dam was a partially controlled, concrete, gravity, central spillway type, with rolled earth fill abutment sections joining the valley sides. The top length is 663.5 feet, and the base maximum width measures 73 feet.

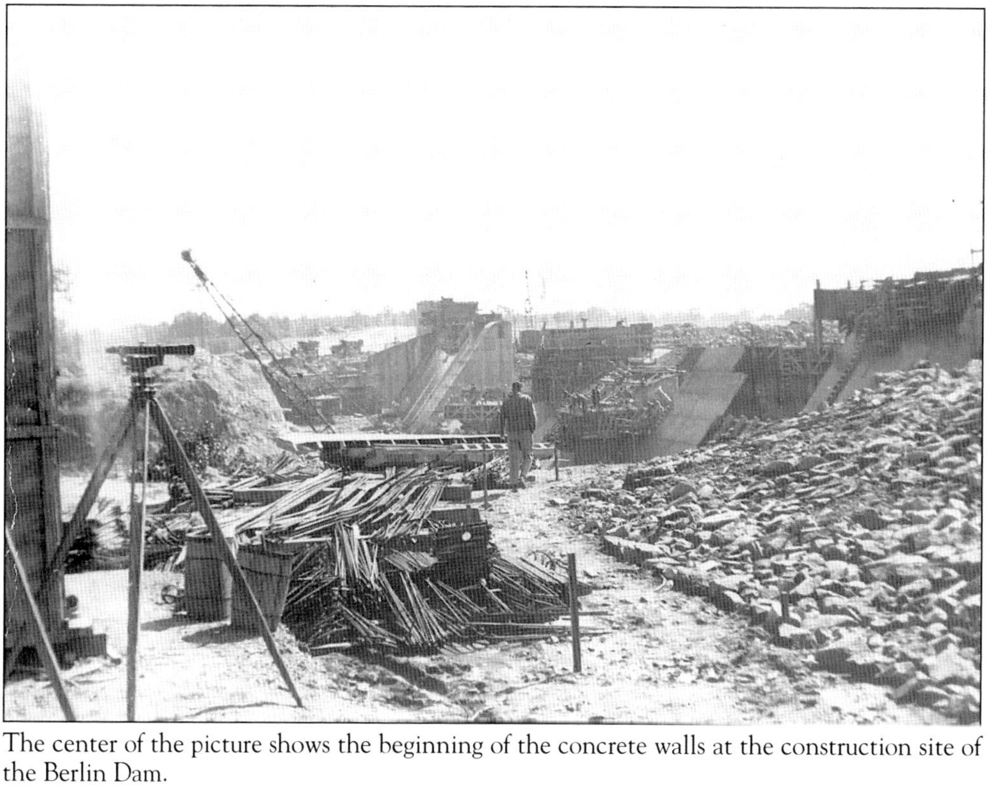

The center of the picture shows the beginning of the concrete walls at the construction site of the Berlin Dam.

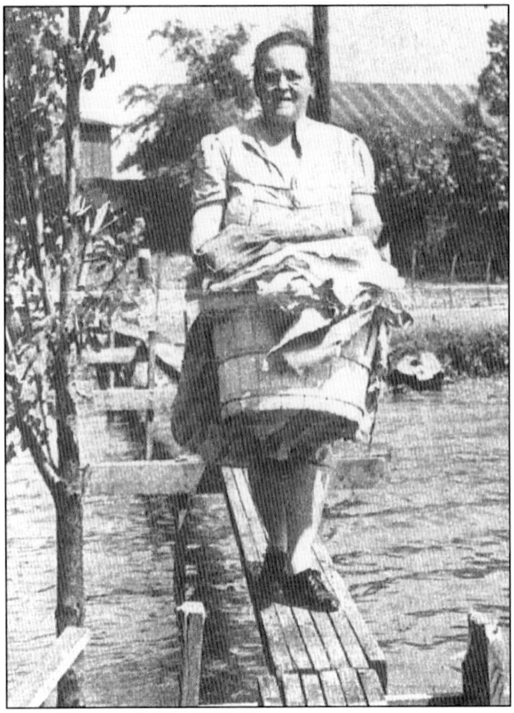

The water from the new Berlin Dam had risen to surround the home of Ross and Ethel Burkey McEldowney in 1943. Mrs. McEldowney was forced to walk the wooden planks to hang up the laundry. A price agreement was reached for the farm. Their house, pictured below, was moved to Berlin Station Road on rollers pulled by tractors. The family lived in the house, currently owned by James & Dianne Millard, as it was being moved.

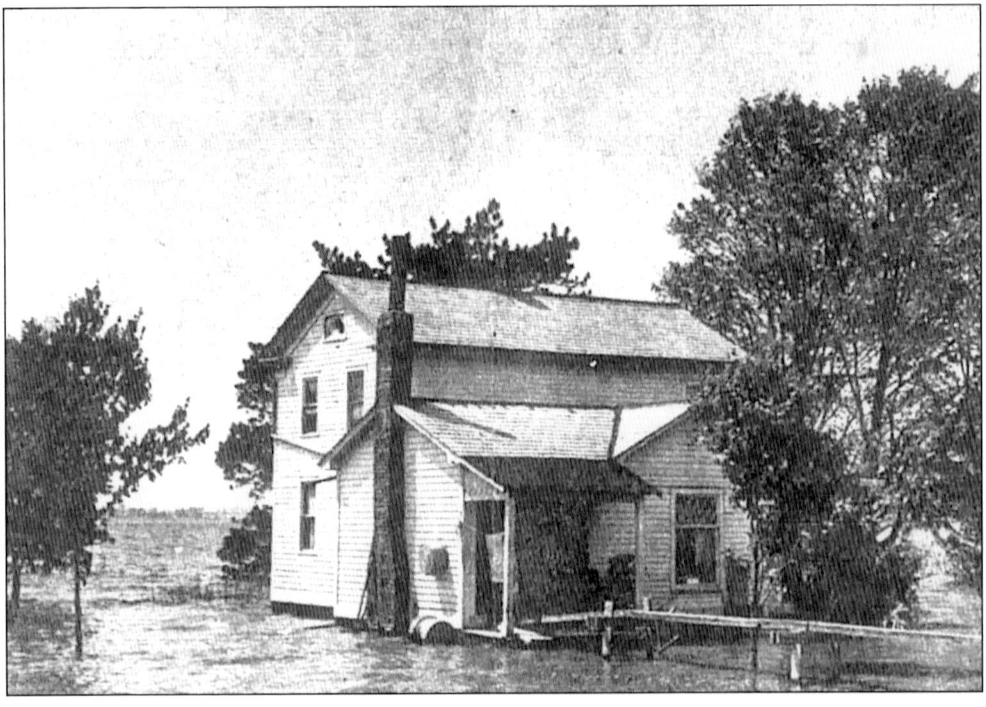

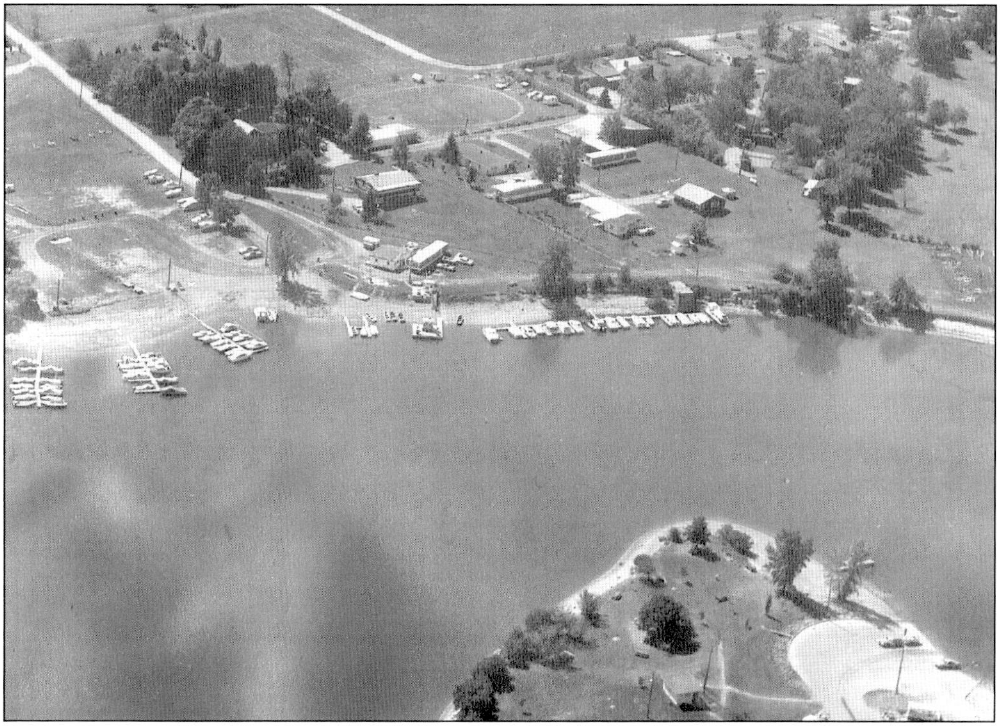

At the top of this photograph is a view of the Dutch Harbor Marina, located on Berlin Lake. The marina is presently owned by Duke Katterheinrich. The land at the bottom of the picture is known as McEldowney's Island.

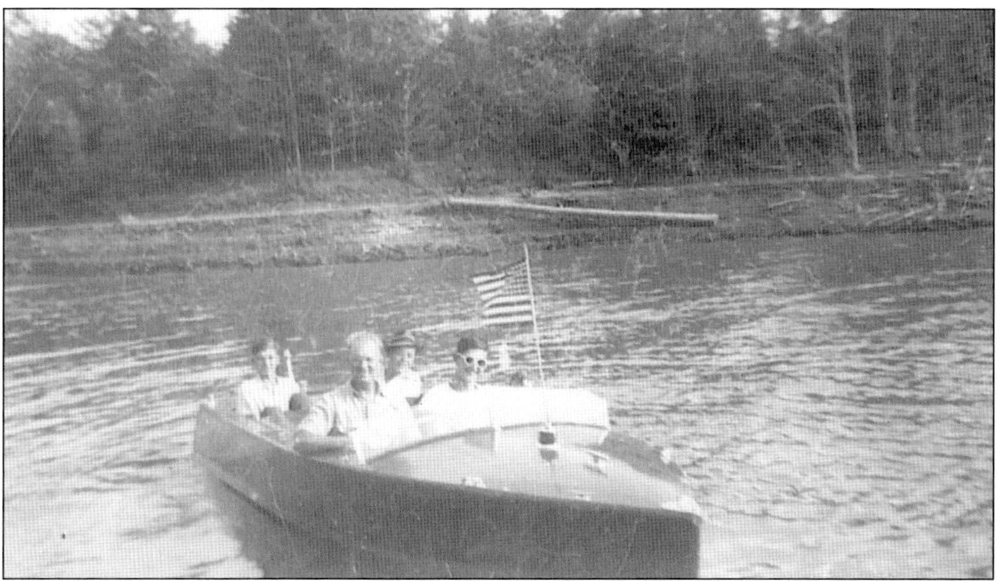

This is believed to be the first boat ever to cruise the lake. Pictured from left to right in 1943 are Bennard Burkey, Earl Shilling, Harold Hartzel, and Lester Burkey. Boating continues to be a popular sport on Berlin Lake, with motor boats, pontoon boats, sailboats, jet skis, and fishing boats found in abundance during the summer months. Camping and swimming are also enjoyed by the area's residents and visitors.

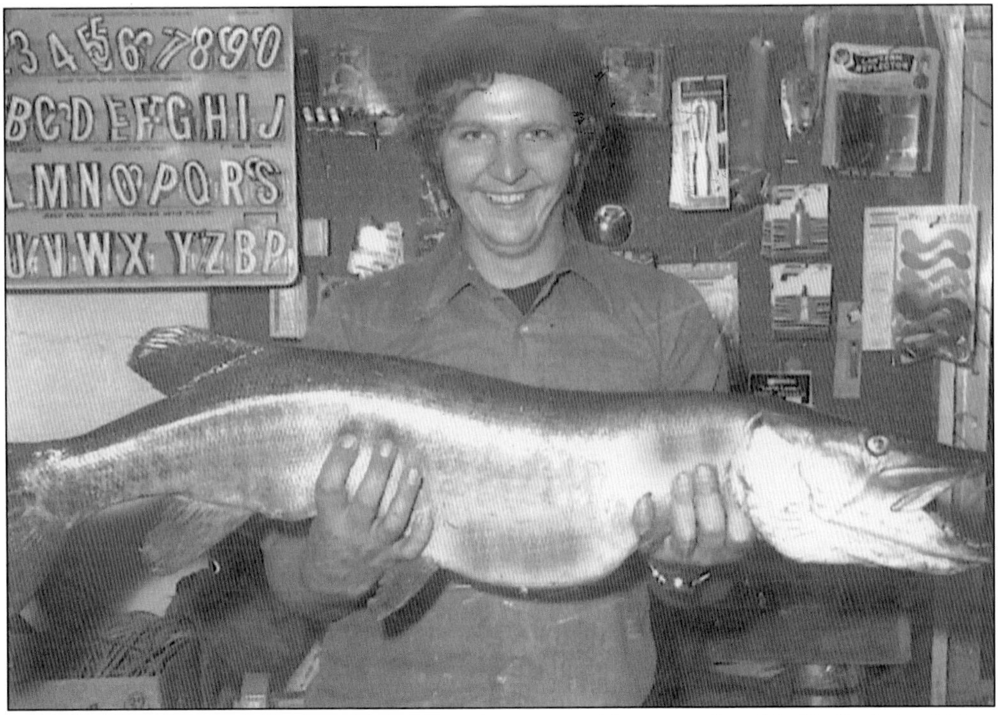

A wide variety of fish, including the large muskie pictured here, are found in Berlin Lake. Other types include large and small mouth bass, catfish, carp, crappie, walleye, and blue gill.

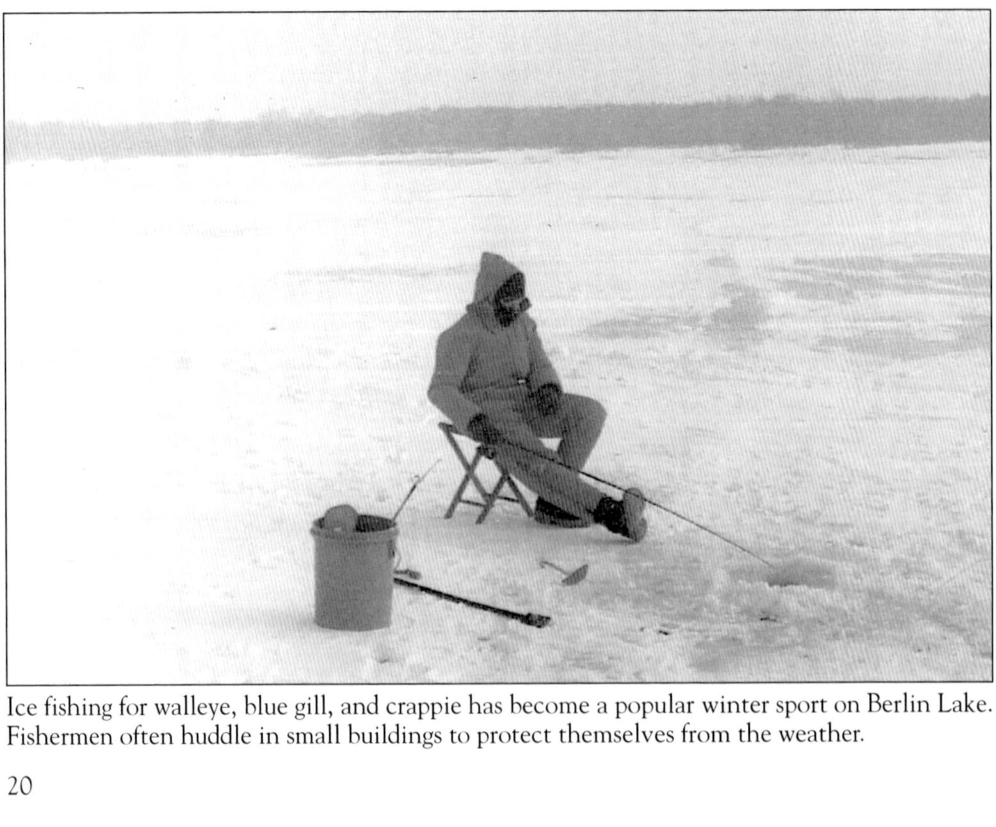

Ice fishing for walleye, blue gill, and crappie has become a popular winter sport on Berlin Lake. Fishermen often huddle in small buildings to protect themselves from the weather.

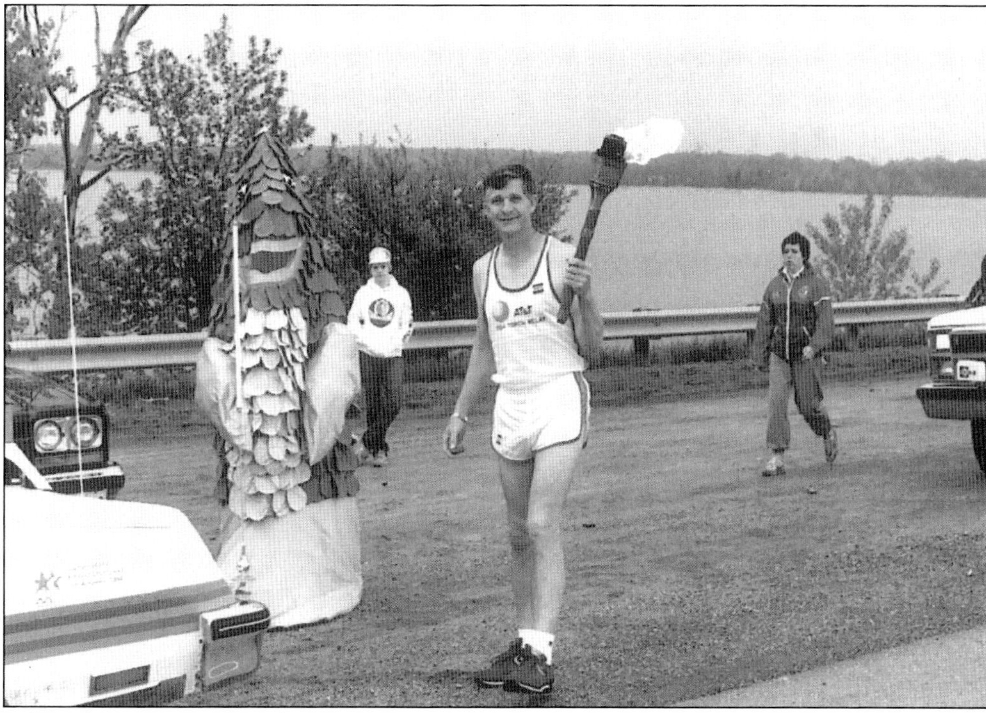

When the Olympic torch-bearer ran across the bridge over Berlin Lake, Freddie the Fish, park mascot, was there to greet him. Freddie passed out badges that read, "Don't drown; it will spoil your day."

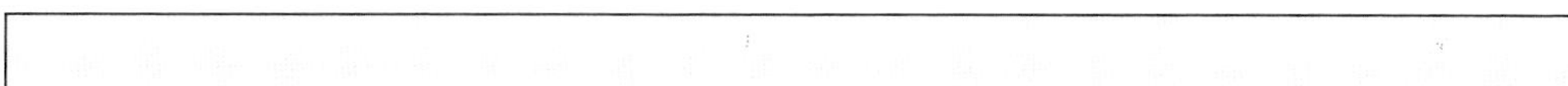

This administration building is located at 7400 Bedell Road, with Pete O'Connell serving as resource manager since 1997. The lake and dam areas fall under the U.S. Army Engineer Pittsburgh District, which oversees the camp grounds, boating area, and dam operation and maintenance. About 25 people are employed in the summer months and approximately 12 through the winter.

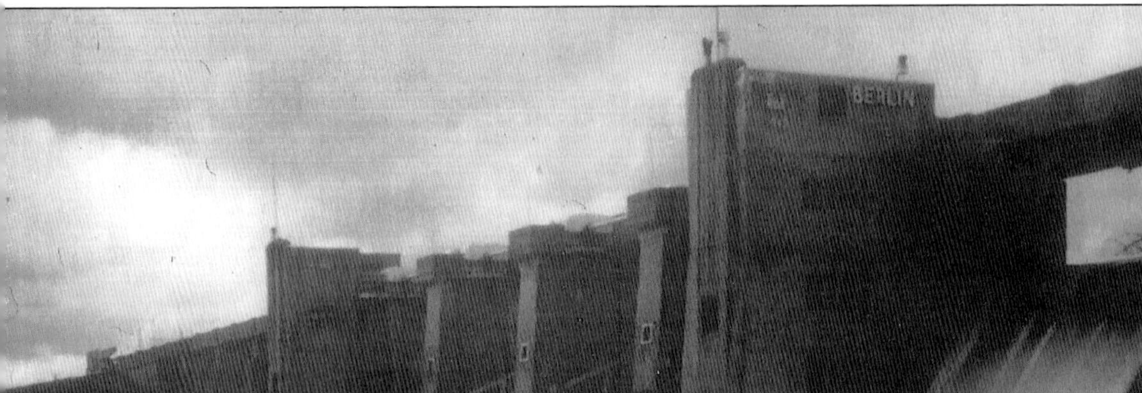

This May 13, 1996, photograph shows the first uncontrolled flow over the spillway of Berlin Dam, which lasted one day. The water is ordinarily released through three valve-controlled sluices that are three feet in diameter. They are located in the controlled section of the spillway. A stilling basin rests immediately downstream from the controlled portion of the spillway. Its purpose is to absorb the energy developed by the discharge of the water. The small concrete dam that forms the stilling basin, located 700 feet downstream from the main dam, is nine feet high and 241 feet long. The land required for the construction of the dam and lake includes 7,990 acres, 6,931 of which are owned by the federal government. The remaining 1,590 acres are privately owned lands subject to flowage and easements agreements.

Two

Berlin Centre Station

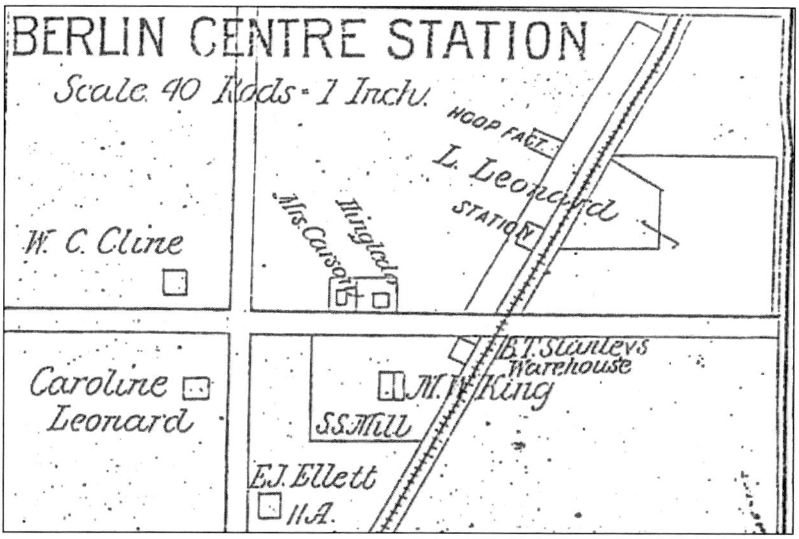

The above map shows the Berlin Centre Station area in 1899. Berlin Township's Business Directory for that year included Central Hotel, Nathan Rakestraw proprietor; B.T. Stanley, shipper of wool, hay, and grain, and dealer in general merchandise; Maple Grove Shropshires; E.J. Ellett, breeder of thoroughbred Registered Fancy Shropshire Sheep; H.E. Shilling, farming and milling with the latest improved rollers; W.E. Carson, physician and surgeon; W.K. Hughes, physician and surgeon; Mervin W. King, farmer, planing, feed mills, and custom sawing; R.S. Hawkins, farmer and dealer in hay and straw; Frank White, farmer and manufacturer of Jersey butter; Chester Bedell, farmer and real estate dealer; L.F. Kline, farmer and breeder of trotters; Charles Swartz, farmer and teacher; Henry Burkey, farmer and breeder of Delania Sheep; and J.W. Myers, farmer and stock dealer. It bears mention that some of the represented businesses also appeared in the 1874 directory.

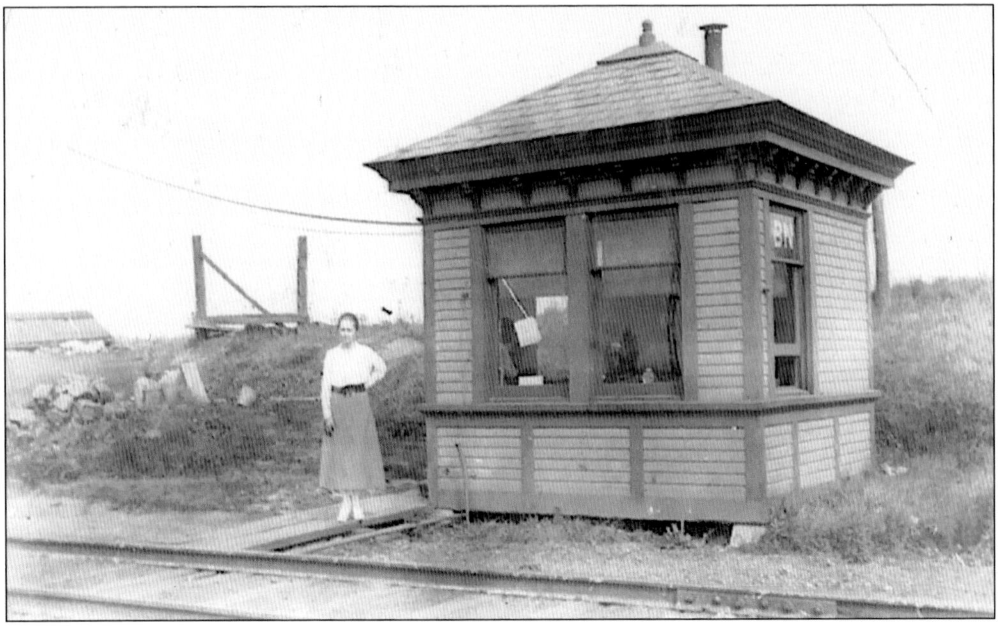

In 1882, land was purchased to build a railroad from the northeast to the southwest corner of Berlin Township. A few years later, the railroad began running trains between Niles and Alliance. Pictured here is the first building to mark the station. Records indicate E.J. Ellett, with the Ashtabula, Niles, & Alliance Railroad, as the station agent for several years. George Shrader became the agent for the railroad around 1912.

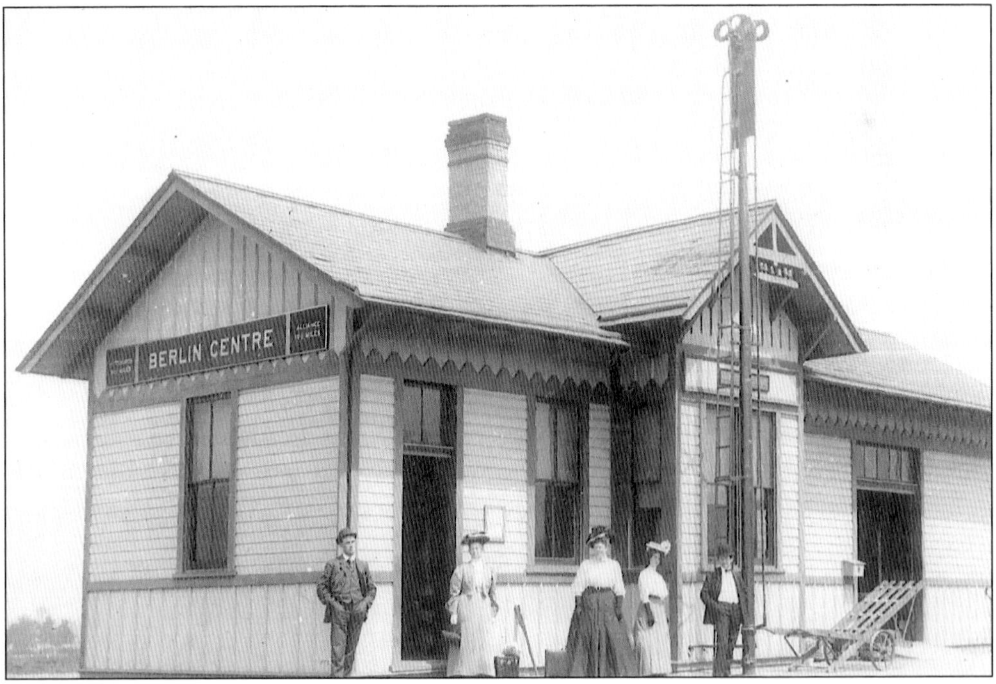

Passengers wait for the train at the Berlin Centre Station located on Berlin Station Road. The Ashtabula and Alliance Railroad ran trains twice daily, and later became part of the Pennsylvania Railroad line, now run by Conrail.

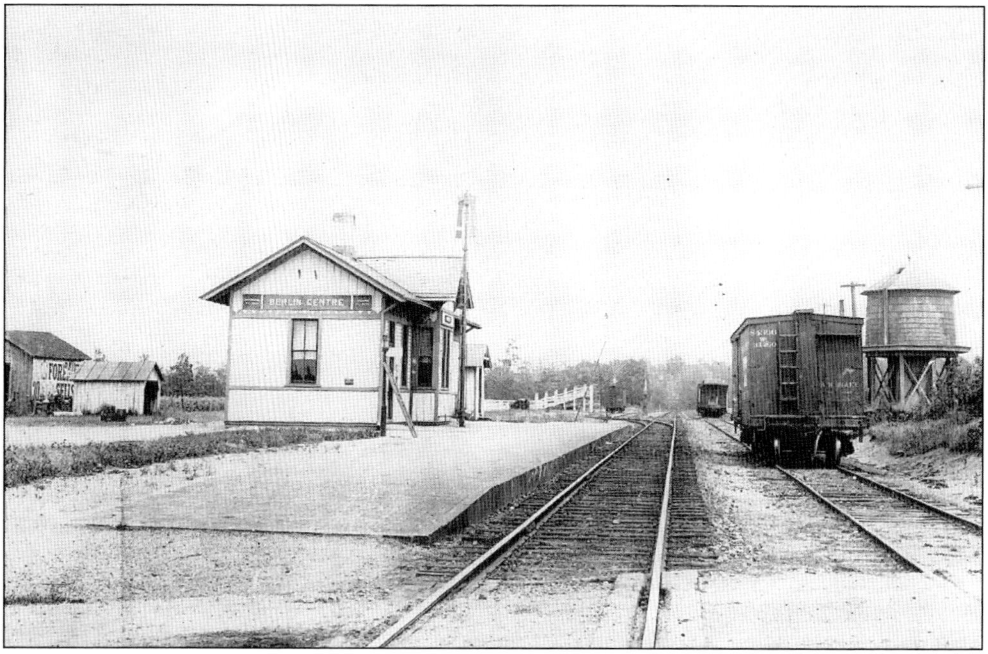

In 1916, when this picture was taken, the Berlin Centre Station featured a passenger ticket office, weight scales, cattle loading chute, telegraph office, and water tower. A man was employed for several hours each day to pump water for the steam engines into the tower beside the station. A small mill pond served as the water source.

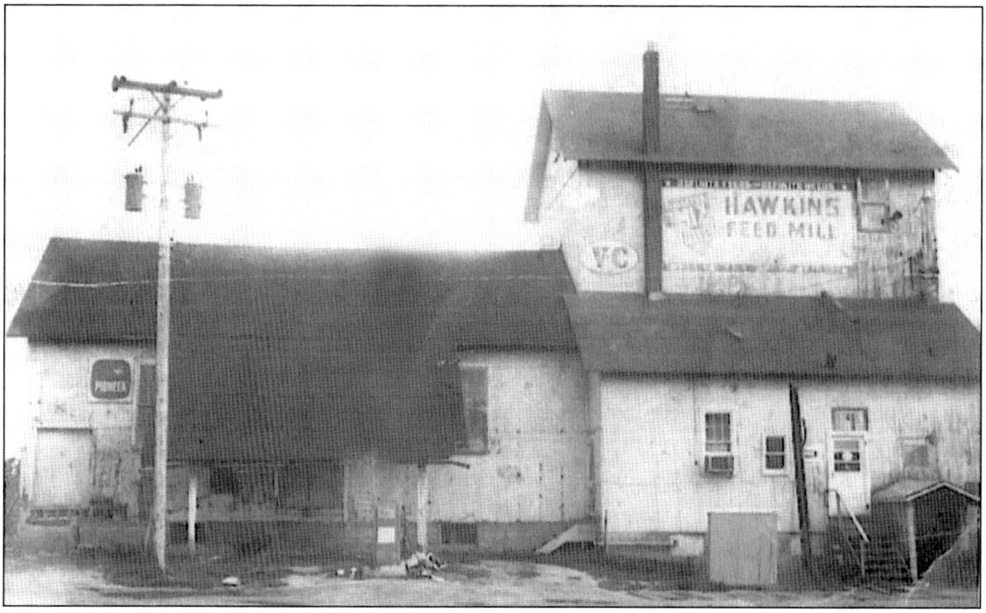

This feed mill was built around 1900 for Mervin King. In 1912, L.E. Hawkins purchased the mill and installed modern machinery. The facility was eventually passed down to his son, Richard Hawkins, who transferred the business to his own son, James Hawkins. This was the place for loading grain at harvest time and providing fertilizer at planting time. Grain was ground and mixed for the farmers. A price-list for the store appears on the following page.

Lynn E. Hawkins | L. E. Hawkins | Richard D. Hawkins

The Hawkins Store & Mill, Inc.

THE HAWKINS MILL

Custom Grinders & Mixers of Feed

Dealers in

Feed, Grain, Seed, Coal, Fertilizer,

Wool, Cement, Sand, Etc.

Berlin Center, O. 3—13—1930

MARCH

PRICE LIST

SUBJECT TO CHANGE

	Cwt.
PURINA Omolene	$2.65
PURINA Chick Chow	3.25
PURINA Startena	4.65
PURINA All Mash Starter	4.20
PURINA Chick Growena	4.00
PURINA 34% Cow Chow	3.30
PURINA 24% Cow Chow	2.85
PURINA 20% Cow Chow	2.75
PURINA 16% Cow Chow	2.60
PURINA Calf Chow, 100 lbs.	5.25
PURINA Calf Chow, 25 lbs.	1.40
Hawkins' 20% Dairy	2.40
Hawkins' 16% Dairy	2.05
Hawkins' Laying Mash	2.80
PURINA Chicken Chowder (mash)	3.50
PURINA Chicken Fatena L. C.	3.00
Gluten	2.00
Oilmeal	2.90
Cottonseed Meal	2.50
Wheat Bran	1.85
Wheat Middlings	2.00
Hominy	2.00
Corn and Oats Chop	2.10
Distillers Grains	2.60
Salt	1.00
Diamond Gluten	2.75
Tankage	4.25
Meat Scrap	4.00
Oyster Shell	1.00
Charcoal	3.00

Special At Car

CASH FERTILIZER PRICES

16%	$19.80
20%	23.80
10-10	27.45
14-4	24.93
2-12-2	27.97
2-12-6	31.93
2-8-10	32.50
4-24-4	50.55
Bone	43.50

	Cwt.
Peat Moss	$3.00
Rolled Oats	4.00
Alfalfa Leaf Meal	3.40
Dried Buttermilk	9.00
Seed Oats, per bushel	.82
Corn (shelled)	1.97
Wheat, per bushel	1.40
Rye, per bushel	1.20
Buckwheat, per bushel	1.30
Scratch (Conkey)	2.45
Our Own Scratch	2.30
Cracked Corn	2.30
Growing Grains	3.00
Conkey Horse Feed	2.40
Chick Feed	3.00
Conkey's Laying Mash	3.30
Growing Mash	3.20
Crate Fattener	3.00
32% Dairy	3.00
24% Dairy	2.80
20% Dairy	2.50
16% Dairy	2.30
Coal (per ton—delivered)	4.50
Sand (ton—delivered)	2.80
Gravel (per ton—delivered)	2.80
Cement (per sack)	.70
Bonemeal	3.30
Candied Copra	2.85
Cod Liver Oil (per gallon)	1.75
Clover Seed	Special price this month

George Kendall Chicken Farm for sale—Located four miles north of Berlin Center, Ohio. Six room house, running water, electric lights, two-car garage, two hen houses.

See B. E. Woolf for pure Tom Barron S. C. White Leghorn Chicks, hatching eggs, custom hatching or started chicks. We highly recommend these chicks.

This sheet will be mailed to you each month in accord with our policy of service and quality feeds. In order to keep our prices as low as possible, we are going to pass on to you what we save when you pay cash.

It will save you money to buy with cash.

~~$1.00 TON OFF FEED PRICES FOR C~~ASH

TWO PERCENT CASH DISCOUNT

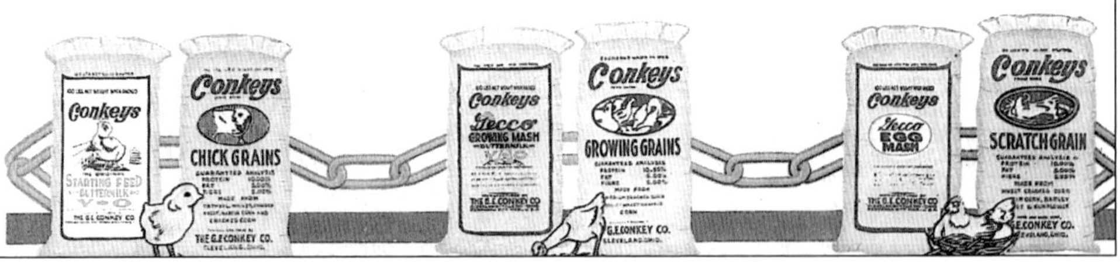

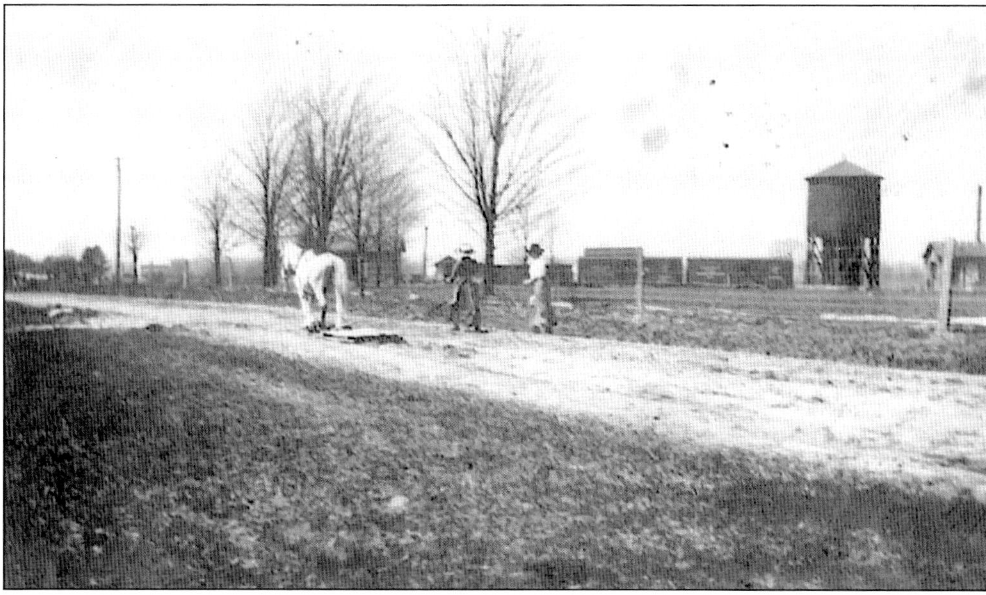

Because steam engines and freight trains were increasing in size, the water supply from the station's mill pond soon proved inadequate. Ross Hawkins conceived the idea of damming up the springs on his farm to provide water to fill the tower. He sold his idea to the railroad and entered into a lease shortly thereafter.

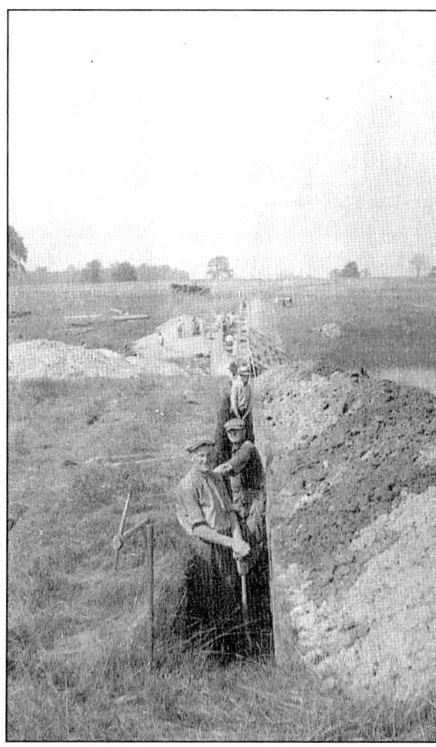

In 1918, a ditch for the pipeline, which extended nearly 3/4 of a mile to the water tower from Hawkins Lake, was dug by hand. The construction of the lake and water line took approximately three months. Gravity flow helped fill the tower at the railroad.

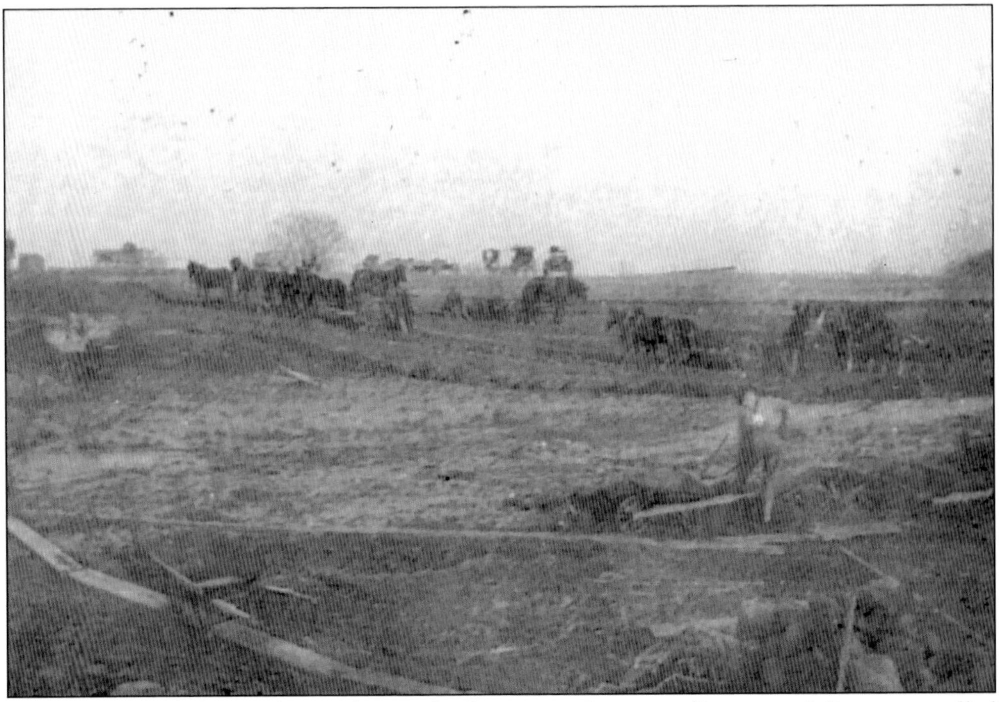

A 5 acre lake bed for Hawkins Lake was dug by men with teams of horses and slip scoops called "wheelers." Each man who provided a team of horses was paid $1 an hour, considered good pay for the times. As many as 20 teams and 20 men were employed at the same time.

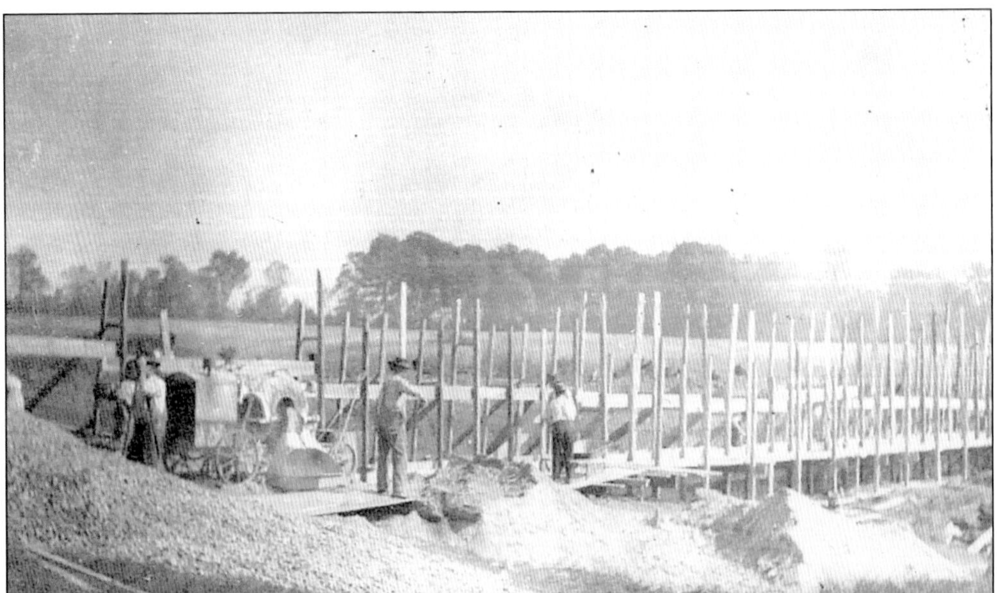

Cement was mixed and poured by hand to form a solid wedge-shaped dam 24 feet high for Hawkins Lake. A tower was installed in the lake with a walkway off the dam. Inside this tower, valves were installed to control the flow of water.

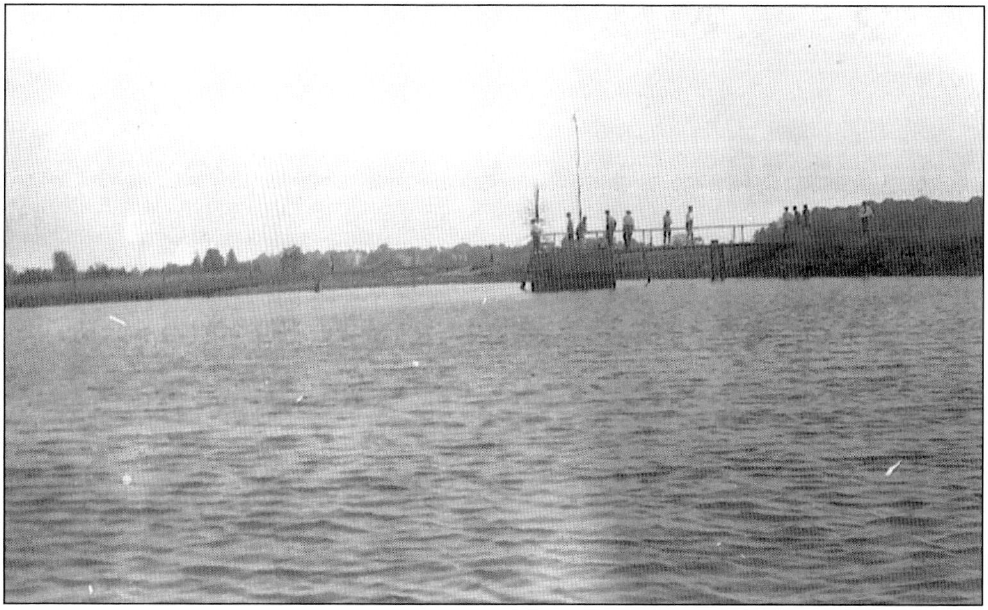

The cement walkway and tower were also used for recreational purposes at Hawkins Lake, so a diving board was installed on top. A screen once fell from the end of an interior pipe, filling the railroad water tower with thousands of fish. A truck was required to remove the fish from the tower and pipeline.

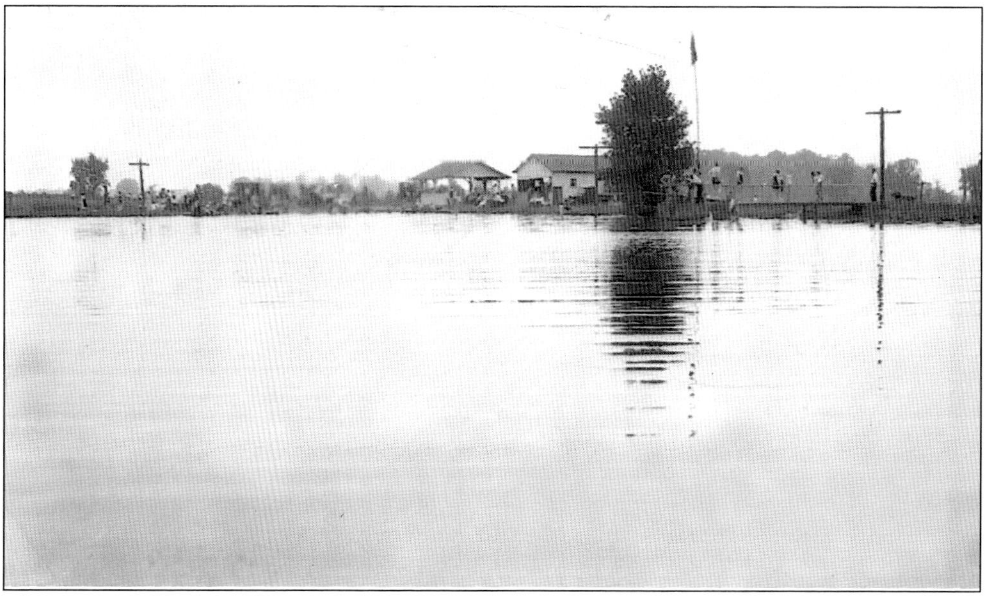

The Hawkins family also developed the lake for recreation, a new concept at the time. For a fee of 25¢ per car, people could swim, fish, and utilize the facilities of several different picnic groves. Many firms from the Youngstown area held company picnics there. In early days, chicken dinners were served at the pavilion on Sundays.

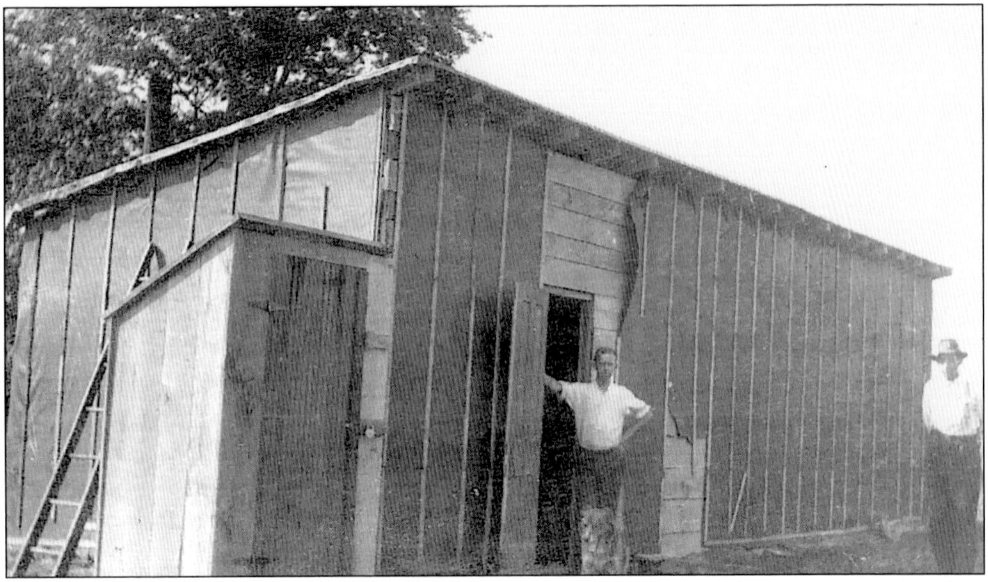

Hawkins Lake provided ice for harvest during winter months. The ice blocks were stored packed in sawdust, then sold commercially year-round from this icehouse on the north side of the lake.

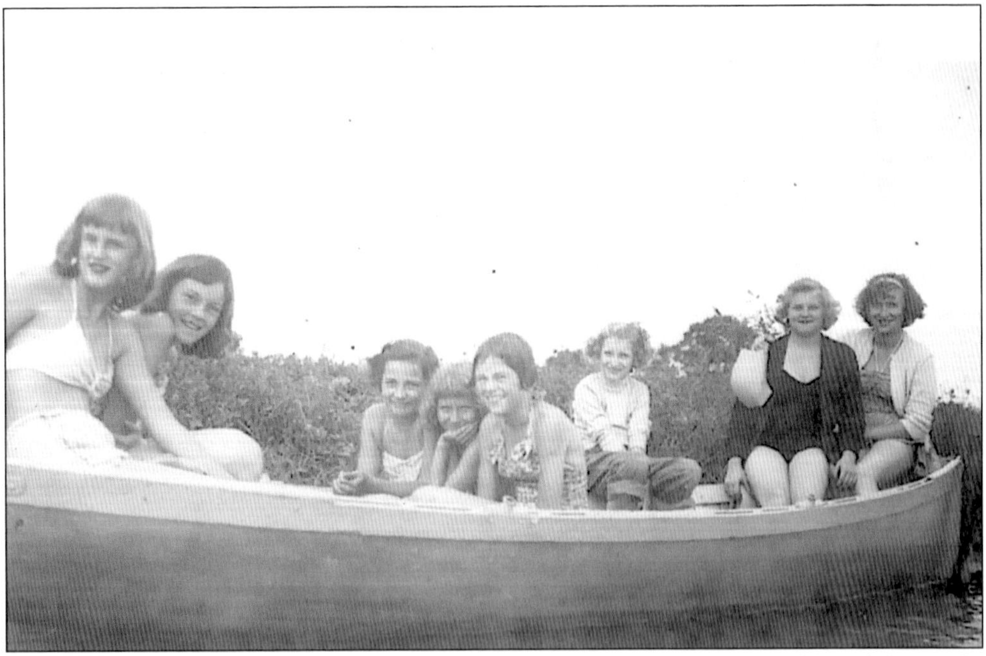

Girls enjoy a ride in a rowboat on Hawkins Lake during the 1950s. Pictured from left to right are Darlene Miller, Joann Hawkins, Carol Truitt, Judy Keeler, Margarete Vickers, Lucille Grondeski, Marlene Miller, and Sylvia Vickers.

Three

BUILDINGS AND HOMES

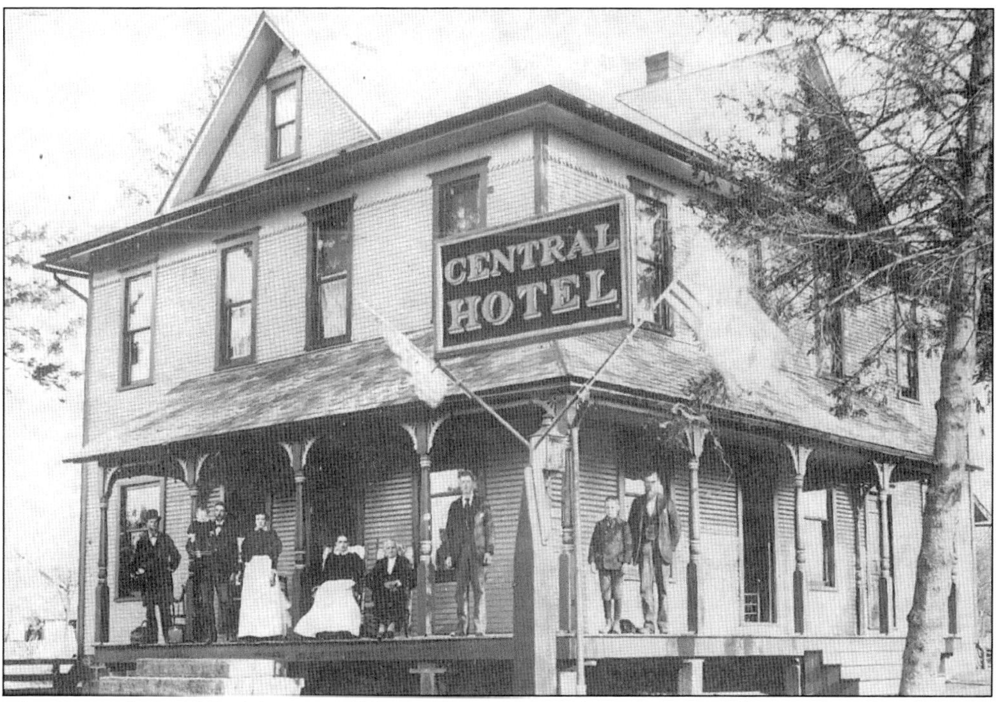

The Central Hotel building is still located on the northwest corner of Routes 224 and 534 in the center of Berlin. Original proprietor Nathan Rakestraw is pictured on the right of this c. 1900 photograph. The hotel was built to accommodate passengers from the railroad.

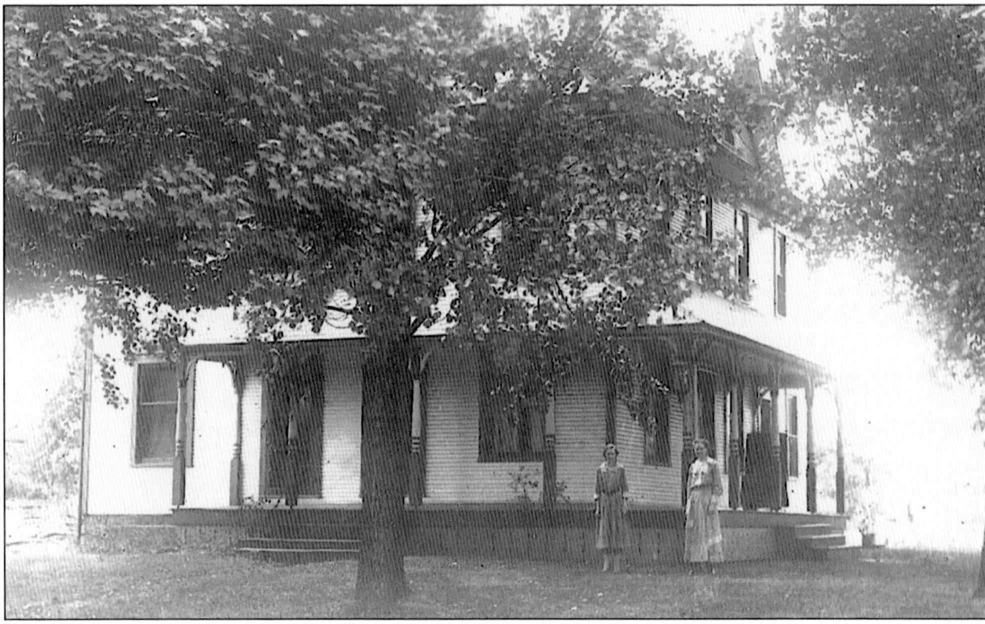

Built in 1898 by Nathan Rakestraw, the Central Hotel was located on the northwest corner in the center. Its 1899 Business Directory listing boasted a new building, newly furnished with heaters. A livery and stable were also provided. Horse and buggies transported travelers from the train station to the hotel for a lodging rate of $1 per night. In 1919, the Heiser family purchased the hotel and used it as a private dwelling. Mary Heiser is pictured on the right. In 1978, Joe and Donna Craig bought the building to divide into three apartments. The hotel's registration book, dated from 1899 to 1904, was donated to the Berlin Center Historical Society by the Rakestraw family. A present-day photograph of the building appears below.

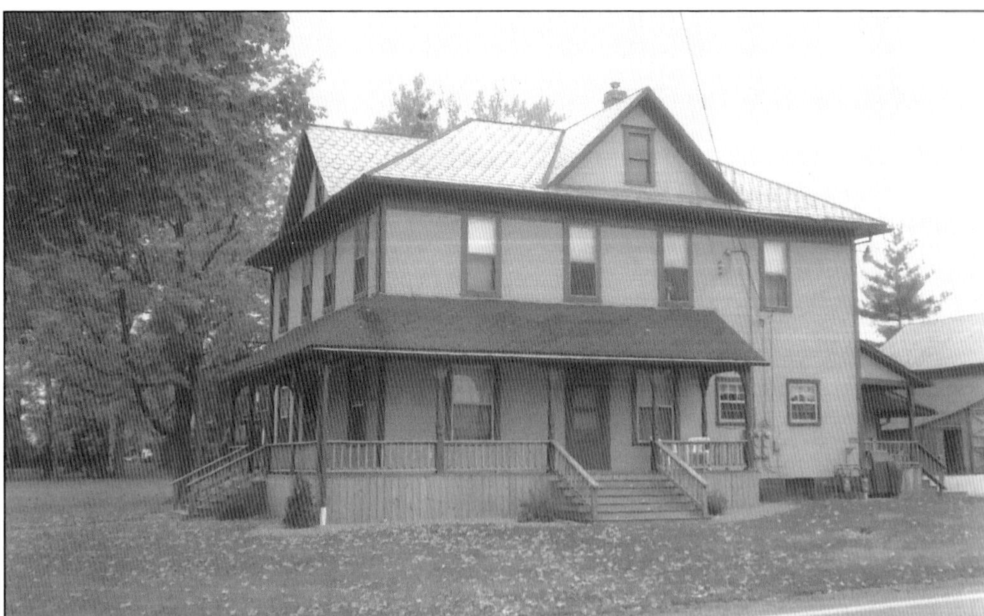

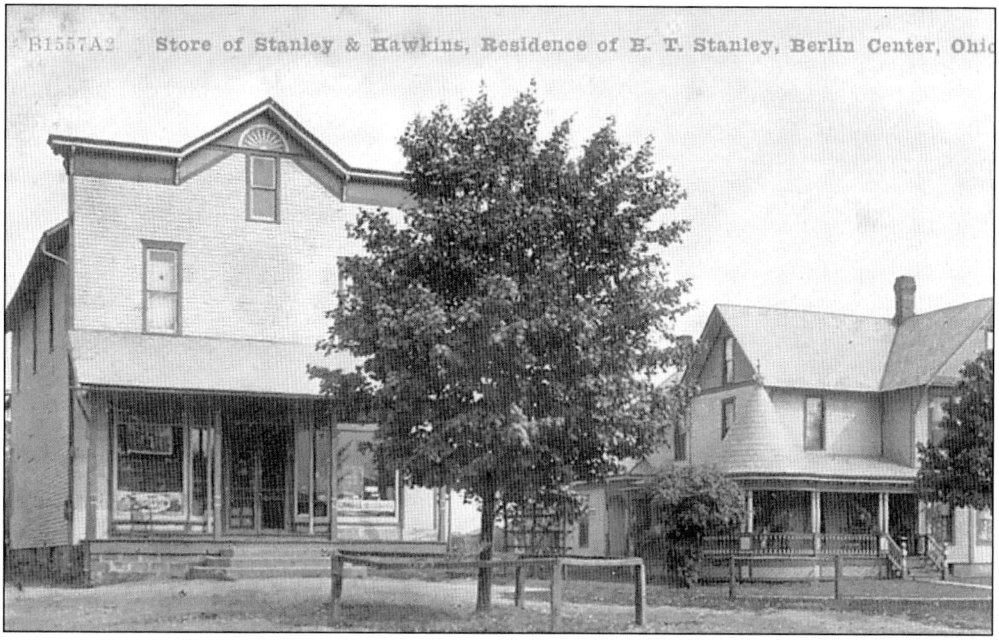

B.T. Stanley bought the general store on the northeast corner of the center in 1877. Fire destroyed the store a few years later, but with the help of friends and neighbors, a new building was constructed in its place. At this time, the store was called "Stanley and Hawkins." In 1912, Larue Hawkins purchased the business, which was operated by his son Lynn as a grocery, locker, and meat market until 1971. At the present time, an antique and collectible store known as "Never Too Olde" occupies the building (pictured below), now owned by Ron and Barb McGarry.

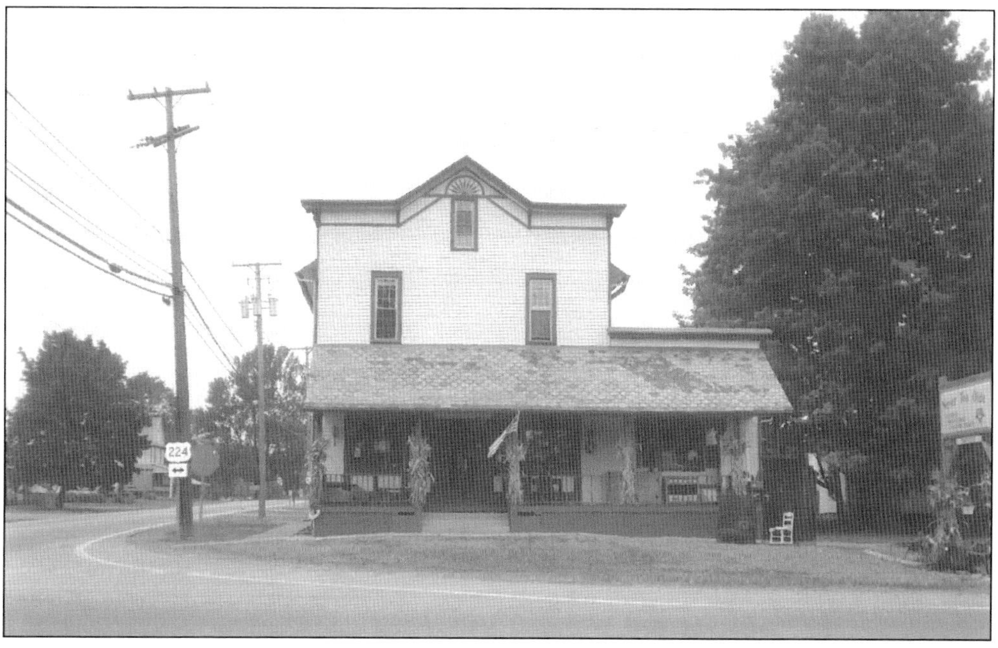

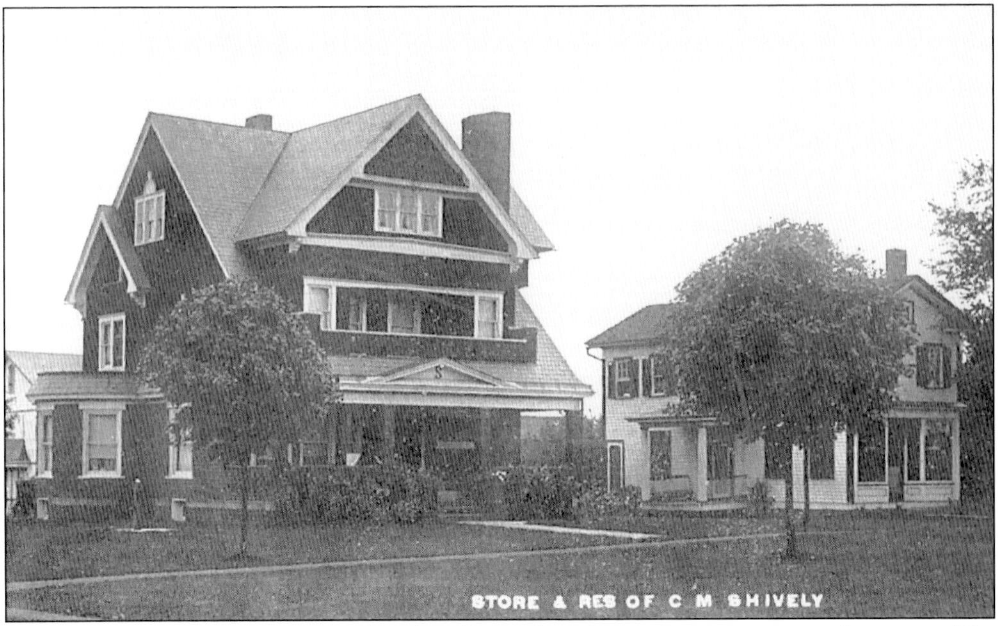

The residence and store of Carey Shively is located on the southwest corner at the center. The house was built in 1904 of gray stone with imported stained glass windows on the stair landing. A barrel in the attic supplied the house with water pumped manually for a wage of 25¢ per day. This was a combination jewelry and shoe store, but Mr. Shively also kept optical supplies on hand. The back half of the store was moved south on Route 534 and converted to a residence (below) currently owned by Lynn and Charlene Fields.

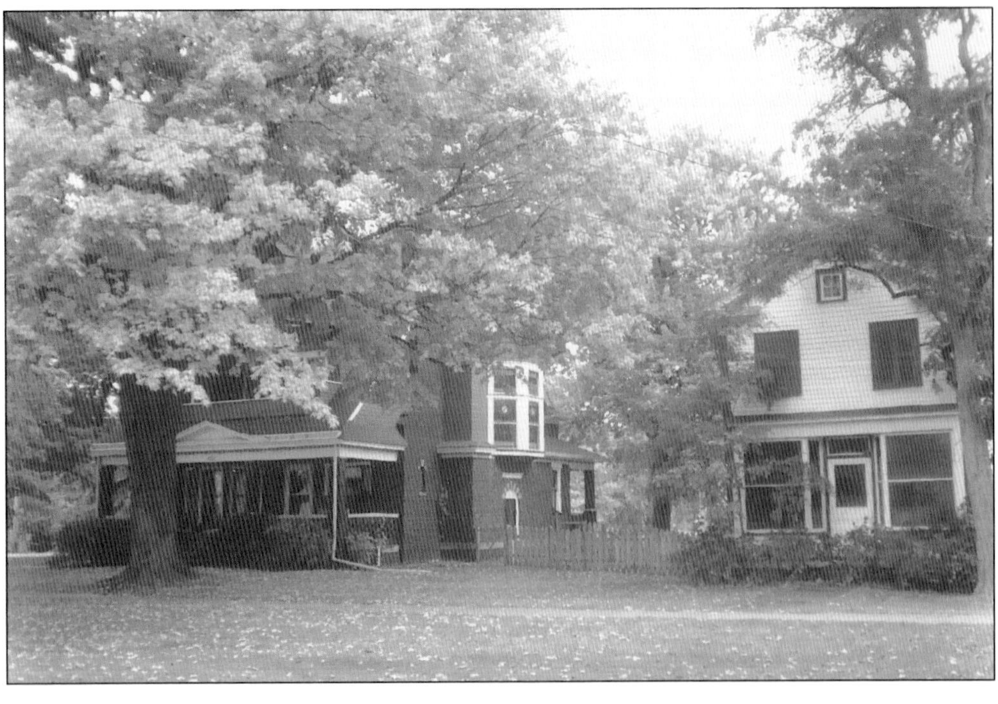

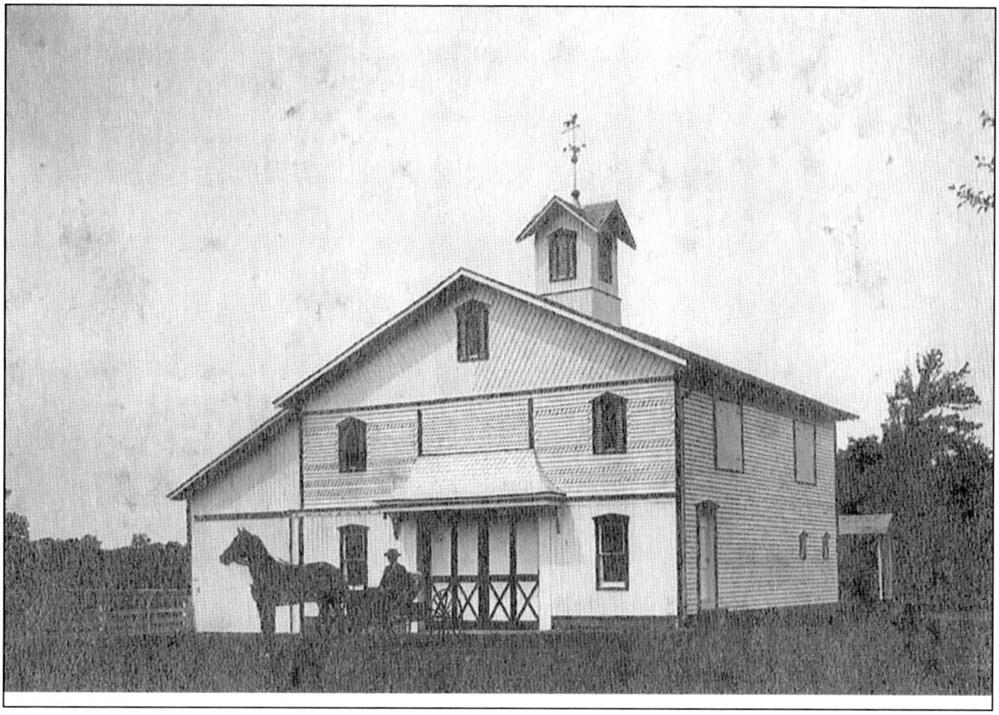

Shown here are two perspectives of the barn and stable on the Carey & Addie Shively property, located on the southwest corner at the center and presently owned by Lynn and Charlene Fields. The 600 gallon barrel, located in the top of the building, gathered water from the roof to be used for the horses. The barrel can still be found in the building.

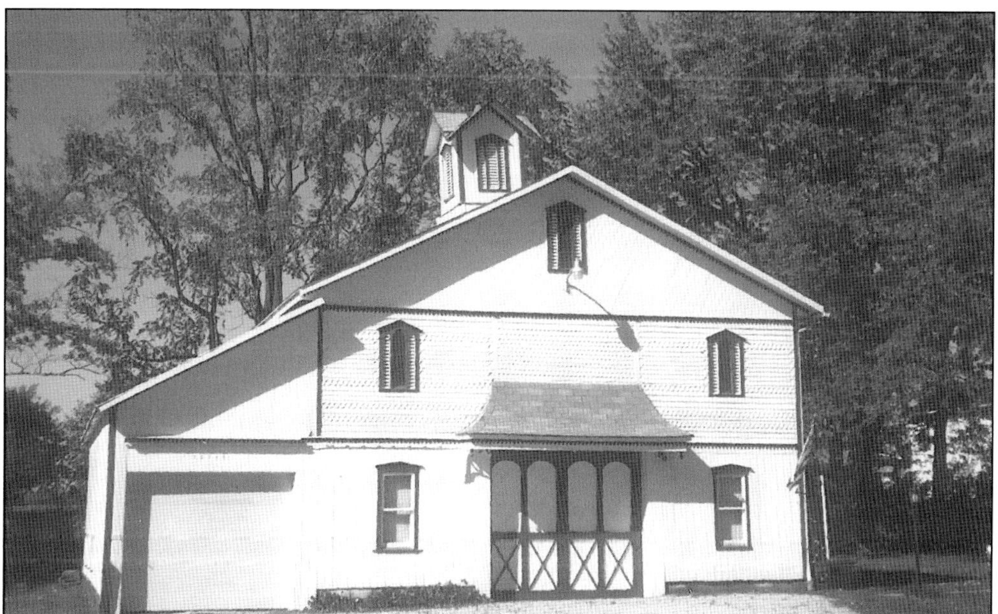

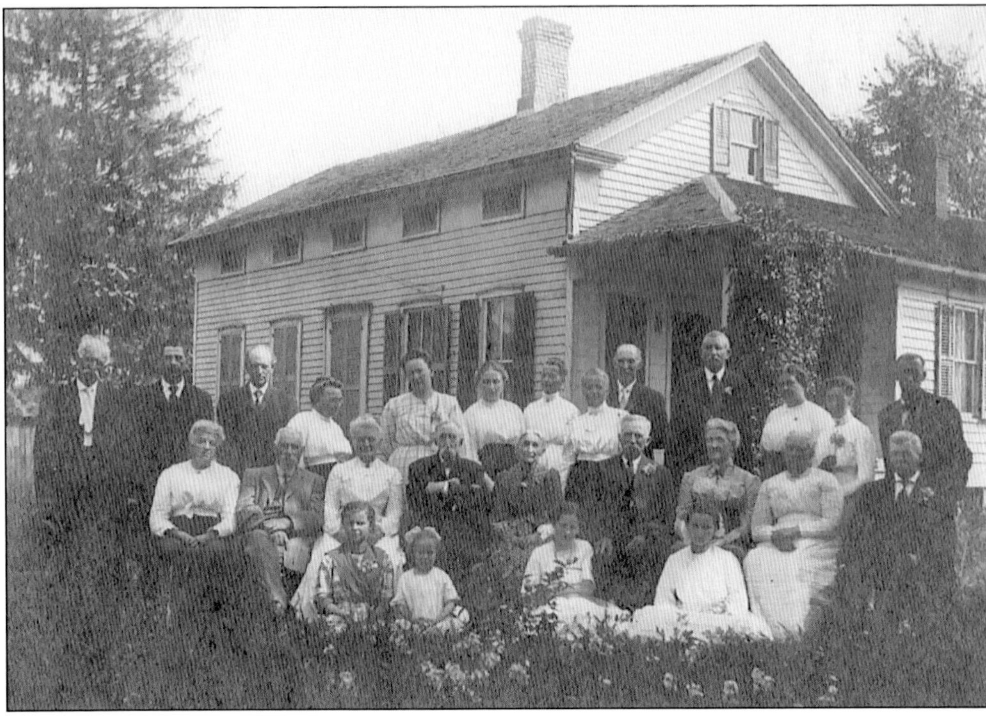

Present at a gathering at Dr. Wallace Hughes's home are, from left to right, as follows: (front row) Theo Smith, Mary Cover, Ruby Shaffer, and Mary Shaffer; (middle row) Augusta Renkenberger, Robert Weasner, Theoda Weasner, Dr. Hughes, Lizzie Hughes, Cecil Porter, Lucy Porter, Larina Beckman, and Walter Vincent; (back row) Theodore Renkenberger, Lawrence Wagner, Mervin King, Sara King, Ida Cover, Edith Wagner, Lucy Vincent, Laura Shaffer, Ollie Hoyle, Sam Shaffer, Addie Shively, Warren Hoyle, and Willes Beardsley

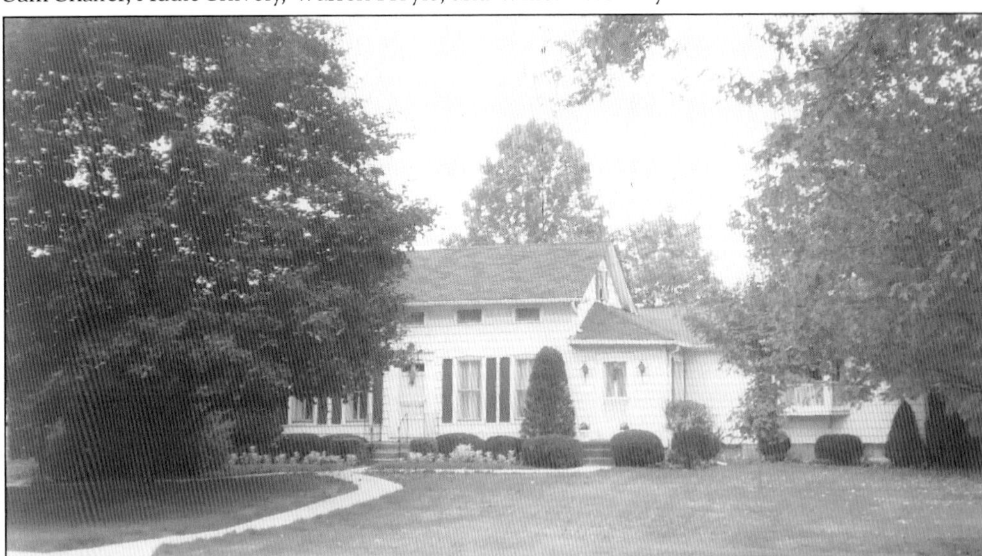

Dr. Wallace K. Hughes built this house, which also included his office. The Olson family owned the home, on southeast corner of the village, for many years. Recently, it was purchased by Nelson and Evajean Williams.

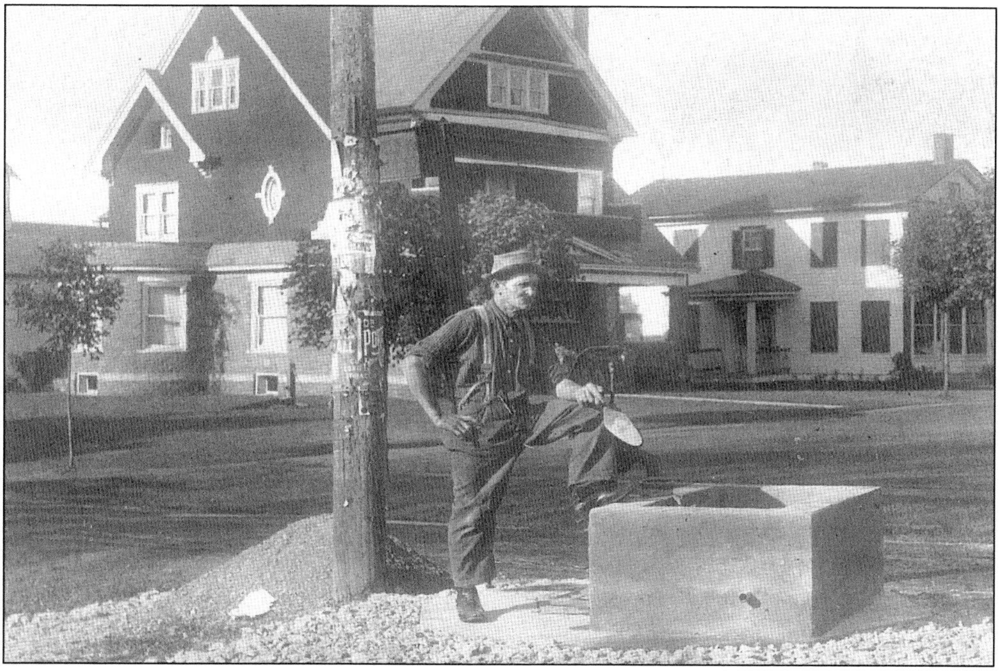

This dug well and pump was located in the center of the village at the intersection of Routes 224 and 534. When the roads were improved, the large horse watering trough was removed and the well covered over. The individual pictured here is Mitch Gunder.

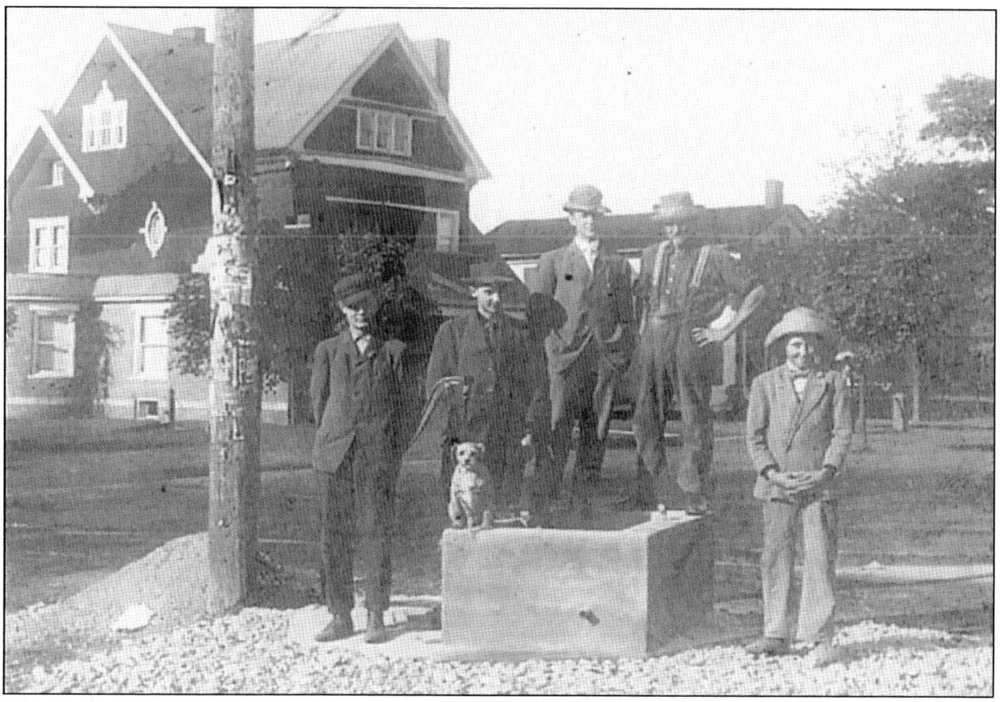

This gathering of local gentlemen is unidentified except for Mitch Gunder, who is featured in the picture above. This was a popular meeting area and valuable means of information exchange. Notice, for example, the posters on the pole.

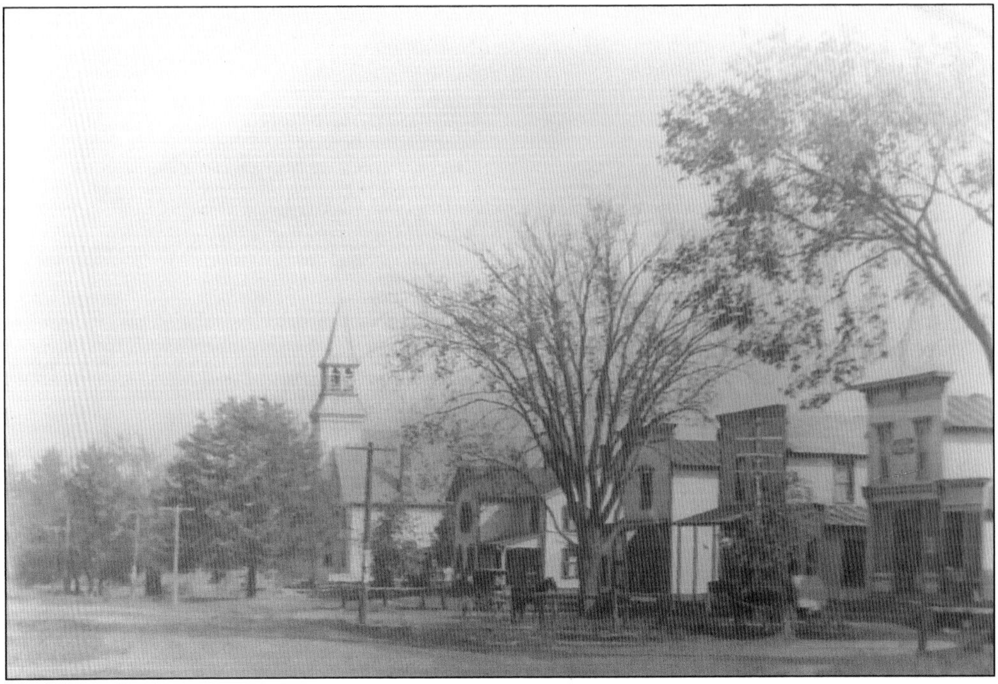

Offered above is an early glimpse of the southeast side of the center, ending with the Methodist Church. On December 29, 1933, when the temperature outside reached eight degrees below zero, a fire started at the rear of the Galbreath and Shively hardware and garage, then spread to the storage building, the lodge hall, and Shrader's Grocery Store. Because Berlin had no fire department, the community was forced to wait for help from other towns. The picture below reveals the devastation. Soon, a new hardware and garage building was erected, and Mr. Shrader moved another building to the same location. The middle lots remain vacant.

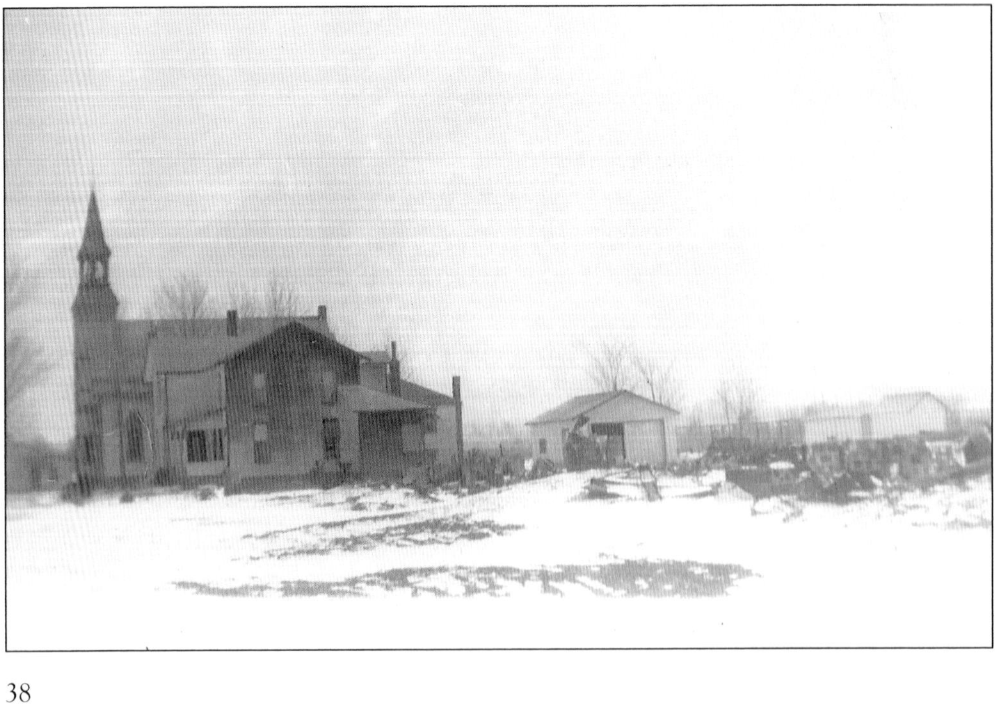

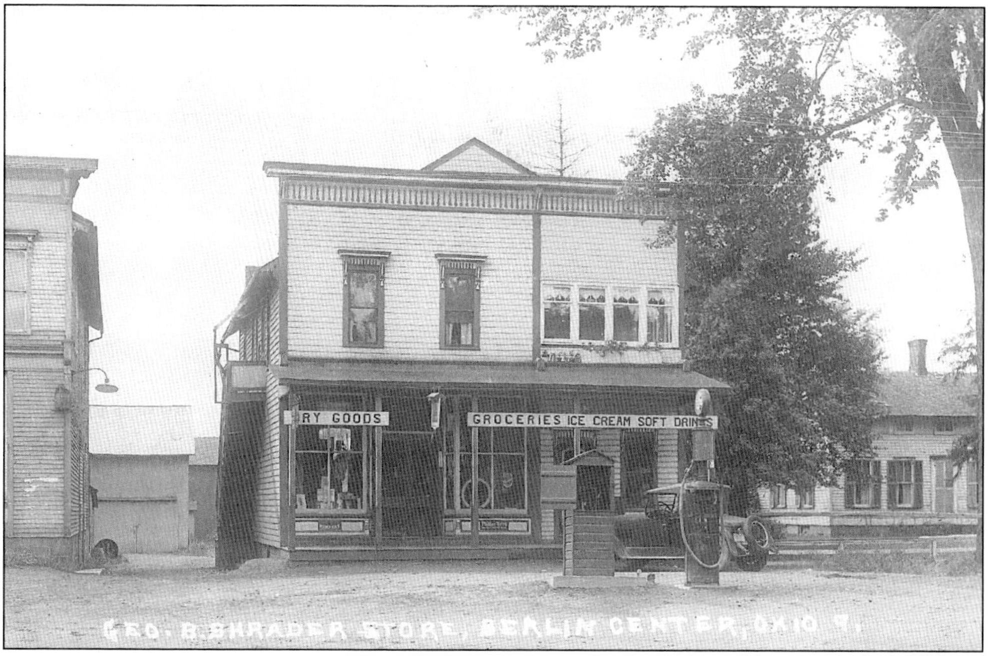

This building housed the Shrader Store, which sold groceries, dry goods, and gasoline in the early 1900s. When the building burned in 1933, the rear structure was moved to house the present store (below), which continues to be run by the Shrader family.

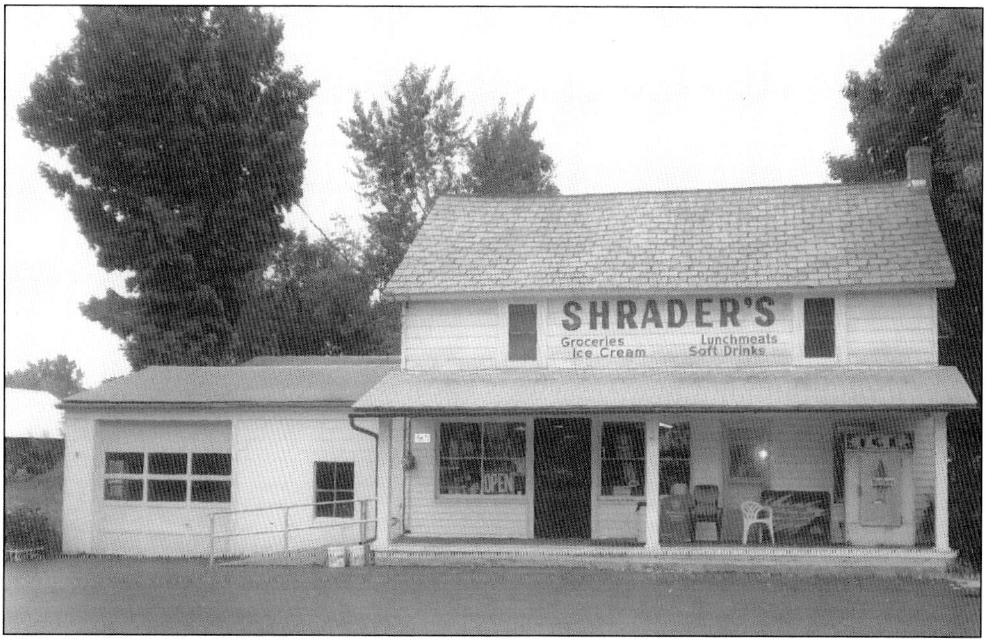

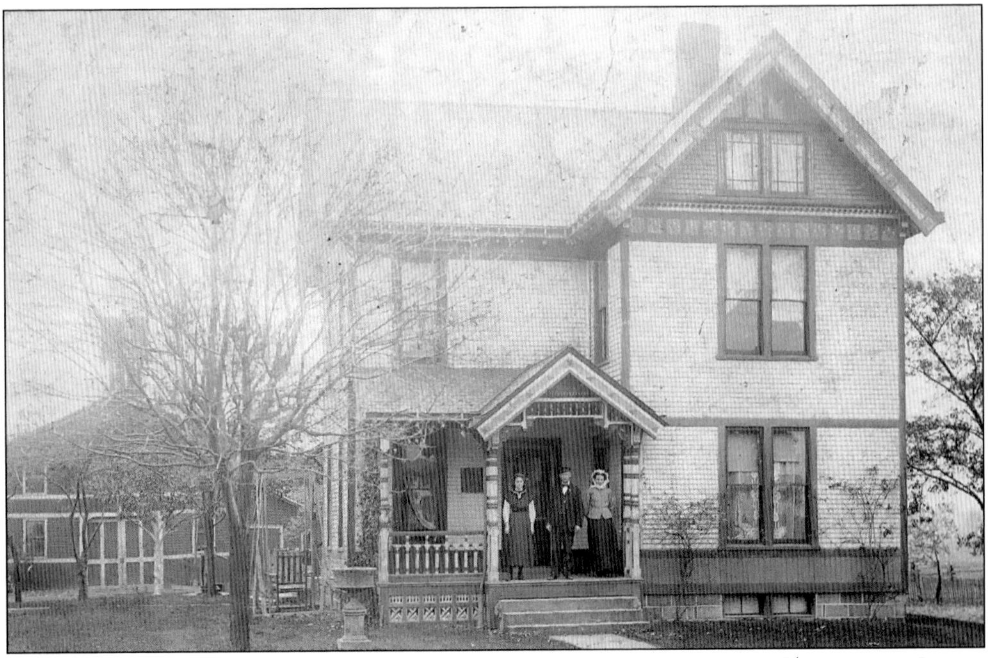

Dr. W.F. and Mrs. Ola Hawkins Carson built this house in 1887 at a cost of $2,500. Dr. Carson practiced medicine and became a physician/surgeon in 1899. Later, owners Dr. Carl and Beulah Petitt Weidenmier added an addition to the rear of the house. Dr. Weidenmier practiced medicine for 40 years in Berlin Center before retiring in 1969. In 1987, the township trustees purchased the building (below), which presently houses the offices of the township and the Historical Society Museum.

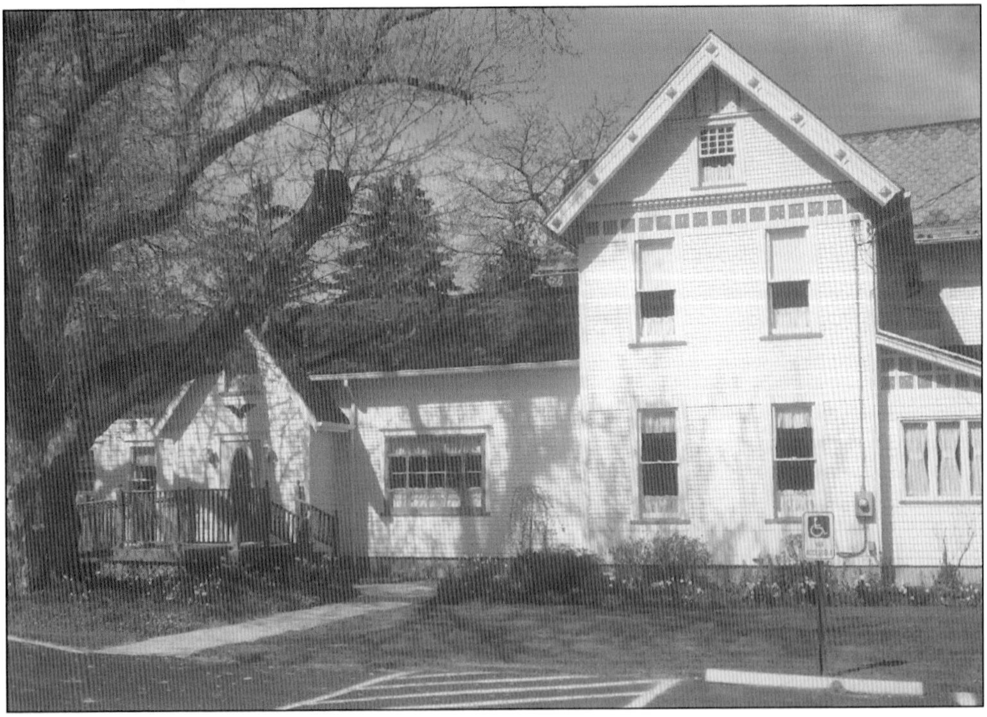

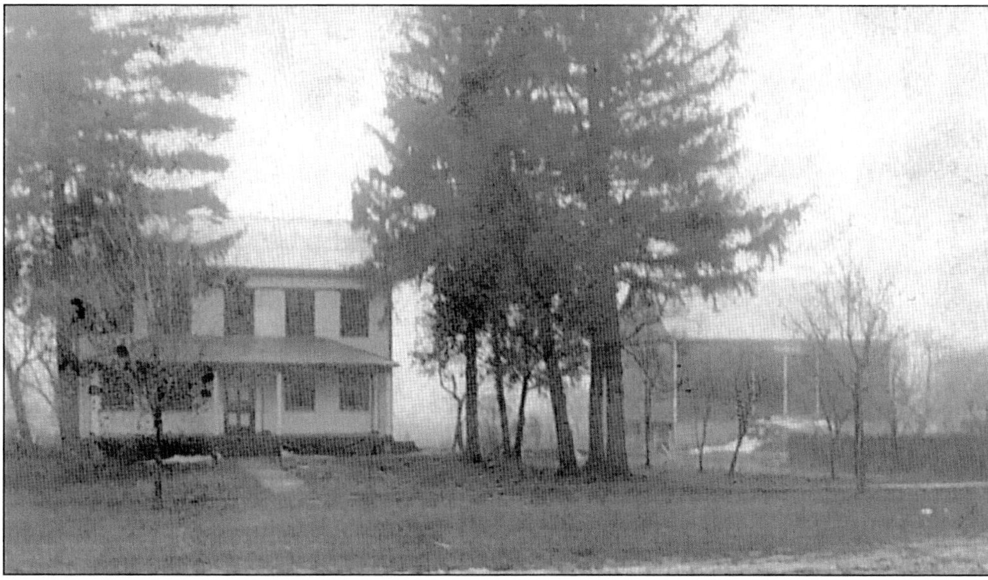

Located on Route 224 near the present fire station, the home pictured here was occupied by Squire and Mrs. Catherine Carson, who also owned the farm land west to the West Cemetery.

George and Catherine Gross Carson were married December 17, 1835. The couple had twelve children, two of which died in infancy. They celebrated their 66th wedding anniversary in 1901. George Carson was known as Squire Carson, and served as justice of the peace in Berlin Township for 50 years. The record book he kept is part of Berlin Township records.

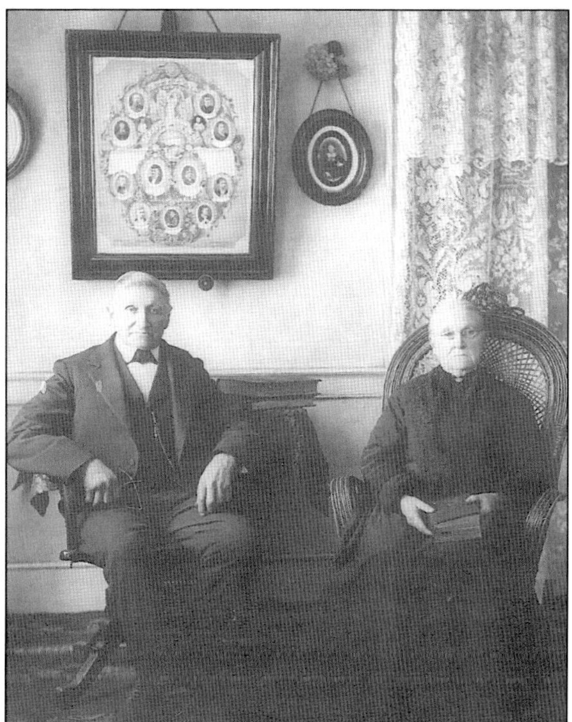

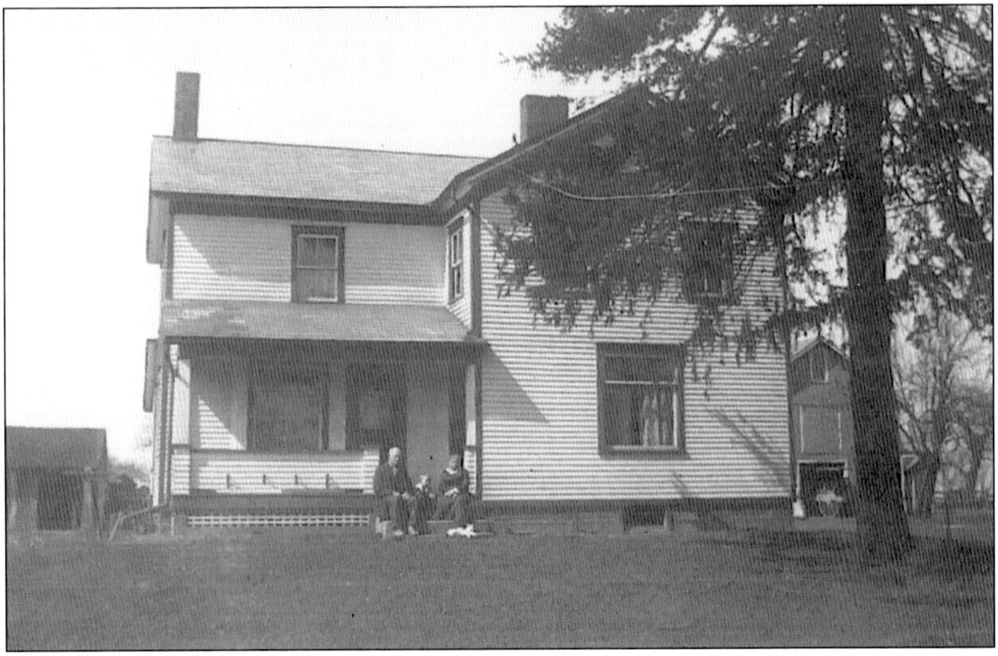

Dr. James and Pauline Brooke Hughes built this house just north of the center. Dr. Hughes practiced medicine in Berlin until his death in 1869. During the Civil War, he offered medical care gratuitously to families of men in the service. He and his wife, who together had four children, were members of the Methodist Church. An able public speaker and highly well-read man, Dr. Hughes contributed to religious and medical journals. The picture below shows the Hughes home as it stands today, owned by Ron and Jamie Adkins.

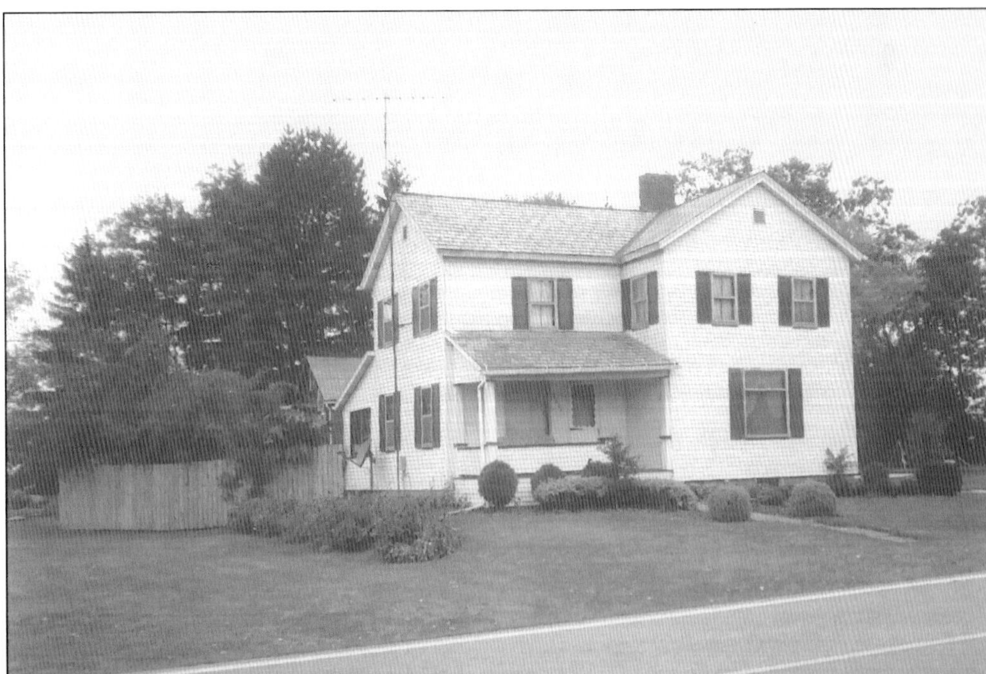

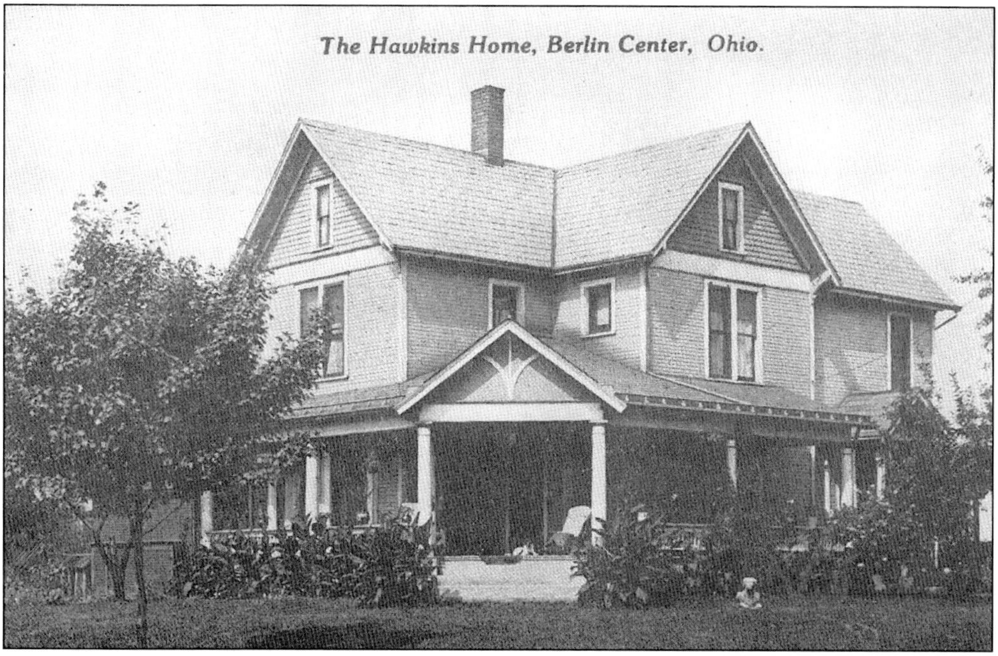

Pictured here are two views of a house built in 1898 by L.E. Hawkins. The top picture was taken in 1914, while the picture below was taken 85 years later in 1999. The current owners are Sandy and George Braymaier, who restored the structure to the beautiful home it is today. The pear tree is still living, but the tree between the walkway and Akron-Canfield Road is gone. Note the absence of electric wires in 1914, as well as the horse under the pear tree and dog on the porch.

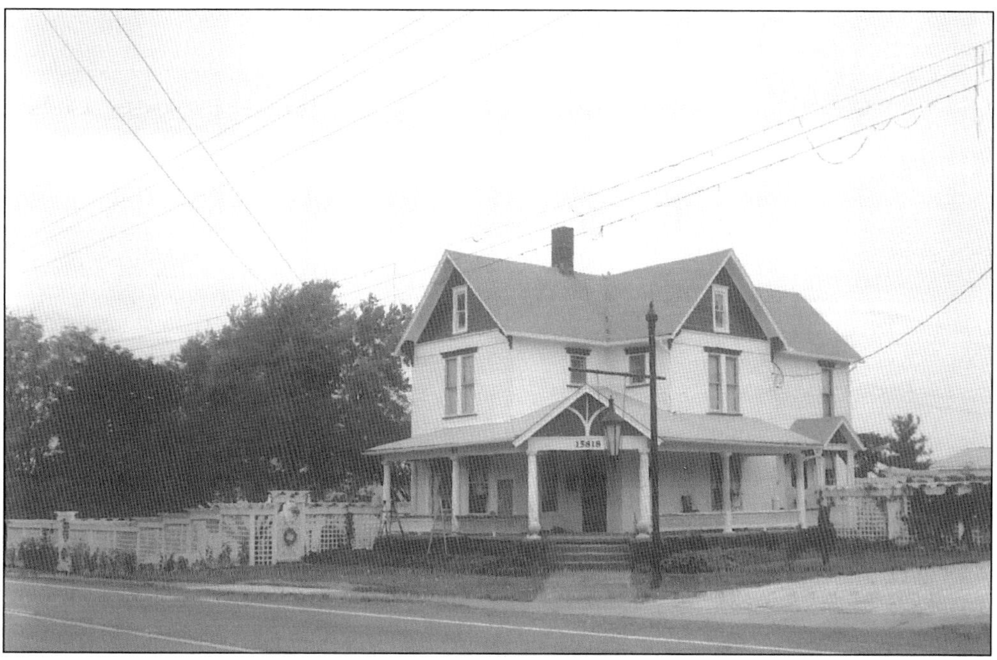

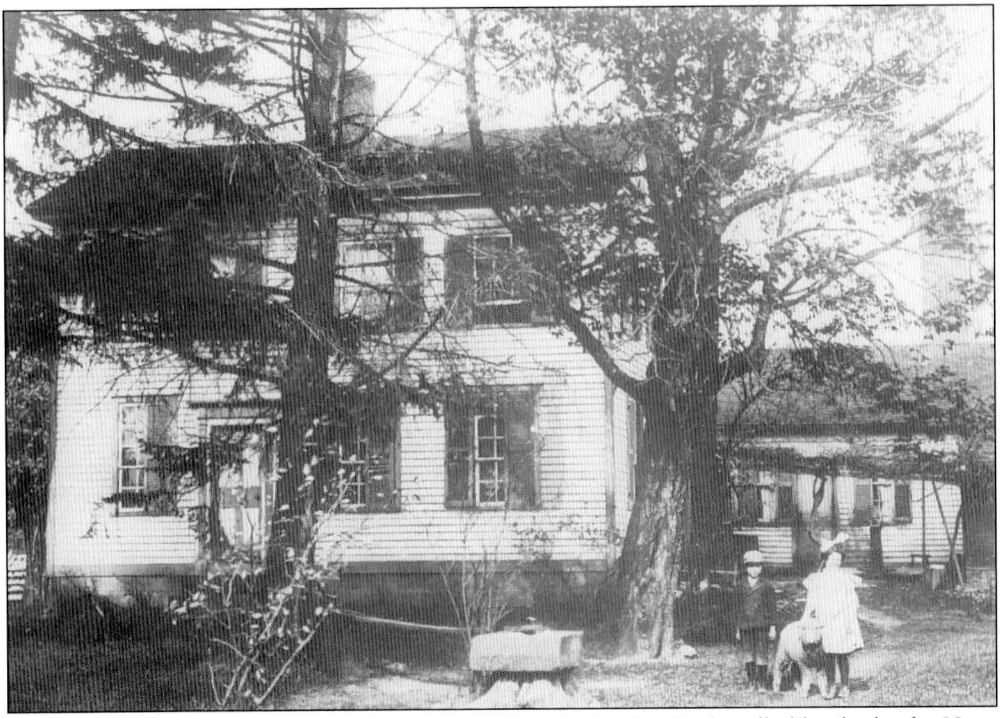

The area's first frame house was built in 1824 by Joseph Coult, who handled land sales for Hart, Mather, and Sell in Berlin Township. W.T. Hawkins owned the home in 1909 when this photograph was taken. The children are Charles Tressel Hawkins and Elma Hawkins, pictured with Snookie the lamb. Below is a current picture of the Coult house, located west of the center and presently owned by the DiRusso family.

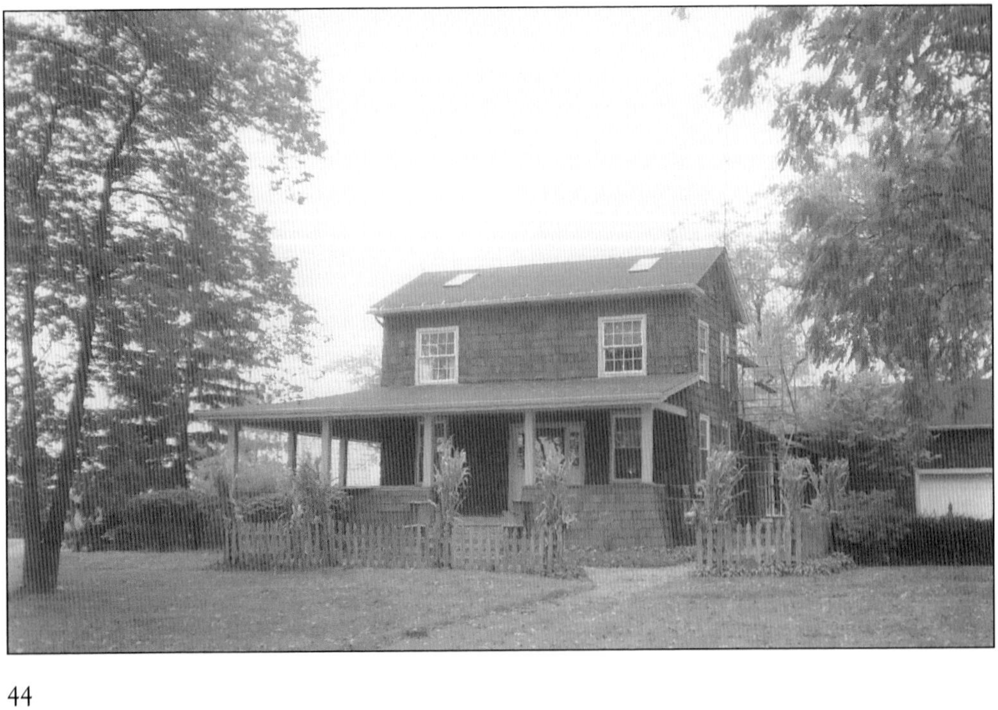

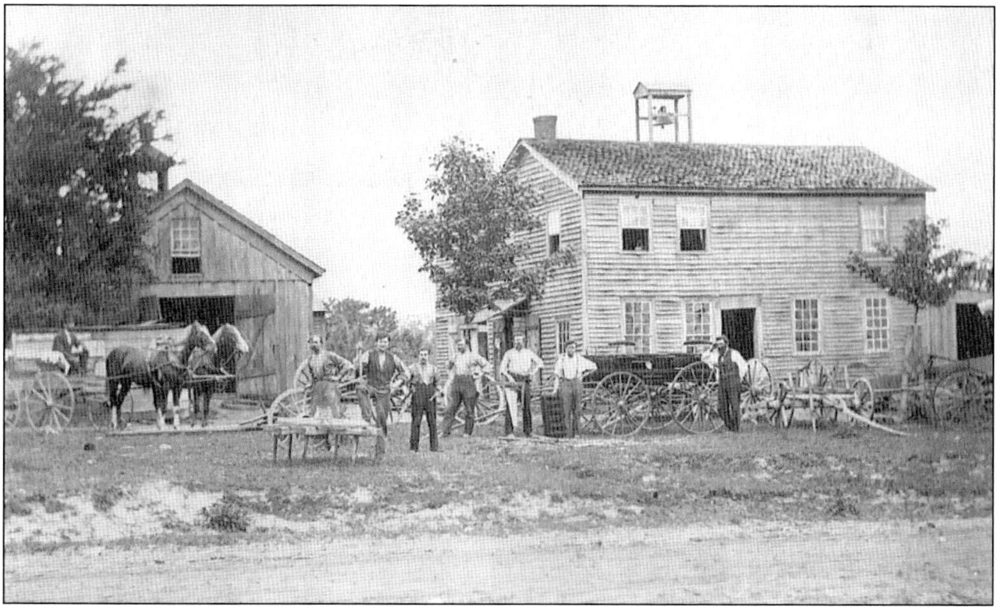

Jacob Mock's Blacksmith Shop and Lewis Mock's Wagon Shop were located on Route 224 across from the present location of the Methodist Church. The Mocks made low wheel piano box buggies and other wagons. The building on the left remains standing today, and the property is owned by Don and Sharon Blosser.

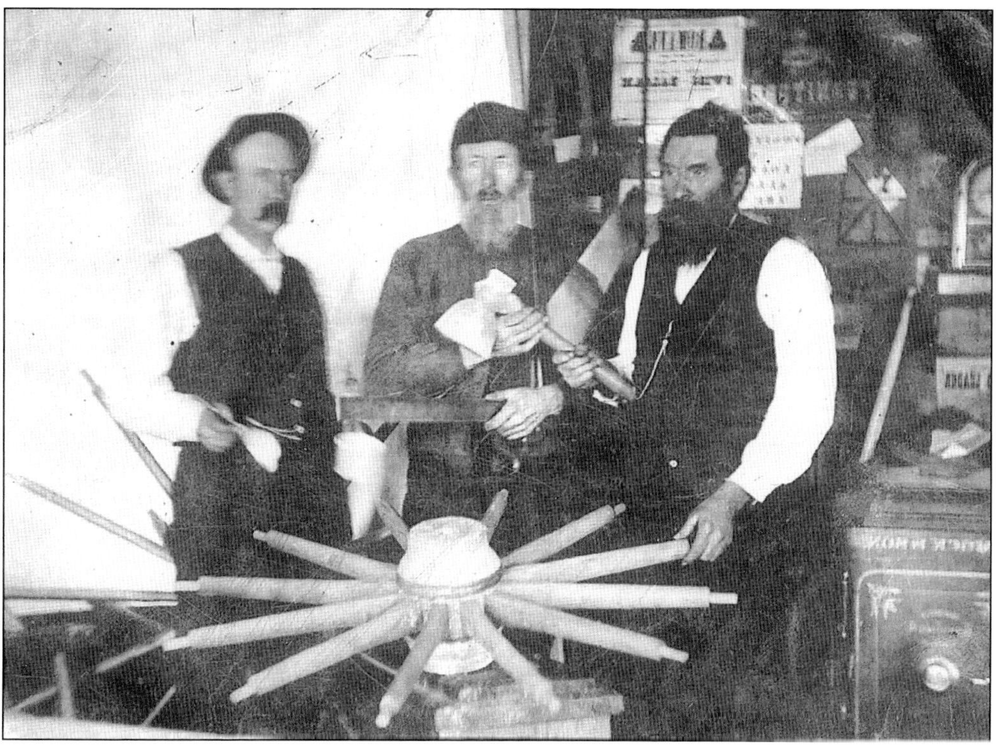

This picture, taken inside the Jacob Mock and Sons Wagon Shop, was printed on a metal plate in reverse. If you hold the picture up to a mirror, the name on the safe can be read.

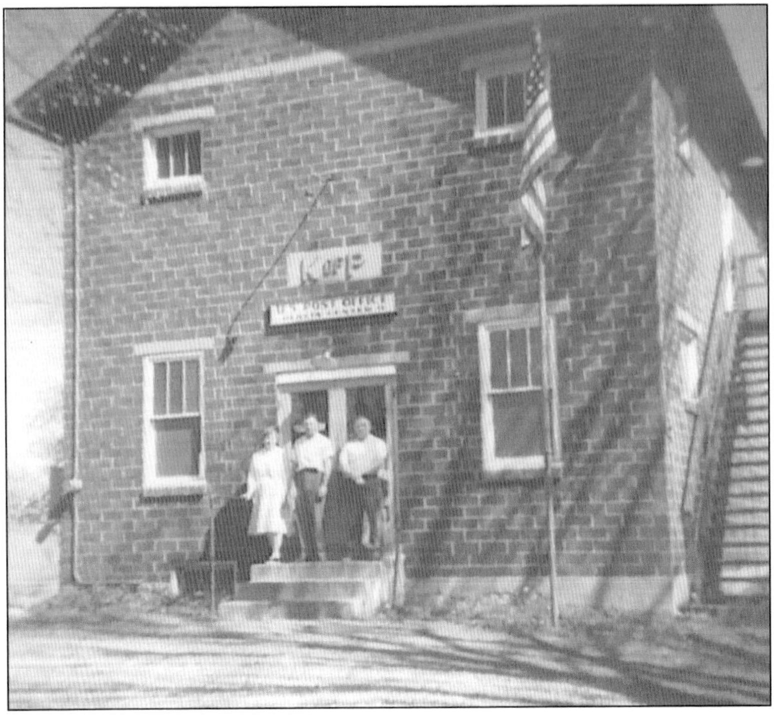

The Knights of Pythias Lodge, active for many years, was located across from the Methodist Church. When Hawkins Store closed, the post office relocated to the front of the lodge building. Because of dwindling membership, the lodge transferred their members to North Jackson, and in 1991, Jesse Meek bought the property and converted the building to apartments. Pictured above are postal workers Janet Kille, Delmus Woolf, and Postmaster Earl (Sandy) Smith. Below is a modern version of the building.

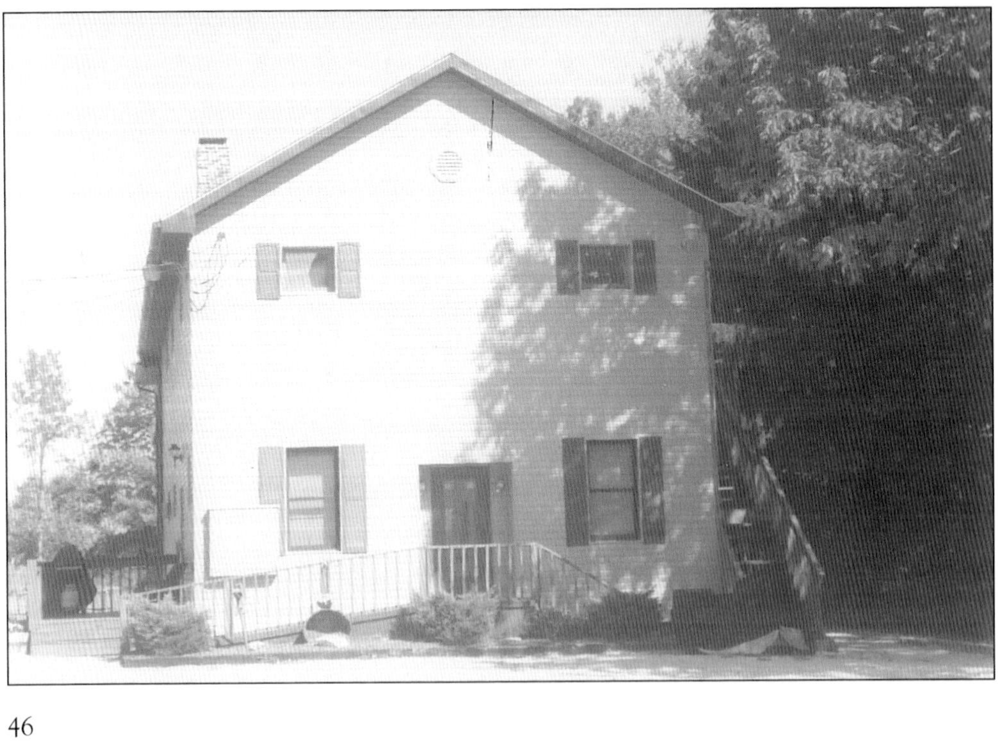

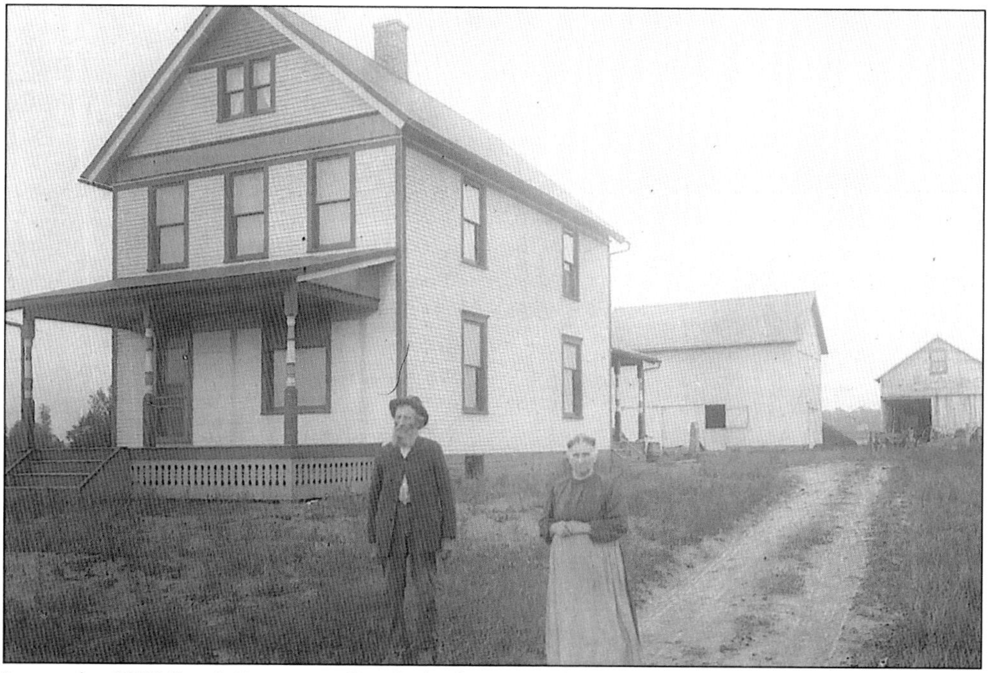

Located at 7275 South Pricetown Road, this house was built by David Harmon in 1908. Pictured in front of the house are David and Emmaline Harmon, grandparents of Addie. Many changes have been made to the house, grounds, and out-buildings by the present owners, Ken and Ruth Craig Canankamp. Pictured below are the Canankamps with their refurbished home, which they purchased in 1960.

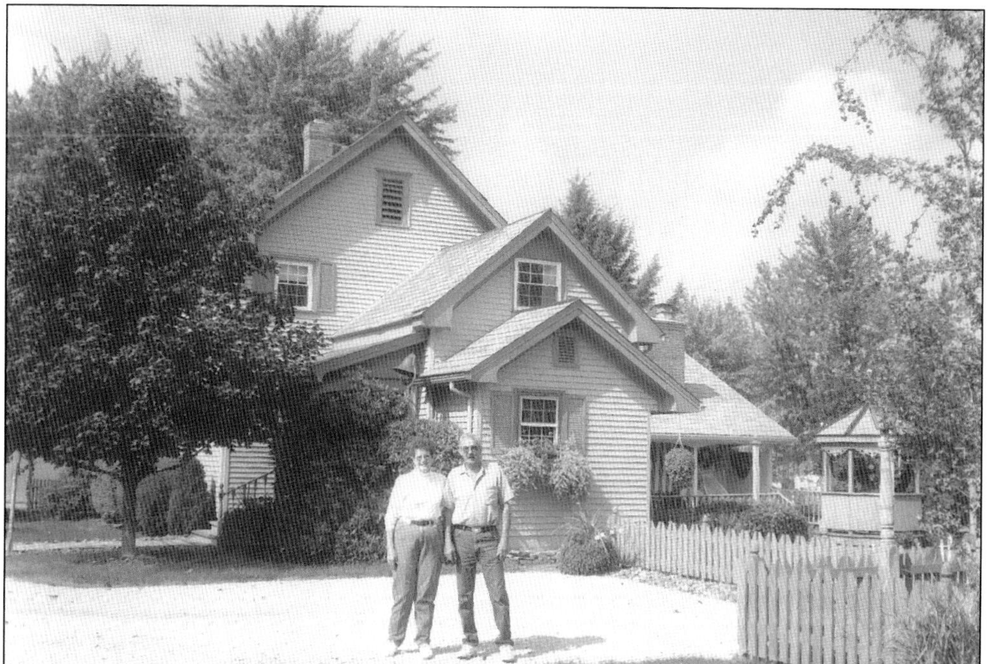

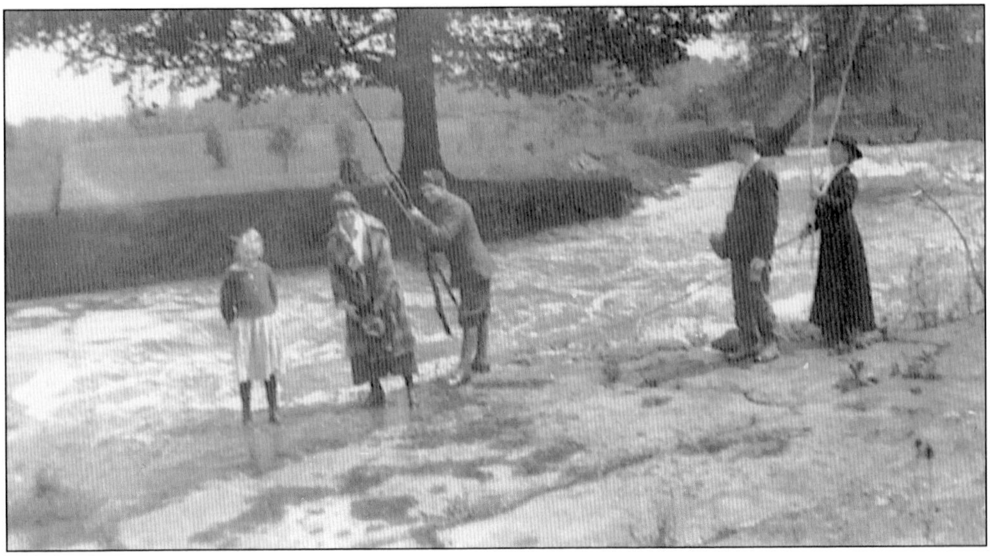

The Bert and Madge Shively home was located at 17270 Berlin Station Road. Pictured above are Roberta Ruggles, Nellie Ruggles, Bill Brooks, Frank Green, and Mabel Green beside the Turkey Broth stream which runs through the farm. Today the property (pictured below) is owned by Bert and Madge's great-granddaughter and her husband, Tina and Lee Smith.

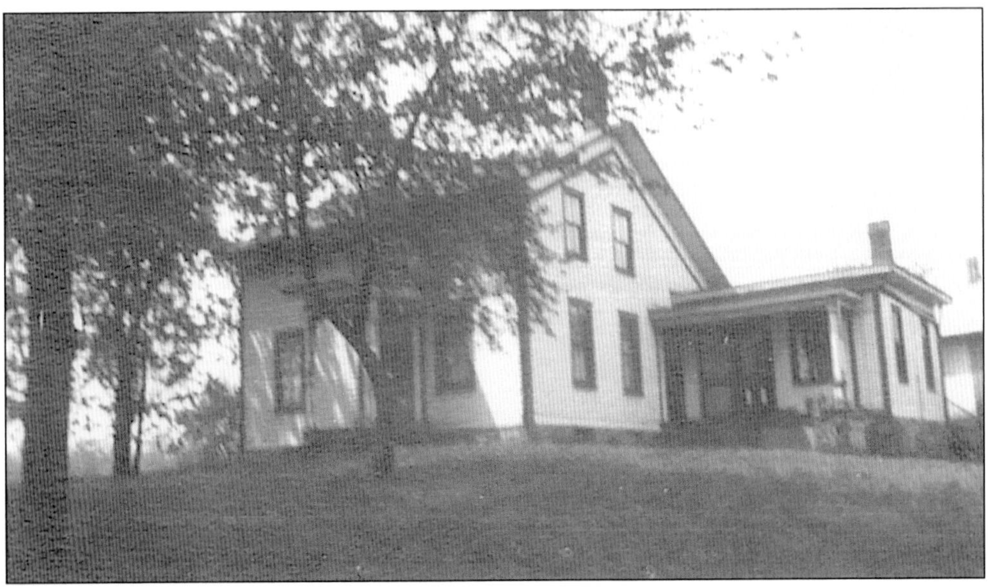

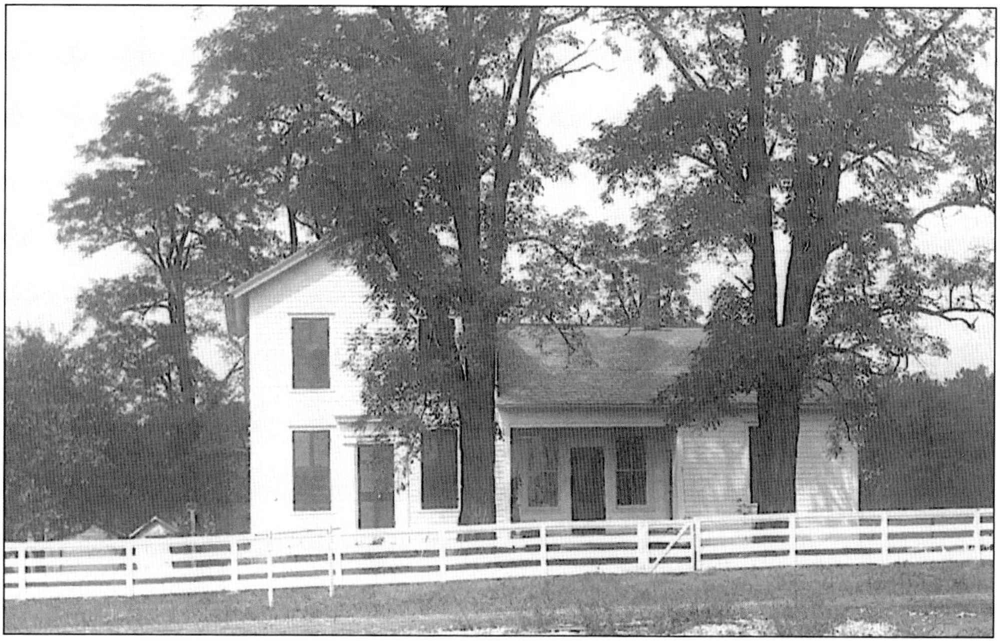

The Wood Felnogle Farm was located on Route 534 at the west end of Hoyle Road. After this home burned, it was replaced with a Sears-Roebuck Catalog house, which was recently remodeled. The barn pictured below was located where Shenandoah Road now intersects Pricetown Road.

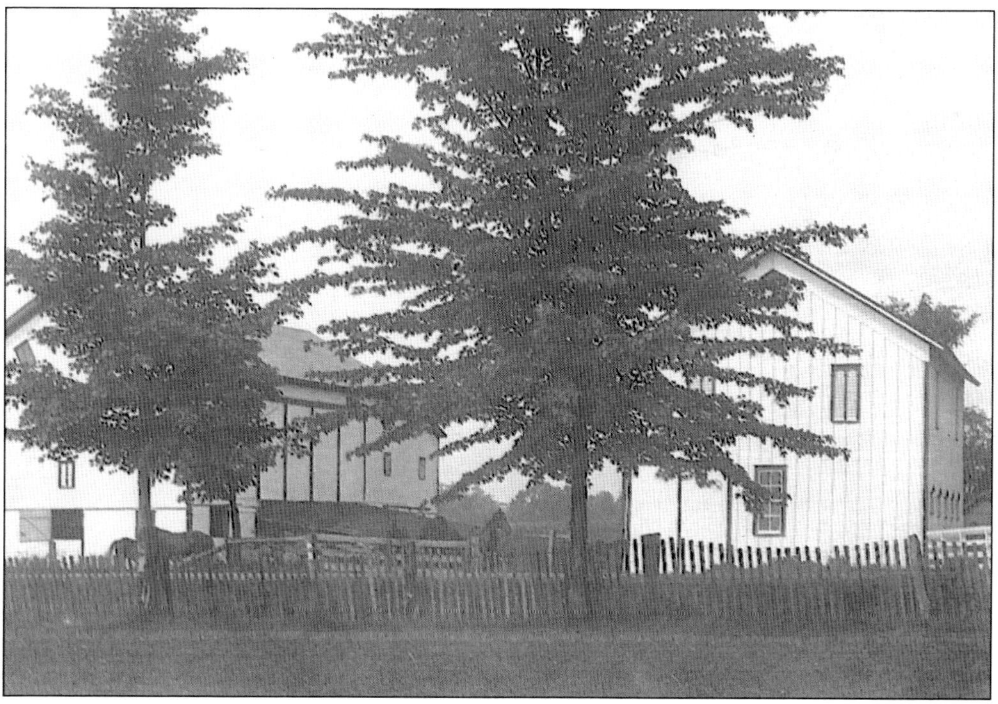

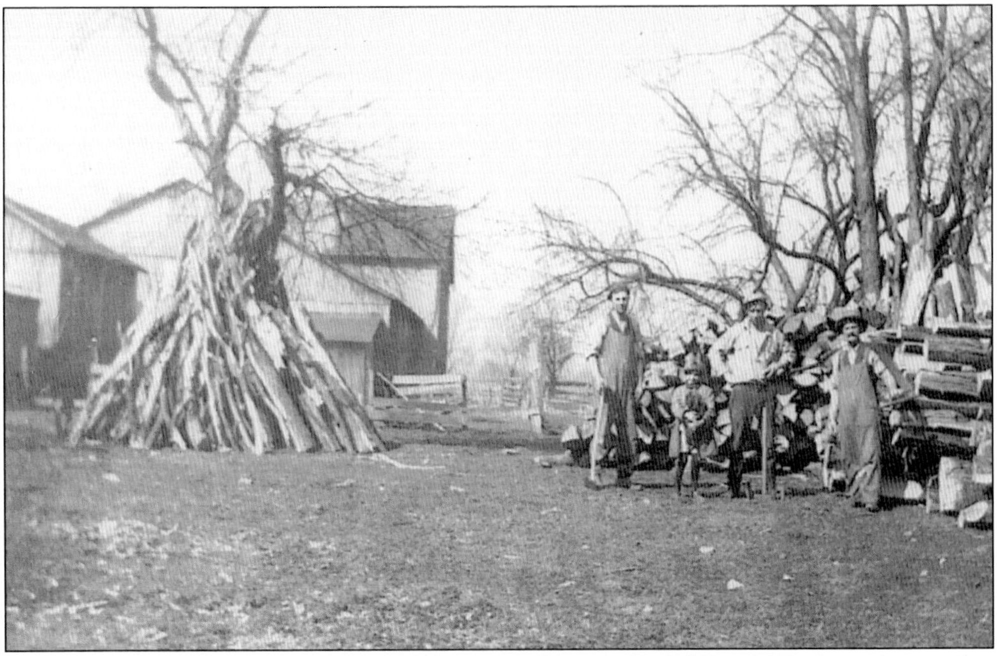

Pictured here is the former Lemuel Bedell homestead at 8424 Bedell Road. The line of ownership also included Earl and Marilla Bedell, John and Mary Hawkins, and the Whitehouse family. The barn burned during the 1970s.

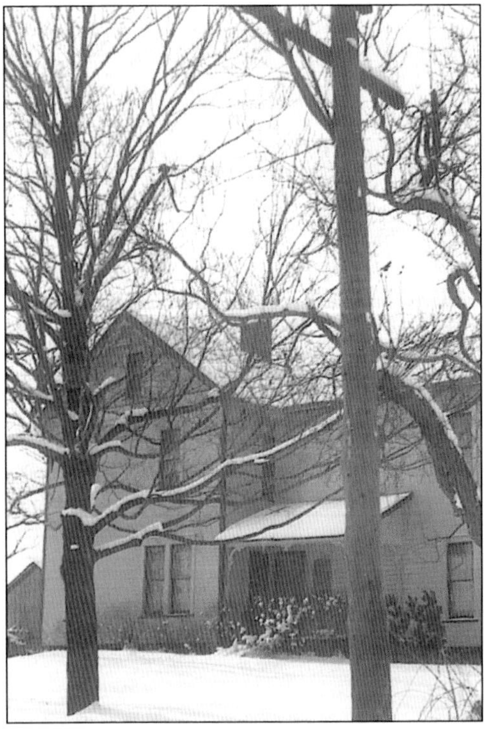

This house is located on the Bedell homestead. The picture was taken when Earl and Marilla Bedell were owners.

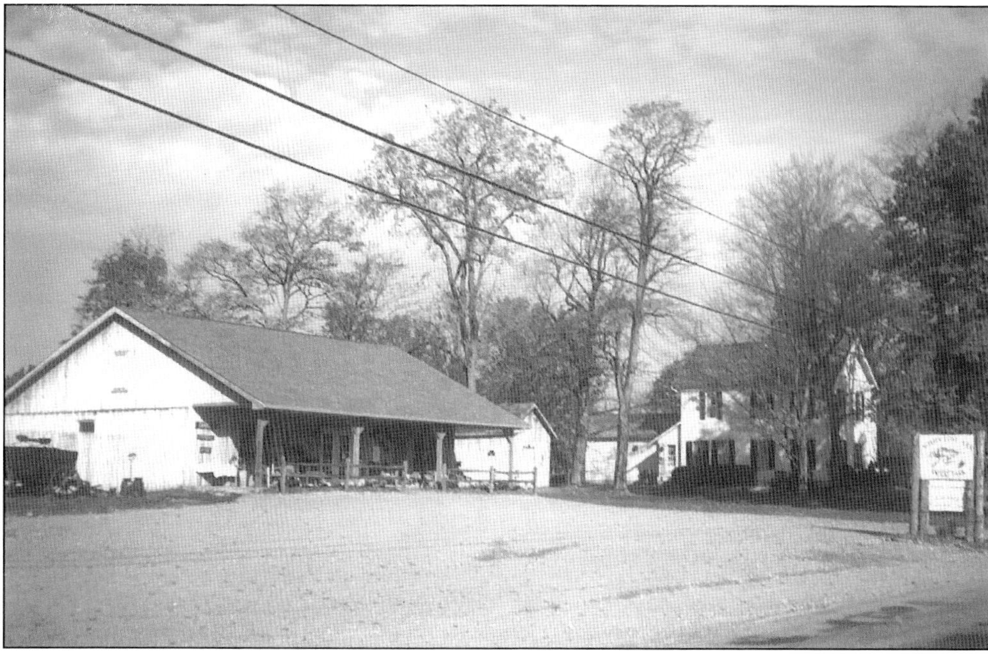

Noah's Lost Ark Animal Park (above) and home at 8424 Bedell Road (below) are owned by Doug and Ellen Whitehouse. They started by raising ostriches, and now have many kinds of exotic animals in a natural zoo setting, which is open to the public.

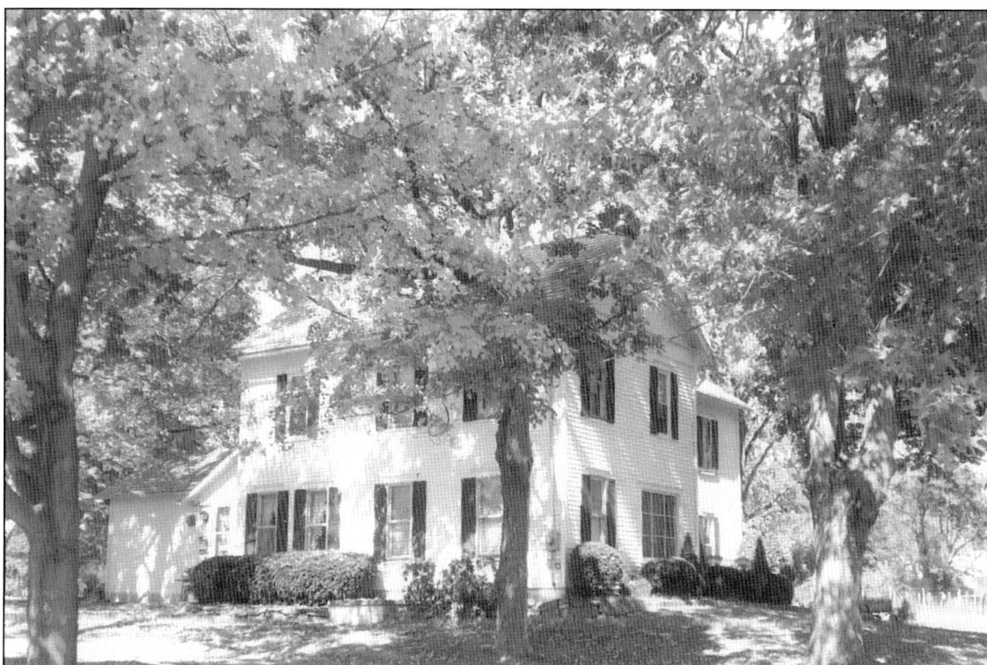

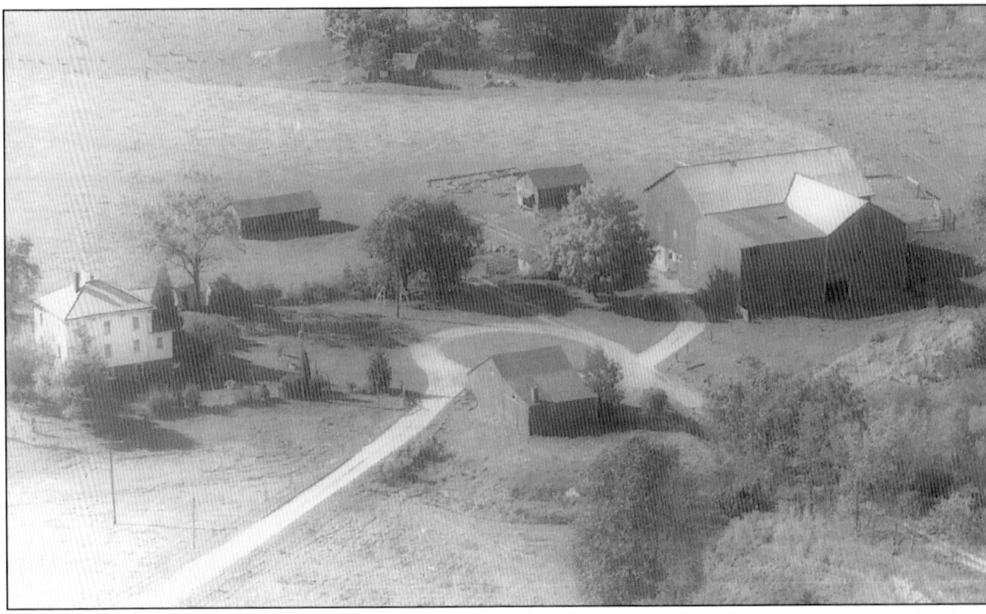

The original homestead of Garrett and Eleanor Packard features a flat, fertile plateau overlooking the Mill Creek that carries the water of Turkey Broth Creek into the Mahoning River. The Packards developed the farm from 1809 until Eleanor's death in 1831. From 1856 until 1914, this home was the residence of Simon and Mary Hartzell. Following Mary's death, Simon sold it to Jacob and Lenora Eshler, in whose family the township's first homestead remains today. A woodcut drawing of the homestead was published in the *Mahoning County Atlas* of 1874.

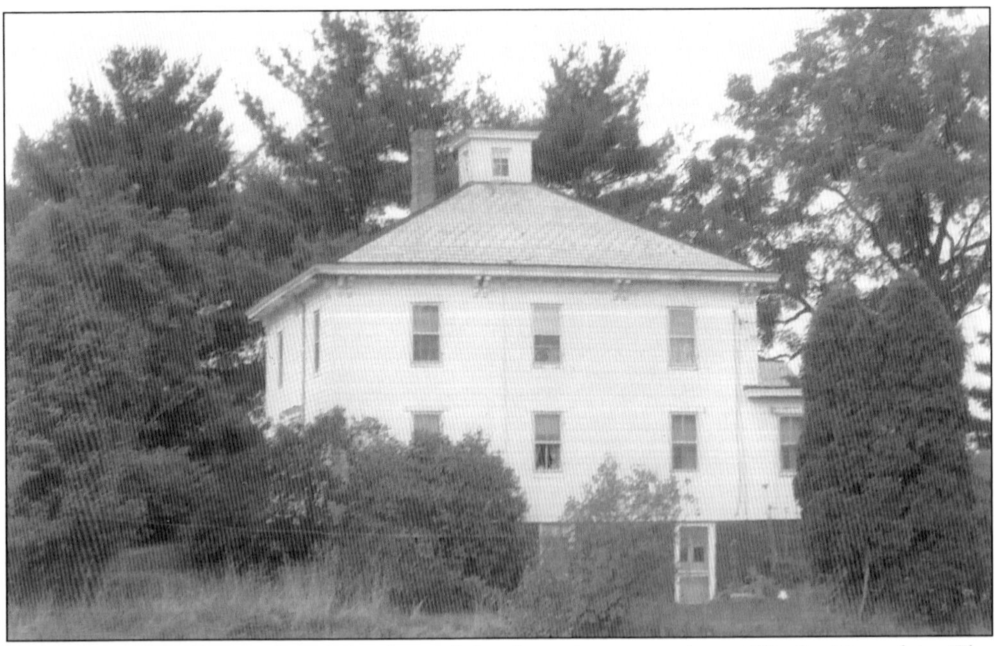

This house, *c.* 1850, stands on the farm of the first pioneer settlers of Berlin Township. The cupola and Victorian Italianate style architecture have made it an easily recognizable landmark in Christytown, the southwest corner of the township for the last century and a half.

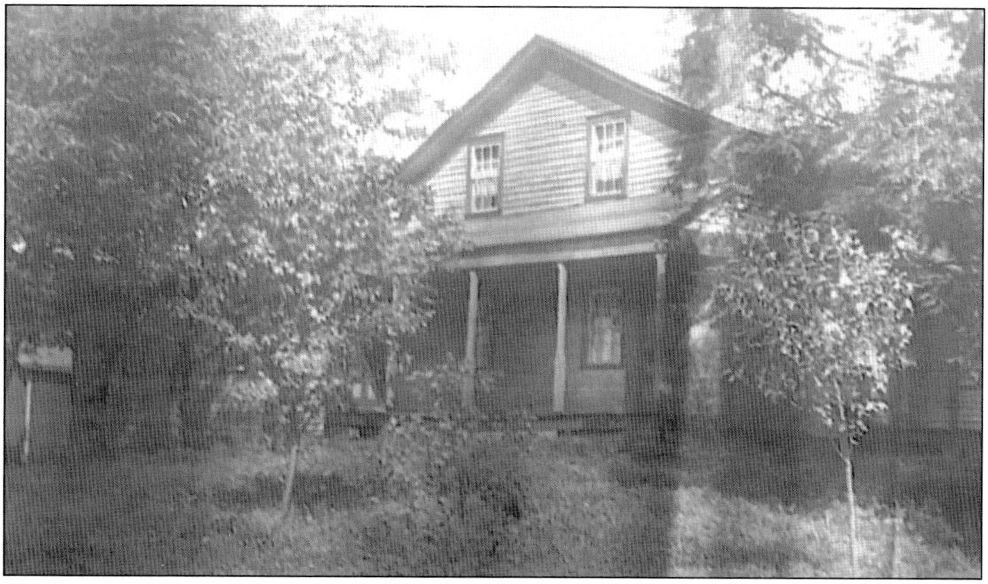

Until the 1980s, this residence, originally known as the Dick Cronick house, was the only home in the village still standing as originally built. It is located east of the center on Route 224 across from the Dairy Isle.

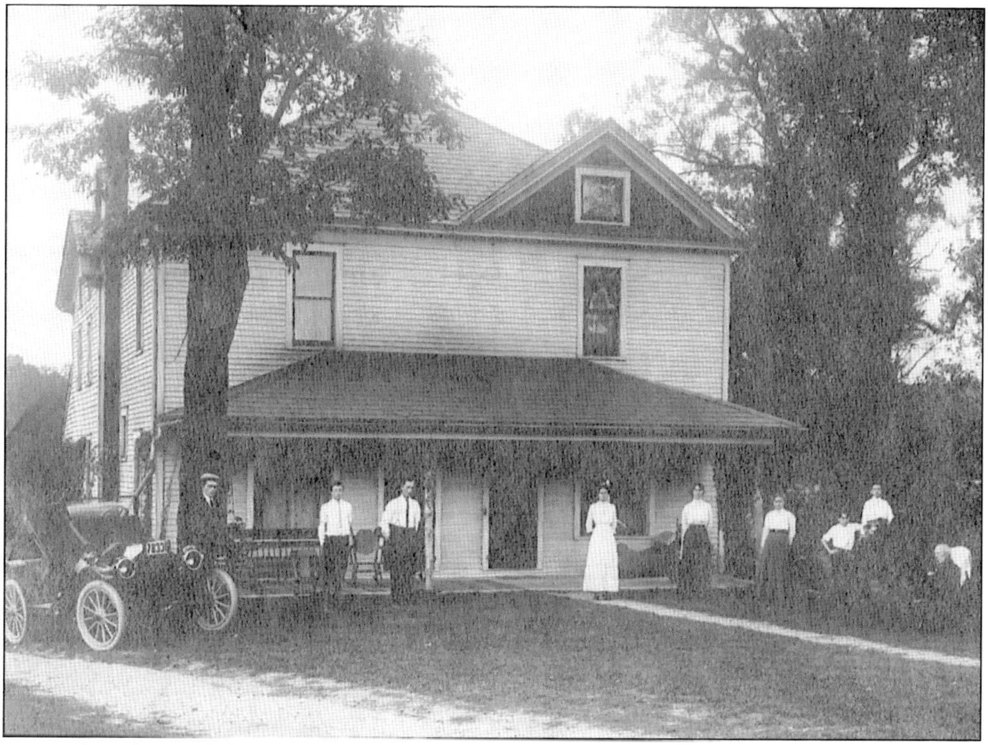

Pictured in front of the Berlin Station Road homestead of Ross and Lenora Hawkins, now owned by Richard Marshall, are, from left to right: Clyde Hawkins, Earl Hawkins, Ross Hawkins, Helen Hawkins, Ethel Hawkins, Lenora Hawkins, and unidentified.

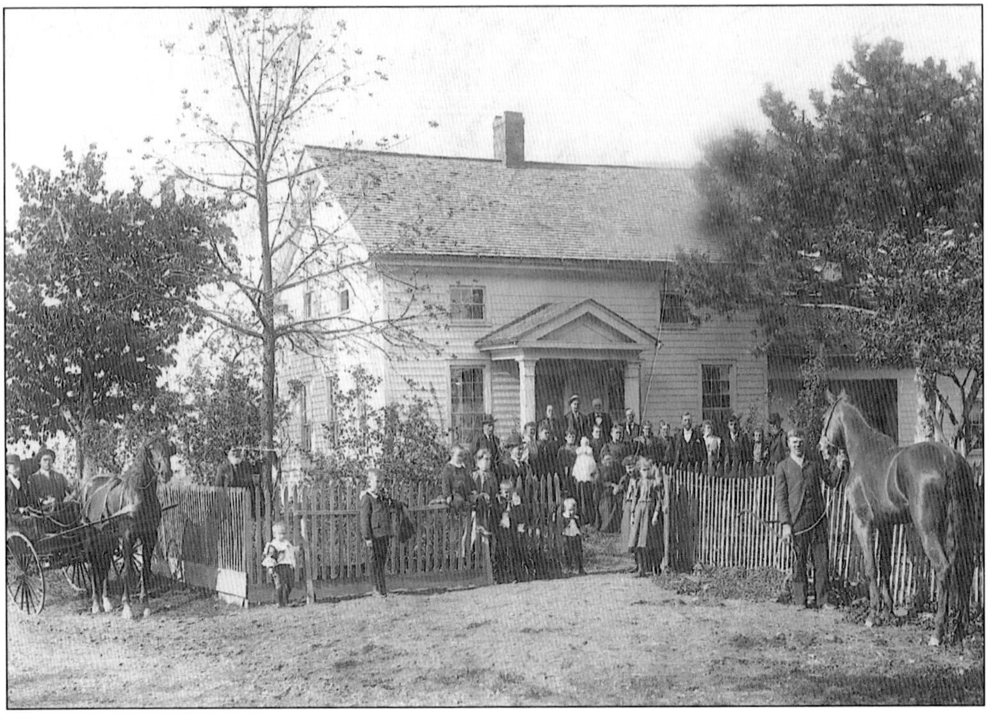

A family gathers at the David Mock home, which remains standing at 16082 Mock Road. An addition has been added to the original house. The young girl in the center by the fence is Pearl Westover (Allen).

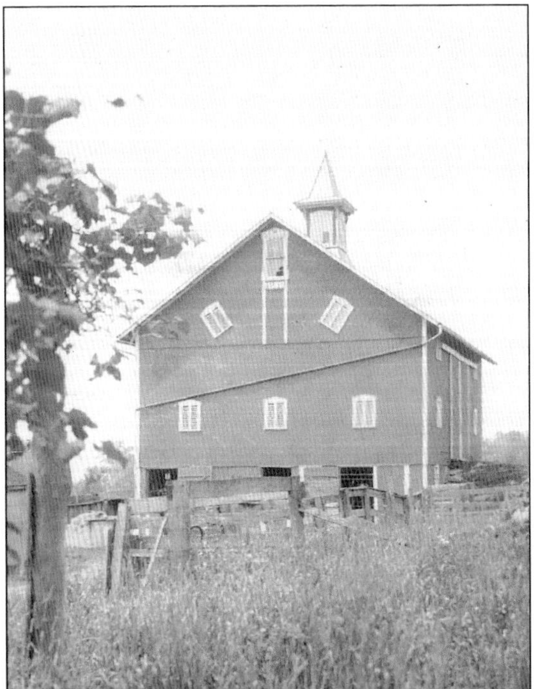

This stately century barn was built on the David Mock farm in 1896.

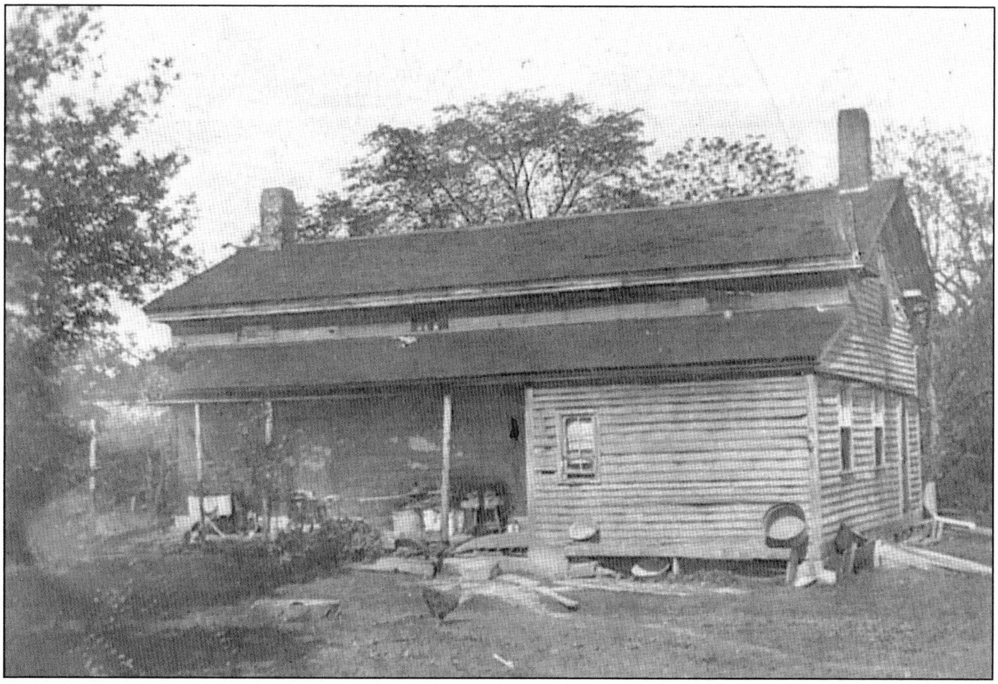

The Hartzell Homestead was located on Bedell Road. Margaret Hartzell's home is built on the land where this house once stood at 5840 Bedell Road.

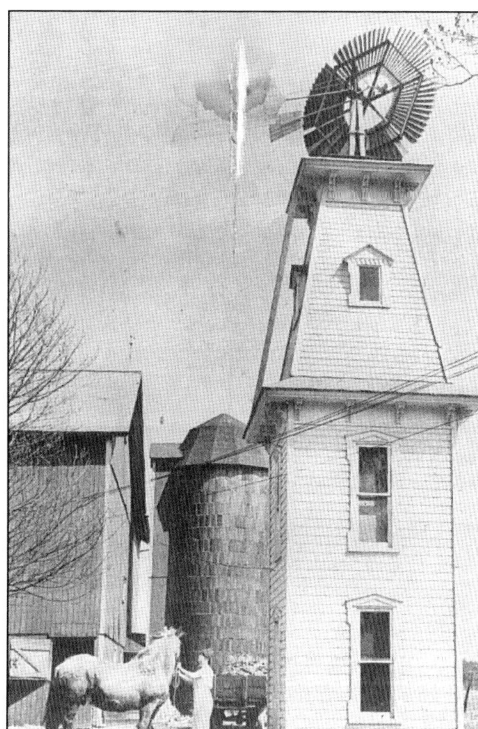

This quaint windmill housing covered a 175-year-old well on the former Charles Dunn farm east of the village on Route 224. It was originally built by Lavosier and Maria DeEtte Hawkins around 1845. John and Cora Diver purchased this home around 1896.

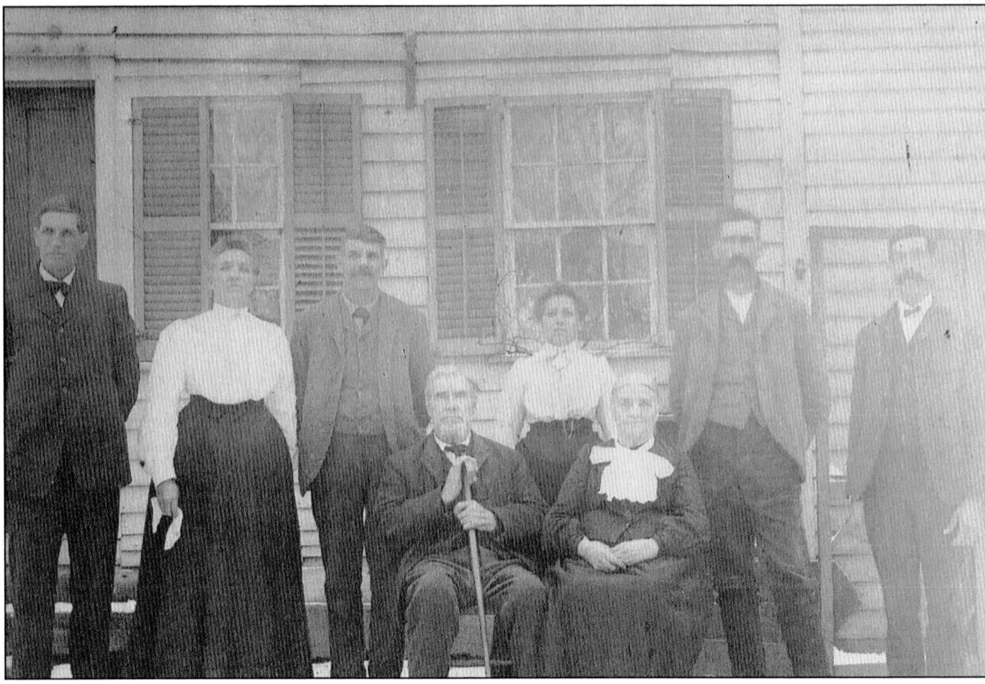

The homestead of Chester and Mary Hartzell Bedell stood on Leffingwell Road near Bedell Road around the turn of the century. Pictured from left to right are Lemuel, Jane, Henry, Anna, James, and Isaac. Seated are Chester and Mary. A daughter, Elsie, was absent from the photograph.

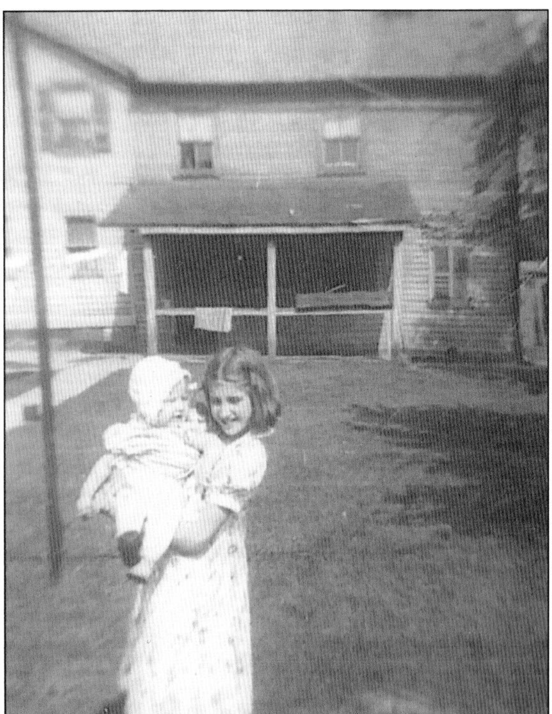

Glenn and Minerva Burkey and their family lived in the Chester Bedell homestead in 1943. Pictured is Caroline Burkey holding her sister Nancy.

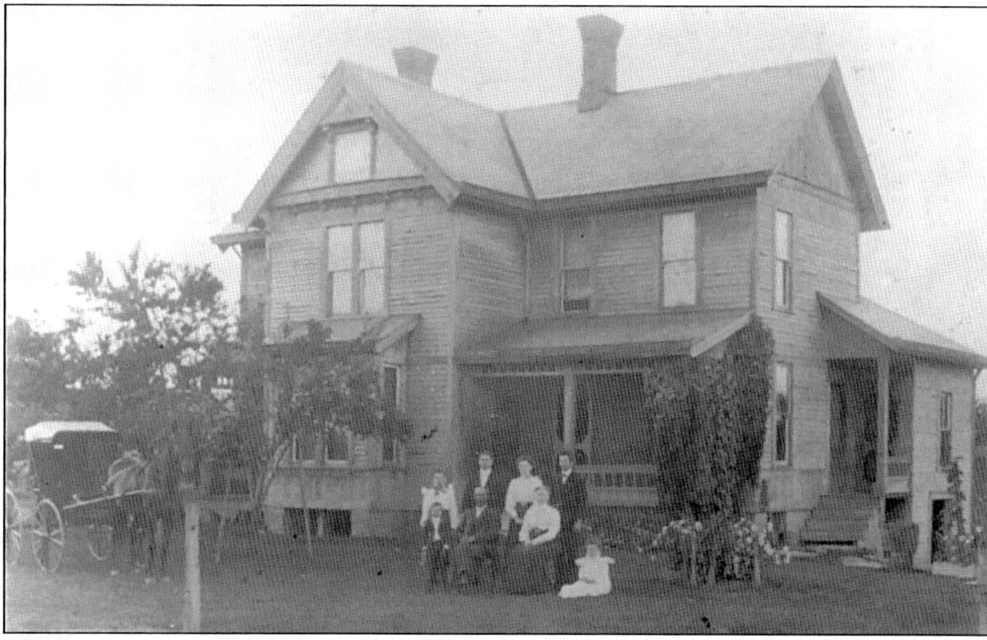

This turn-of-the-century photograph features the Amos and Clara Carson Hoyle home, built by Amos Hoyle in 1885. The family had lived in a log cabin on the other side of Turkey Broth Creek, but changed the path of the creek to claim land upon which to build this house. Pictured are the Hoyle family from left to right: (front row) Charles C., Amos, Clara Carson, and (Emma) Hazel; (back row) Mabel E., Ford E., Maud L., and Earl C. The present owners are Richard and Pam Hoyle, the fifth generation of Hoyles to own this land.

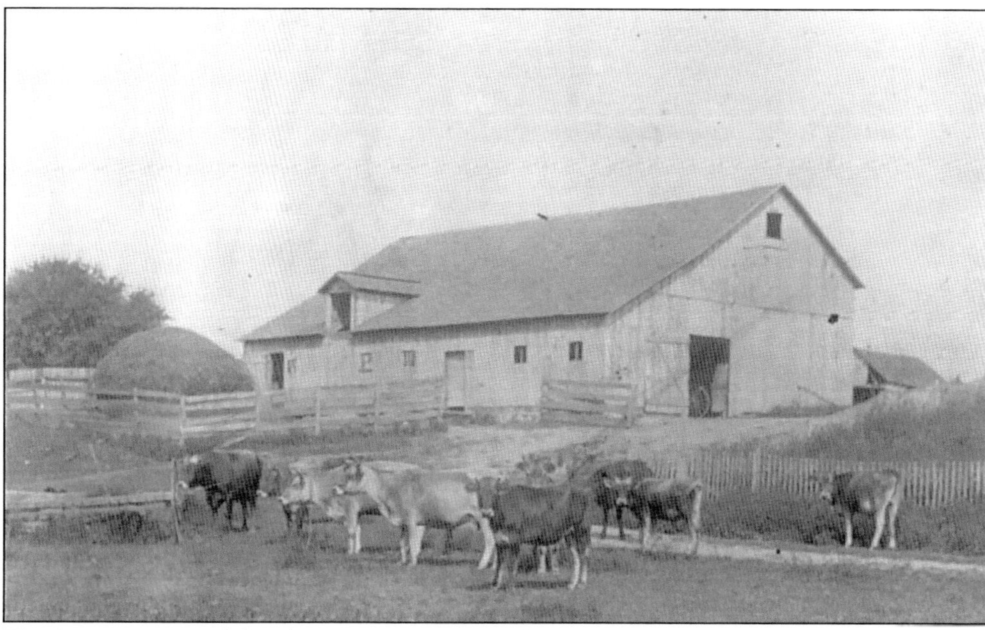

This barn was part of the above Hoyle homestead located on Hoyle Road. When it was taken down in 1999, part of the barn was used to construct a smaller building at the Rick and Coleen Truitt home at 6875 South Pricetown Road.

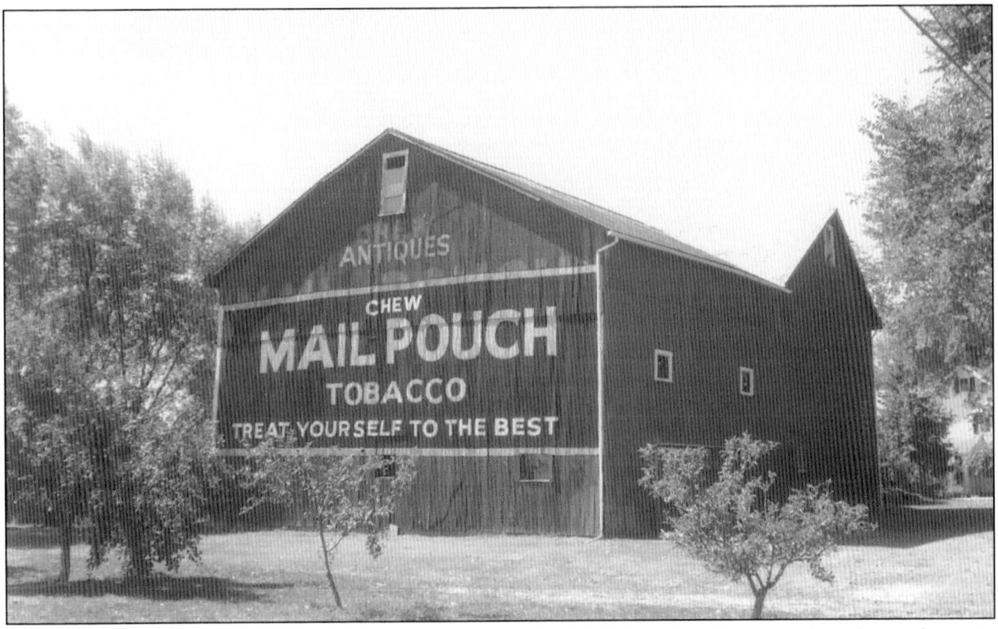

Pictured here is the only remaining advertisement for Mail Pouch tobacco painted on a barn in Berlin Township. The barn is owned by John and Margaret Murvay, and is located at 17287 W. Akron-Canfield Road.

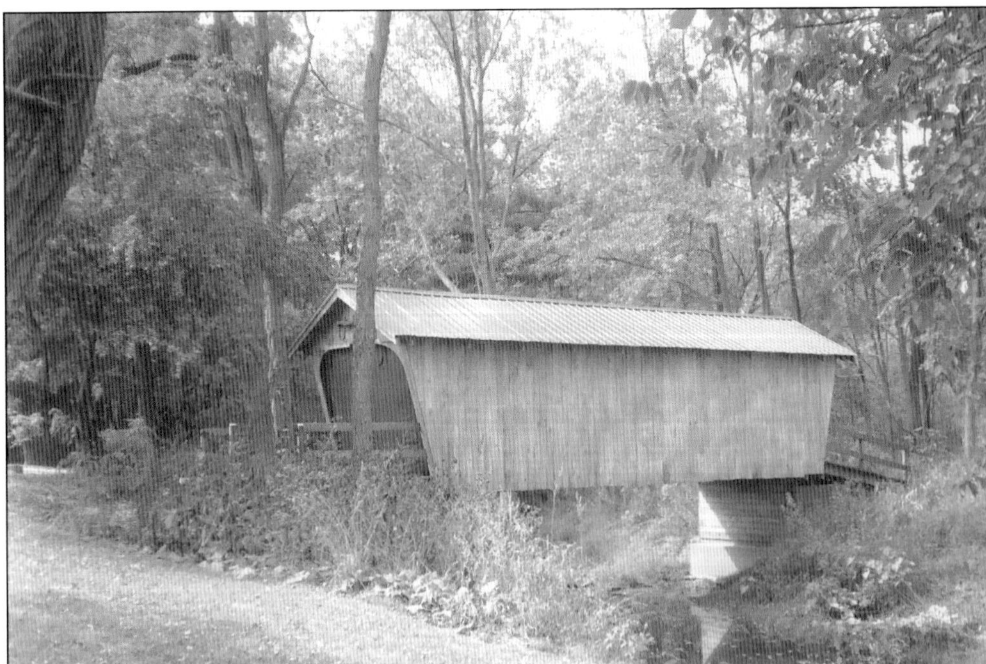

A replica of a covered bridge over Turkey Broth Creek was built in 1998 west of the village on Route 224 (Akron-Canfield Road). It is owned by Howard Wiggs.

Four

ORGANIZATIONS AND CHURCHES

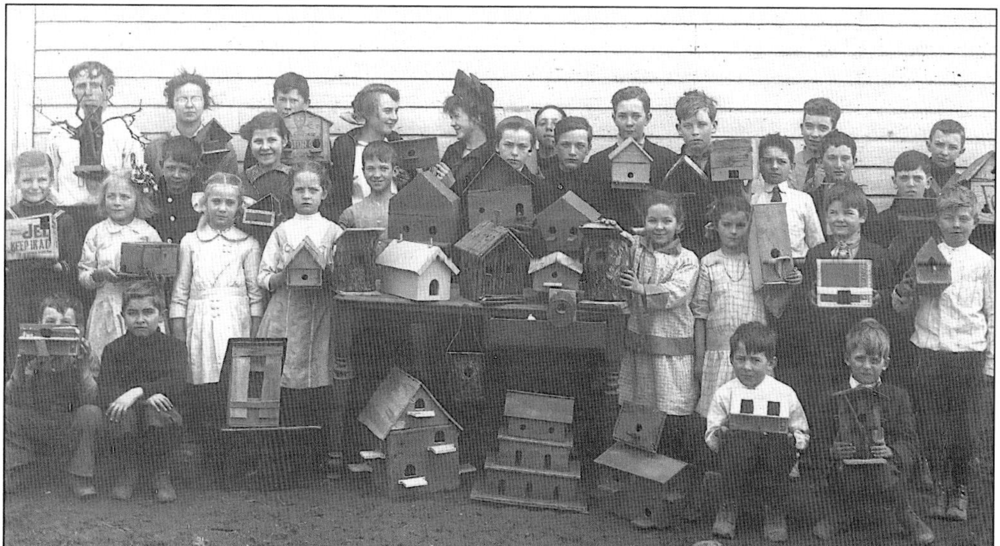

The Berlin Center Bird Club displays their handmade bird houses in 1915. One boy has been credited with making 25 of them. Pictured from left to right are, as follows: (first row) Robert Ruggles, Bennie Killie, Myron Renkenberger, and Orrie Diver; (second row) Violet Kime, Gladen Ruggles, Leta Lewis, Alene Cline, Mary Cover, Lucy Diver, Forrest Newell, and Stewart Burkey; (third row) Myron Hawn, Alice Hartzell, Richard Hawkins, Tressel Hawkins, John Hawkins, Jessie Carver, and Howard Best; (fourth row) Lindley Vickers, Theo Cattell, Layfayette Burnette, Hazel Siddel, Carol Hawkins, Foster Hilles, Frank Cline, Victor Himes, Frank Green, and Wallace Heiser.

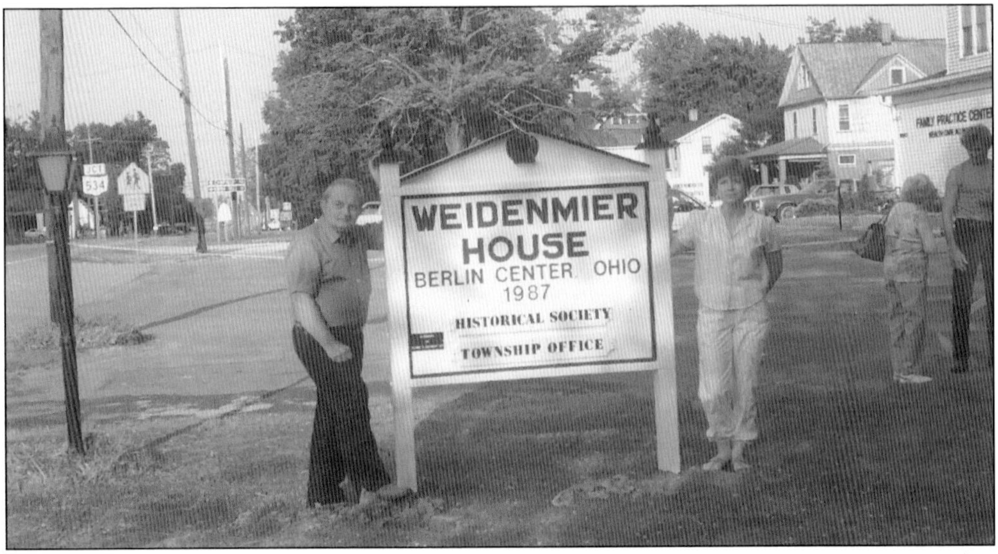

The original Weidenmier House sign was erected in 1991. Historical Society member Joe Ondreko (left) made the sign, and Kathy Moser (right) lettered it. The Junior Delmont family donated the cost of the sign in his memory. Showing evidence of wear, the sign was replaced in 1999 with a newly designed model made of recycled plastic material. The design matched the recycled plastic signs placed by the Berlin Trustees at the four main entrances to the township in 1998.

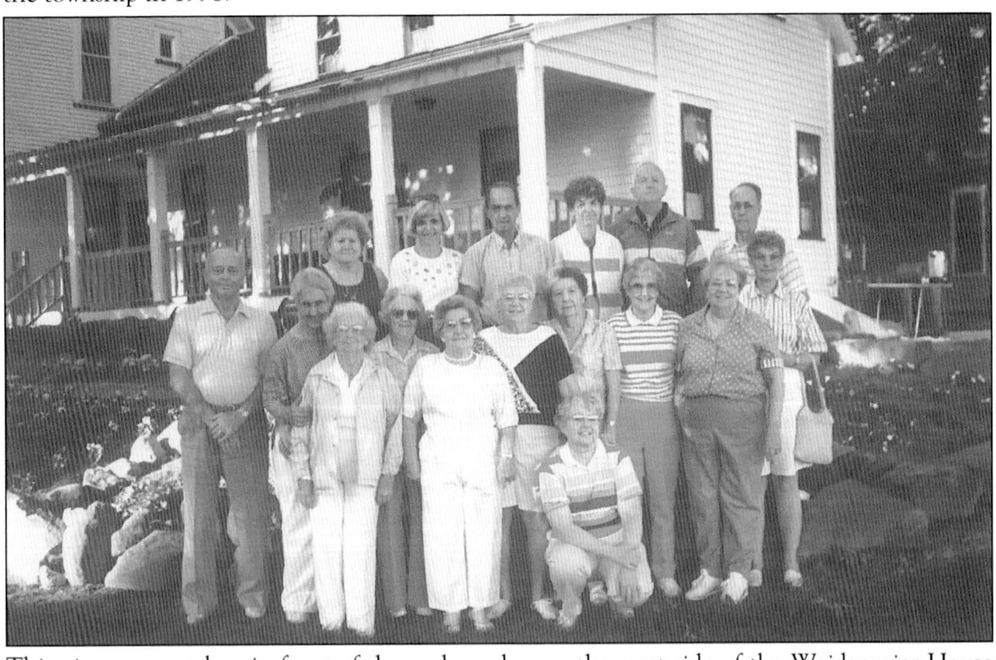

This picture was taken in front of the rock garden on the west side of the Weidenmier House during a 1992 meeting of the Berlin Center Historical Society. Members from left to right include, as follows: (front row) Bessie Eshler, Mary Eshler, and Barbara Hoyle; (middle row) Kenny Engle, Helen Engle, Theresa Thomas, Viola Clark, Peggy Graham (a Florida visitor), Evelyn Obenauf, Gloria Marteney, and Twilla Brown; (back row) Helen Weir, Sandie Engle, Dick Engle, Mary Hawkins, John Hawkins, and Al Marteney.

Shown moving the statue of Chester Bedell to the Weidenmier House in 1993 are, from left to right, Dick Engle, Ivan Hoyle, and John Hawkins. The Bedell family has loaned the statue to the Berlin Center Historical Society for display in their museum.

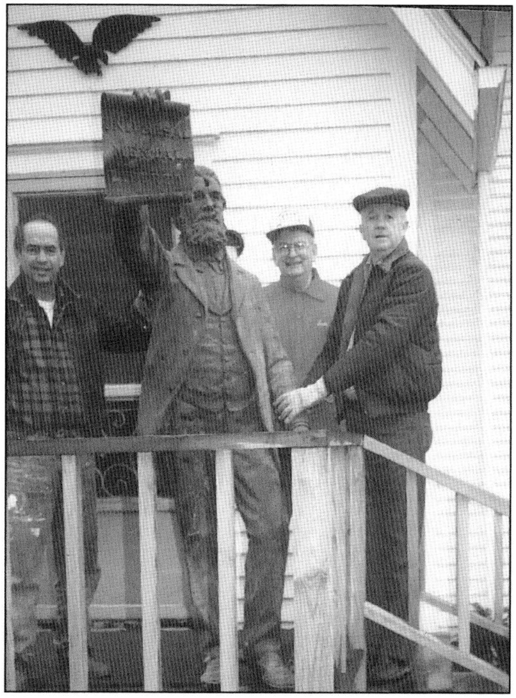

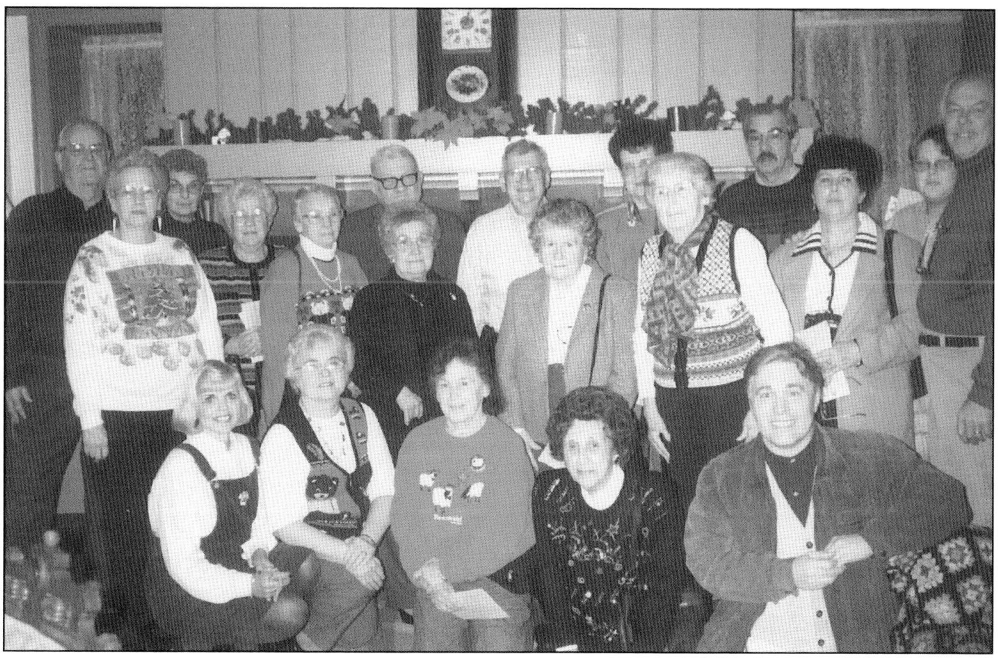

The Historical Society sponsored a tour of the historical Strock Stone house, operated by the Austintown Historical Society. Pictured are, from left to right, as follows: (front row) Sandie Engle, Barbara Hoyle, Jennie Halczak, Genevieve Hutzel, and Ron Eshler; (middle row) Marge Noble, Edith Kale, Helen Weir, Maxine Hilles, and Gerry and Bruce Thompson; (back row) Dick Noble, Twilla Brown, Viola Clark, Grover Griggs, Ivan Hoyle, Ruth and Ken Canankamp, and Winston Thompson.

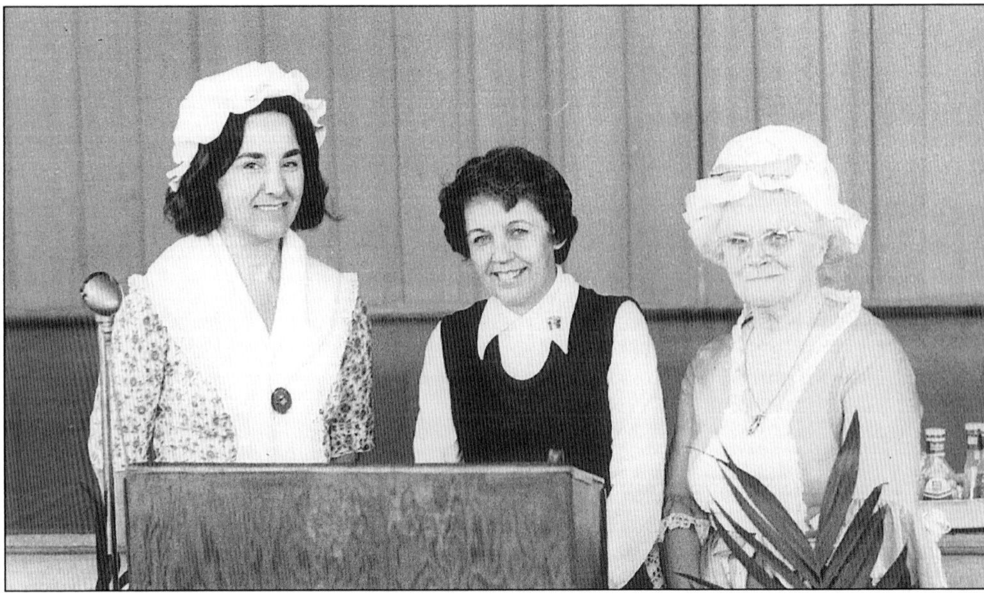

About 190 women attended this Abigail Adams luncheon, held in April of 1976 as part of the bicentennial celebration. Betty Didur had the oldest dress, Sandra Engle the best new colonial dress, and Maxine Hilles the most original dress. Pictured from left to right are Juliann Kreca, luncheon chairperson; Juanita Roderick, speaker from Youngstown State University; and Beulah Weidenmier, general chairperson of the Bicentennial Committee.

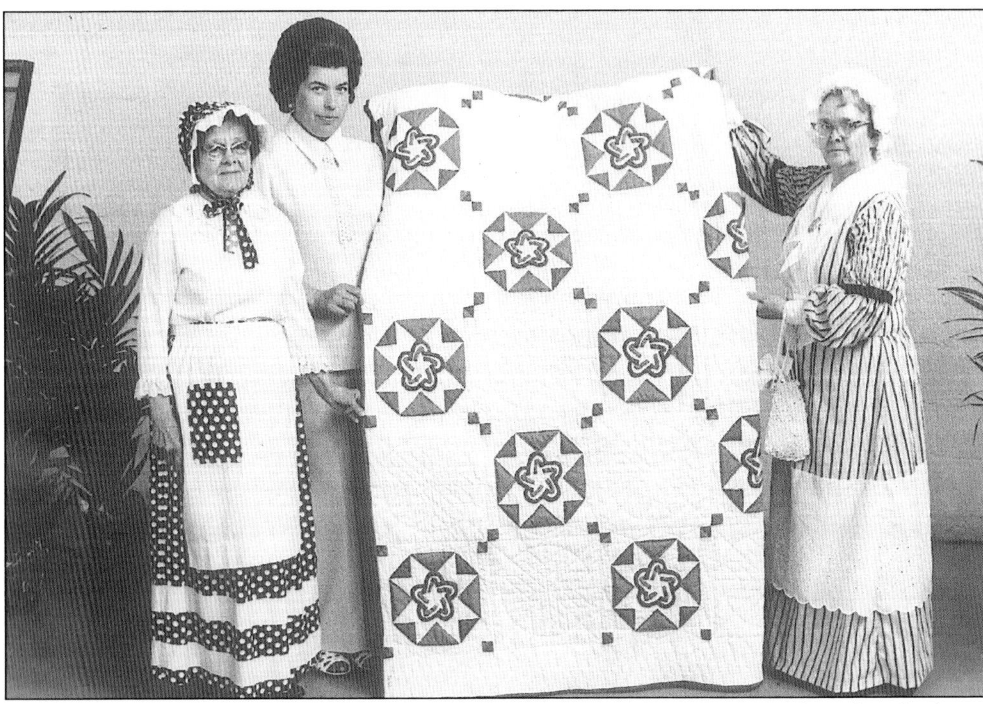

Several ladies of the Mt. Moriah Lutheran Church pieced the Bicentennial Quilt, which was presented to the Bicentennial Committee by (left to right) Christine Hacker, Helen Reed, and Laura Confoey for auction at the Western Reserve School.

In June of 1976, an event of the bicentennial celebration was held at the Western Reserve High School. Frank Green was greeted by Leonard Mace, whose colonial suit was handmade by his wife Carol.

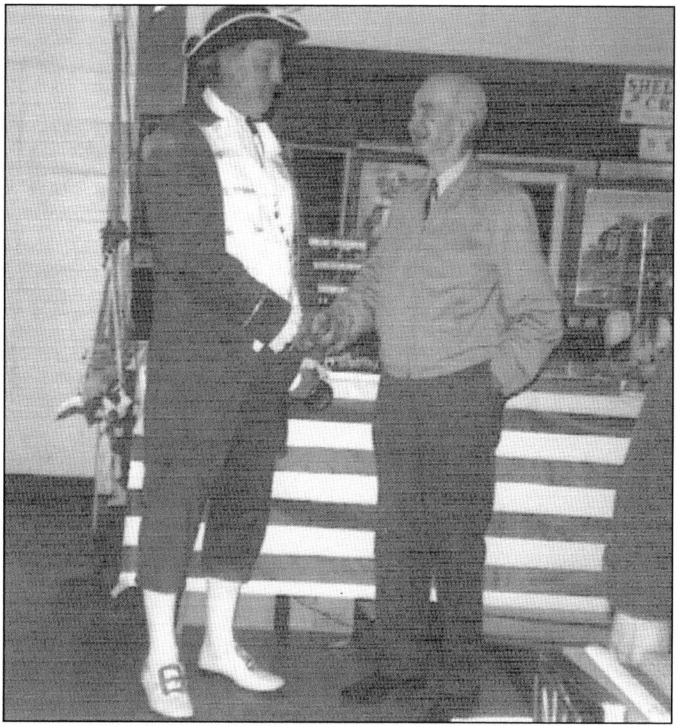

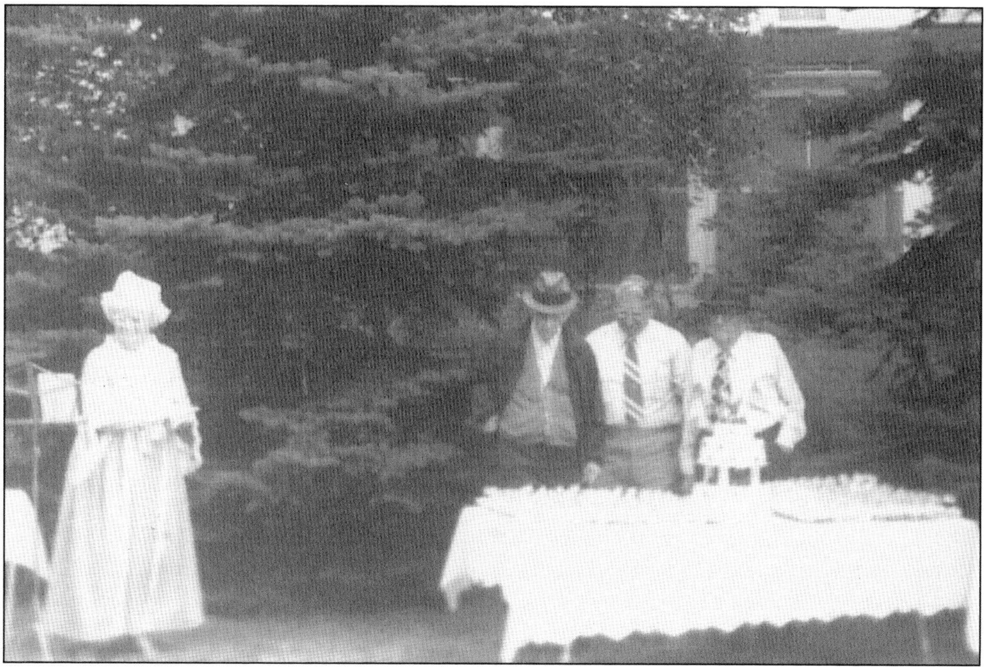

During the Fourth of July bicentennial celebration, a gathering was held at the home of Dr. Carl and Beulah Weidenmier. Many bells were displayed and rung. Pictured from left to right are Beulah Weidenmier, Roy Renkenberger, Myron Young, and Albert Yeager. The gentlemen, both in their nineties, were honored as the oldest residents in Berlin and Ellsworth Townships.

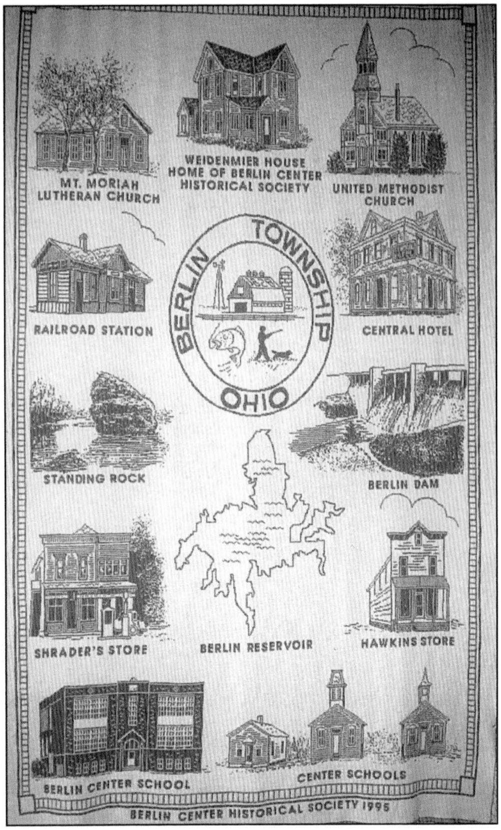

In 1995, the Berlin Center Historical Society designed throws using photographs of various landmarks and early buildings from the township. The cranberry red and wedgewood blue throws sold for $35 each. The historical society was initiated when a group of interested residents gathered at Beulah Weidenmier's house on April 14, 1987. They agreed to serve as organizers, and gained a charter on October 15, 1987. Currently, the historical society holds regular meetings at the Weidenmier House, where the museum is maintained.

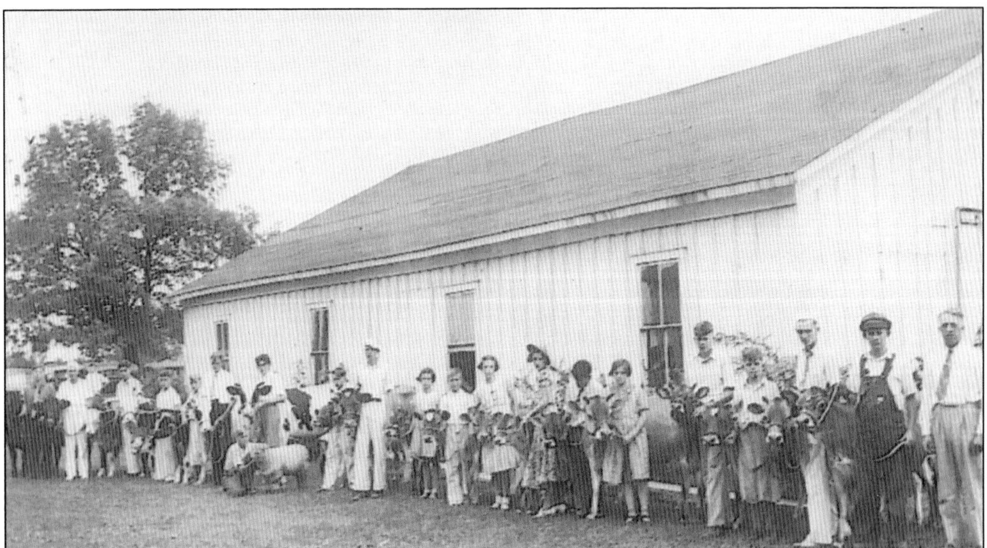

Berlin Busy Boys 4-H Club at the 1937 Canfield Fair are, from left to right, as follows: Dick Noble, Bob Noble, Raymond Anderson, Junior Woolman, Malcolm Obenauf, Robert Coman, Forrest Kale, Dick Bean, Randall Baringer, Calvin Baringer, Marjean Conkle, Virgil Hoyle, Dolores Conkle, Rema Fields, unidentified, Joann Conkle, Jim Craig, Dick Craig, Kenneth Obenauf, Adair Allen, and Russell Ward, advisor.

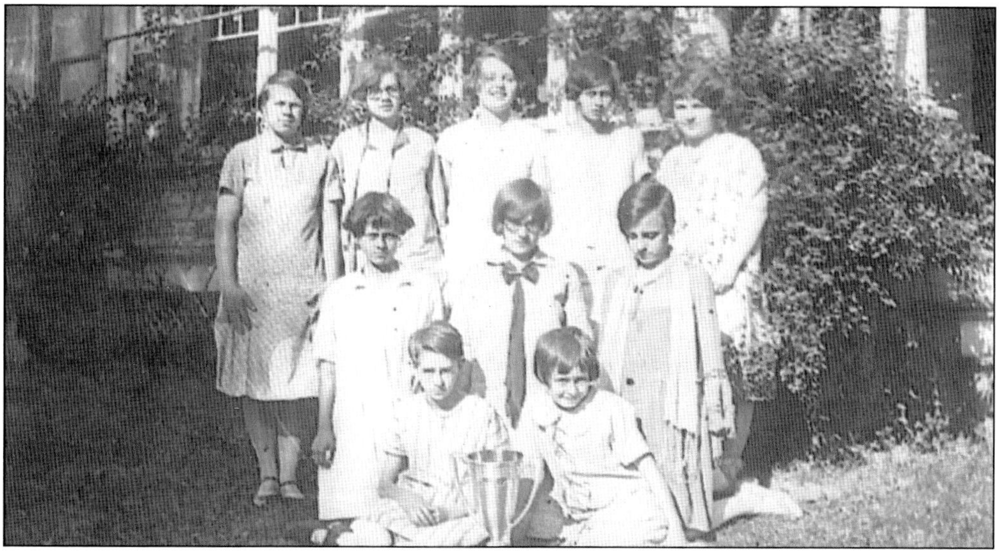

Berlin Happy Workers 4-H Club in 1926 are pictured with their Loving Cup award. Mary Cover served as the club leader, and members consisted of Ethel Stallsmith, Lois Summers, Veva Paxon, Dorothy Stallsmith, Sara Shrader, Mildred Eshler, Virginia Florence, Dorothy Davis, and Celia Goodman (order unknown).

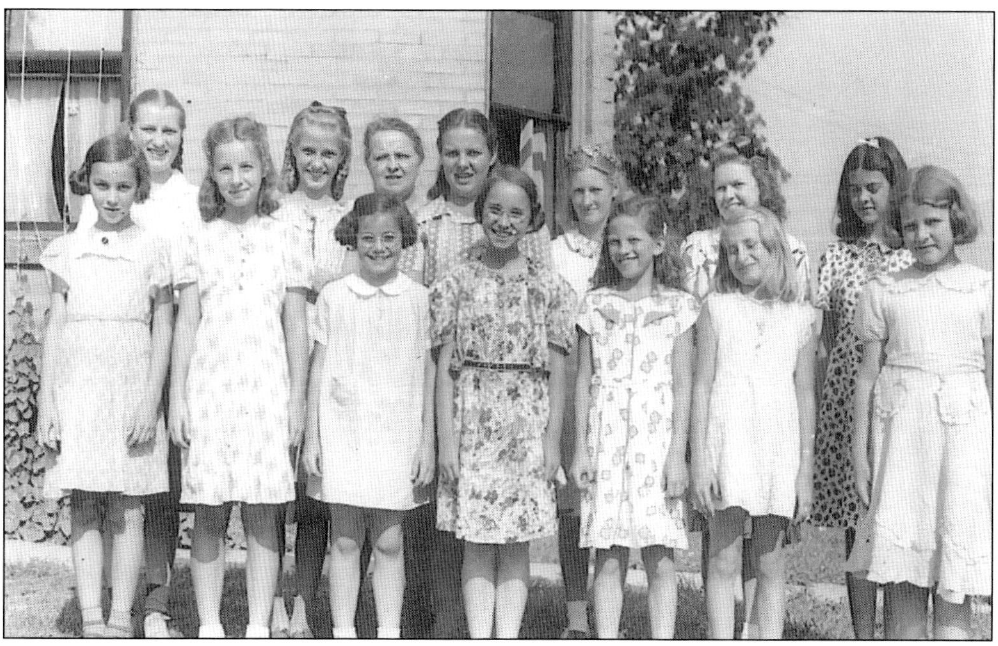

The Berlin Sunshine Workers 4-H Club poses for a 1940 photograph at the Rakestraw home. Pictured from left to right are, as follows: (front row) Joyce Conkle, Veva Hoyle, Gay Nell Conkle, Martha Briet, Janet Rakestraw, Genevieve Simms, and Nina Dudley; (back row) Marjorie Rakestraw, Eloise Rakestraw, Theo Smith (club leader), Opal Smith, Vera Olson, Virginia Bardo, and LaDonna Bedell.

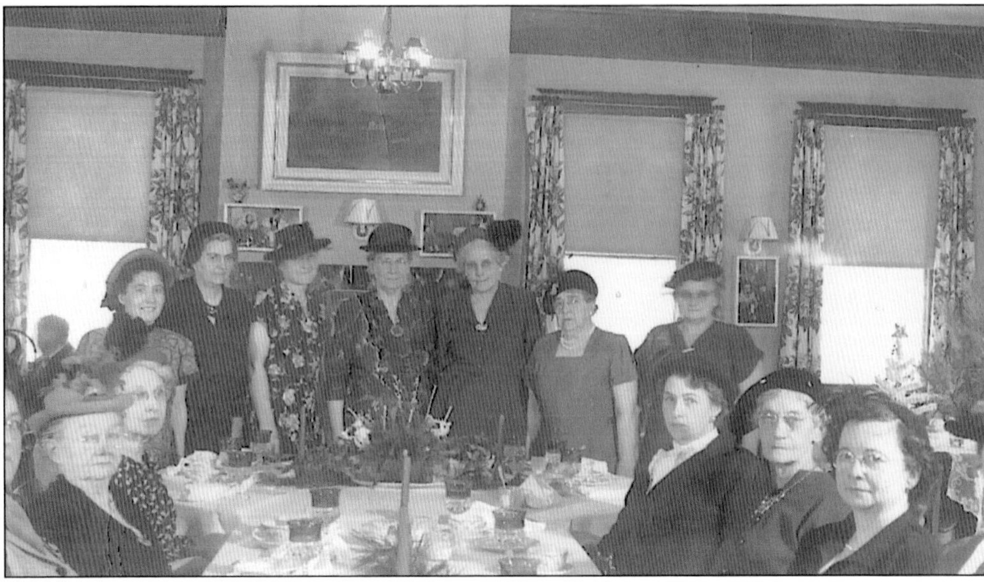

The Christytown Happy Thought Club was begun by Marilla Bedell for the ladies of the Christytown area in 1923. Pictured at this 1951 gathering are, from left to right, as follows: Ethel McEldowney, Nora Eshler, Hazel Myers, Mary Eshler, Marilla Bedell, Elsie Franks, Madge Shively, Phoebe Renkenberger, Rose Bedell, Alice Grimes, Bessie Burkey, Pearl King, Bessie Eshler, and Sally Coleman.

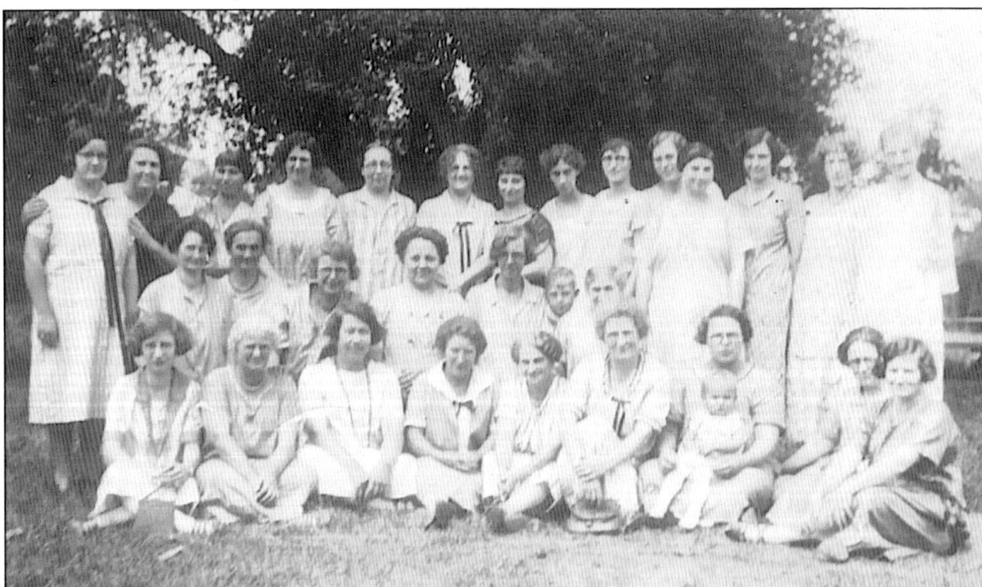

Pictured at a Home Extension Picnic in the early 1900s are, from left to right: (front row) Grace Hoyle, Mrs. Jenkins, Austie Renkenberger, Harriet Phillips, Bird Shrader, Lottie Vickers, Theo and Opal Smith, Ada Summers, and Myrtle Gudgel; (middle row) Mrs. Jenkins, Jessie Keller, Marion Brooks, Ida Lewis, Ruth and Orville Berry, and Laura Renkenberger; (back row) Dorothy Hartzell, Anna Paxon, Eliza and Marjorie Rakestraw, Phoebe Wilson, Amy Smith, Cora Diver, Jennie Durr, Blanch Resslar, Pearl King, Mary Rakestraw, Bertha Shively, Marilla Bedell, Mrs. Riss, and Mary Goist.

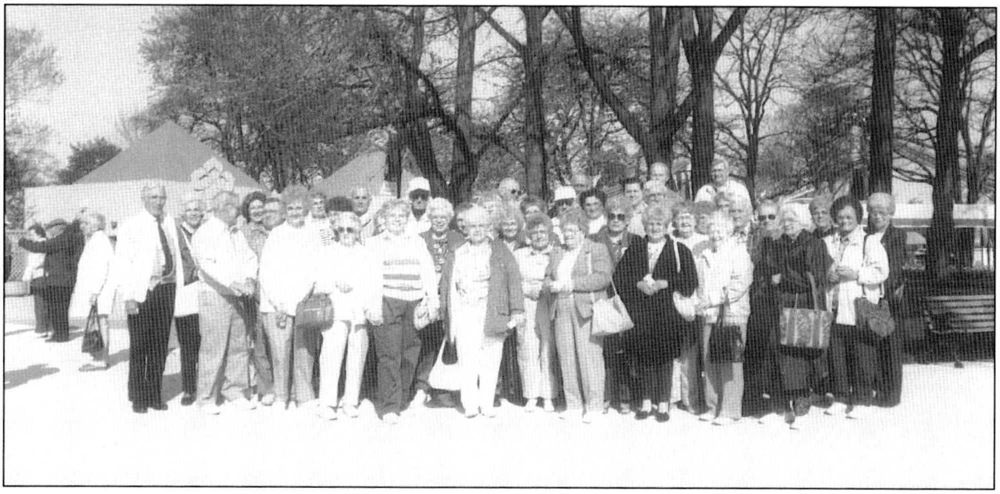

The Silver Threads took a bus trip to the Ameriflora exhibition in Columbus in 1992. Pictured from left to right, are: (first row) Delmus Woolf, Bob Thomas, Ann Myers, Theresa Thomas, Barbara Hoyle, Ethel Weingart, Mary Eshler, Helen Weir, unidentified, Vallaise Bullis, and unidentified; (second row) Mary Woolf, Jack Pricer, Margaret Joslyn, Rachael Oesch, Ruth Boyle, Elma Iddings, unidentified, Dorothy Keller, Gerald Keller, and Lillian Ondreko; (third row) Eleanor Pricer, Twilla Brown, Don Hugli, Adam Myers, two unidentified women, Dick Truitt, Edith Truitt, Joe Craig, George Eckis, Violet Eckis, unidentified, Marjorie Ross, Donna Craig, and Grace Ripley; (fourth row) two unidentified men, Joe Ondreko, and Ivan Hoyle.

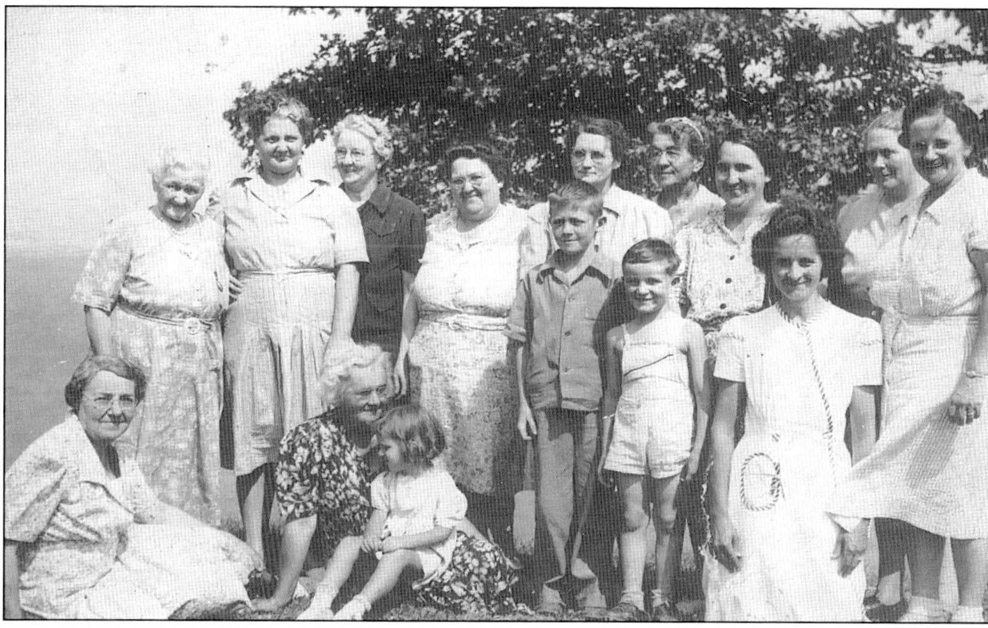

Shown here is a summer gathering of the Pythian Sister Lodge #512 in the 1940s. The Pythian Sisters started in Berlin Center in 1921 when they met at the Linfield Temple of the Knights of Pythian. The group disbanded in May of 1991. Pictured from left to right are, as follows: (front row) Ida Lewis, Jessie Keller, Judy Keller, Richard Hilles, Darryl Hilles, and Alene Klingeman; (back row) Elizabeth Rhodes, Dora Harshman, Laura Kale, Anna Paxson, Grace Hilles, Austia Renkenberger, Annie Briet, Blanch Woolf, and Leora Hilles.

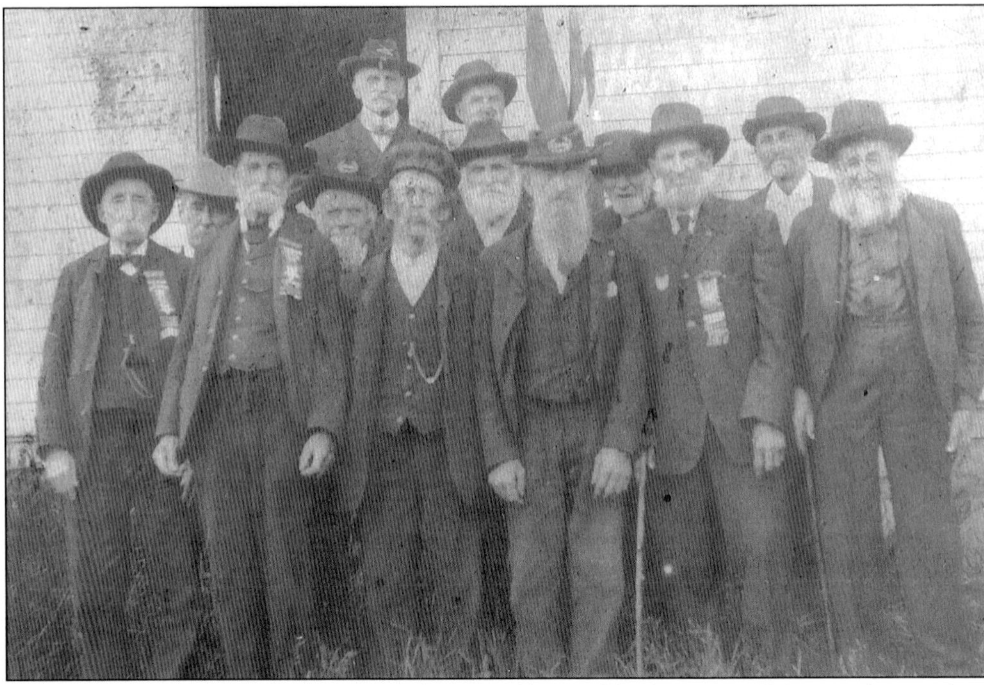

The Berlin Center Grand Army of the Republic Kirkbride Post #600 was chartered on August 19, 1886. Members are pictured above, but not individually identified.

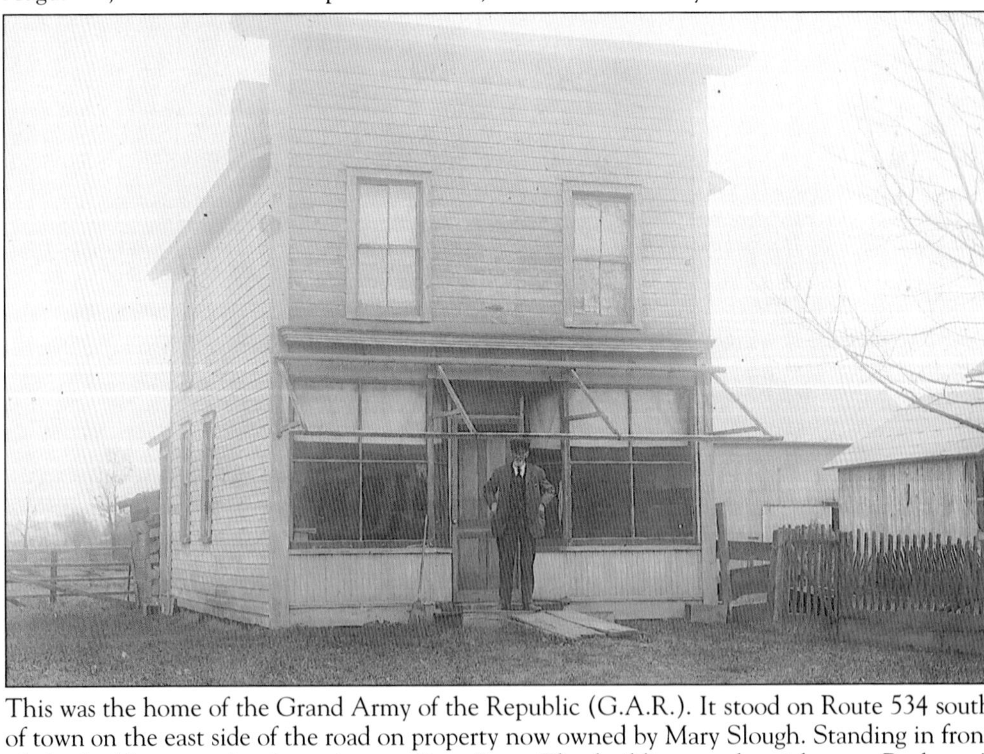

This was the home of the Grand Army of the Republic (G.A.R.). It stood on Route 534 south of town on the east side of the road on property now owned by Mary Slough. Standing in front of the building is a local auctioneer, Burt Durr. The building to the right was Beckman's Ice Cream Store.

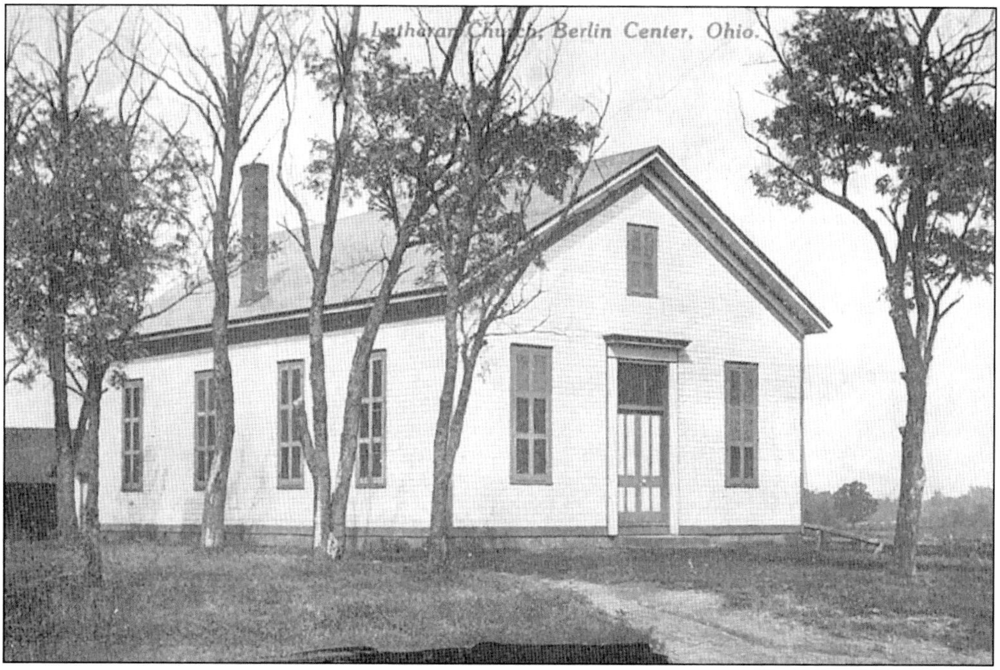

The Mt. Moriah Lutheran Church building was constructed north of town in 1872. The Lutherans had met in private homes and other buildings prior to this time. In 1828, Rev. Henry Hewitt officially organized the congregation.

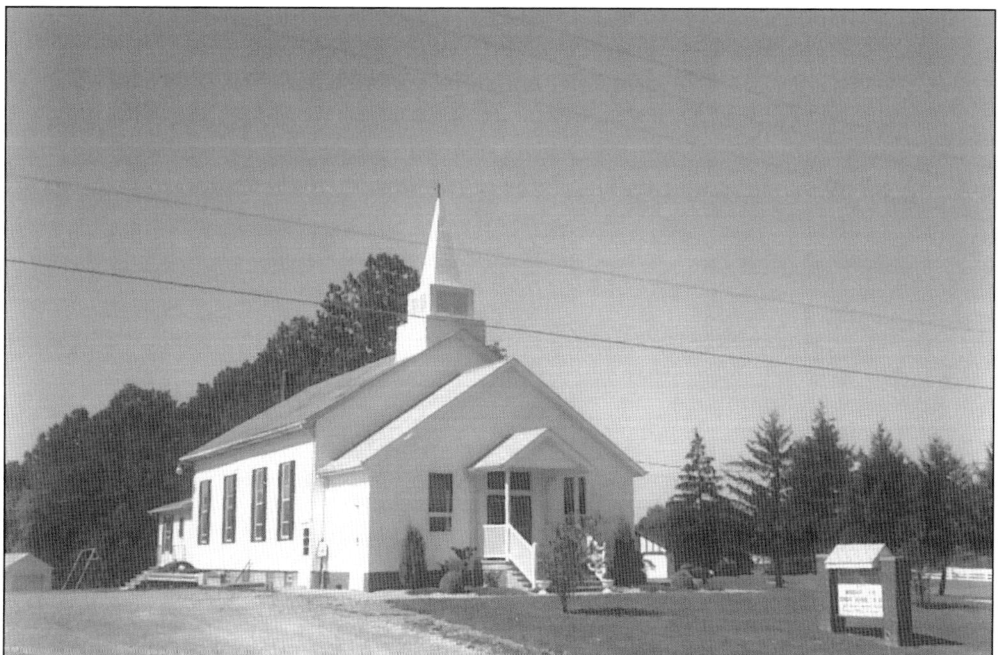

The present building has acquired additions, and is currently being served by Rev. David Phoenix. The building is located at 4626 South Pricetown Road (Route 534).

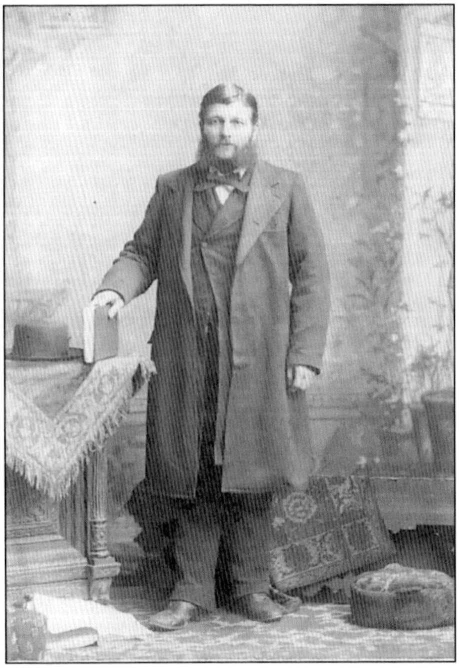

Rev. Elias A. Best was pastor at the Mt. Moriah Lutheran Church from 1890 to 1891. He signed this picture, "Faithfully, Elias A. Best".

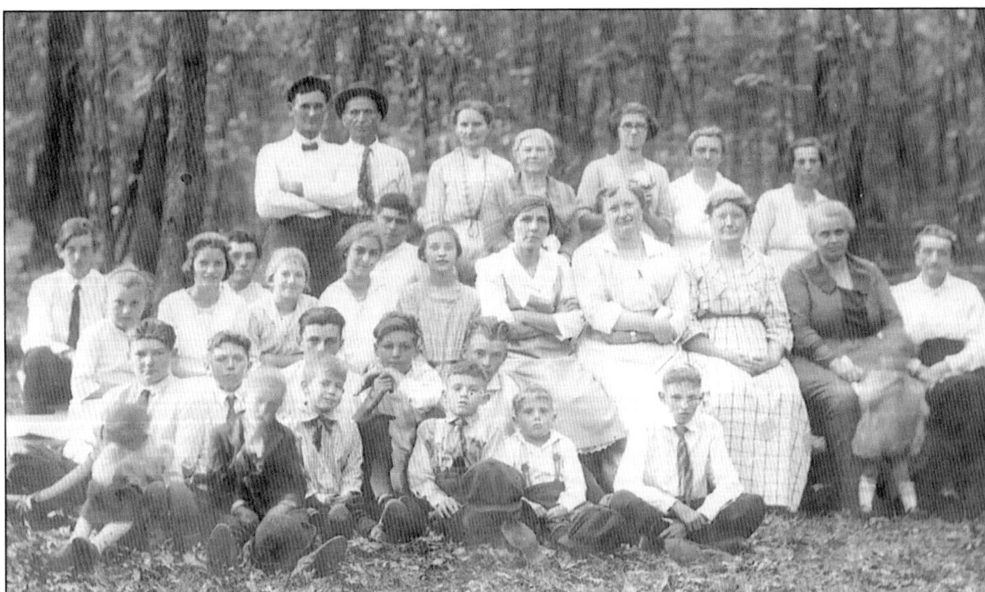

Pictured at this picnic in the early 1900s are, from left to right, members of the Mt. Moriah Lutheran Church Sunday School: (first row) ? Mench, Harold Yeager, ? Mench, John Yeager, Forest Yeager, and Dwight Yeager; (second row) Forest Newell, Richard Baringer, Ivor Shilling, Melvin Baringer, and Orren Burkey; (third row) Myra Shilling, Cathryn Davis, Mary Newell, Helen Baringer, Mary Mench, Etta Baringer, Ola Harmon, Emma Newell, and Mrs. Mench and baby; (fourth row) Vern Yeager, Arthur Yeager, and Delmar Baringer; (fifth row) Clyde Baringer, Ervin Harmon, Mary Heiser, ? Burkey, Pauline Baringer, Fay Shilling, and Martha Yeager.

This Berlin Center Methodist Church building east of the center was constructed in 1887. The previous church, more recently owed by Mr. Houdyshell, had been built in 1839 north of the center on Route 534. Rev. J.R. Shaffer served as minister from 1883 to 1885.

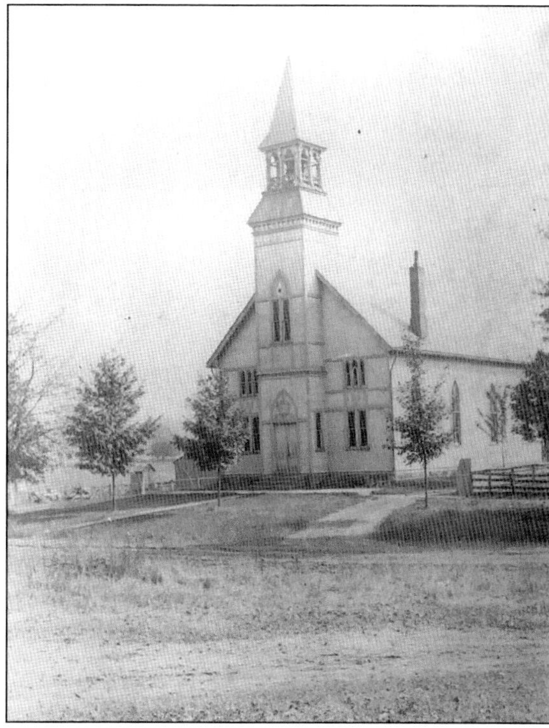

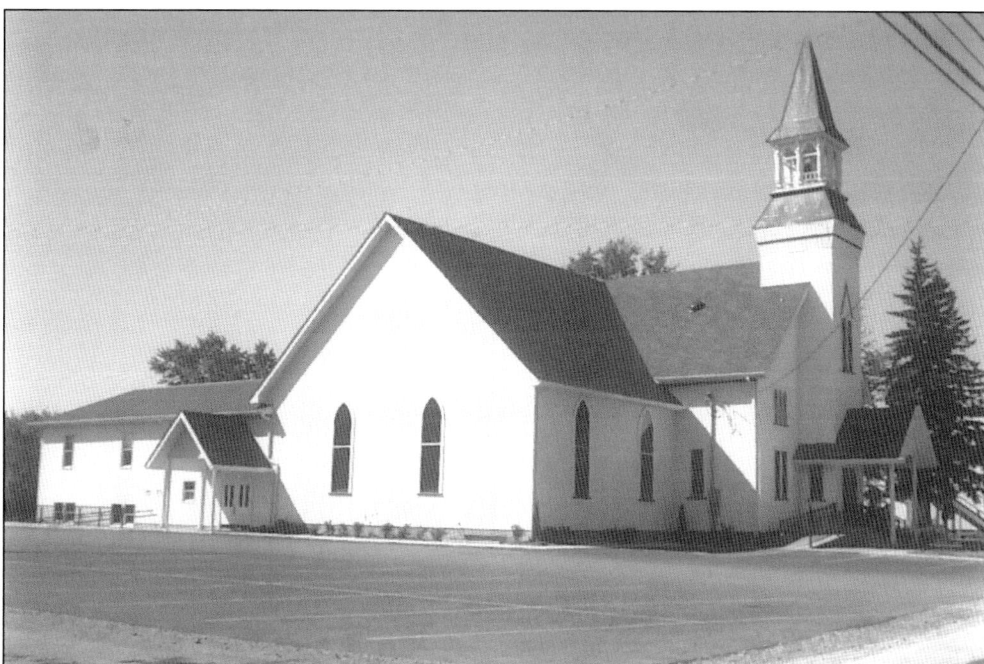

The Berlin United Methodist Church, as it is known today, is located at 15611 Akron-Canfield Road, and dedicated its newest additions in November of 1999. Rev. Russell Libb has served as pastor of the church since 1975.

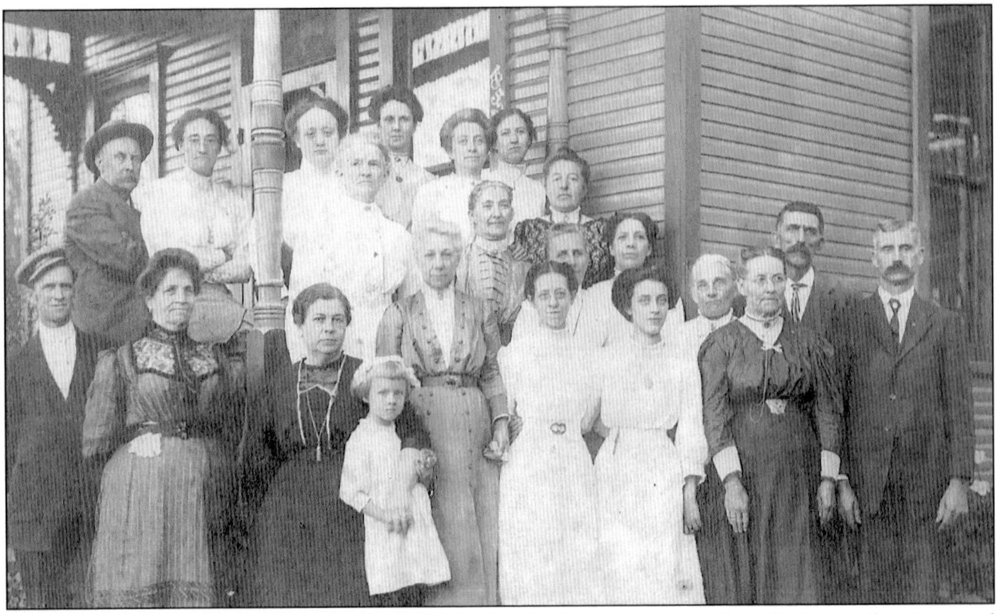

This group picture of the Berlin Center Methodist Ladies Aid is not identified in order. Pictured are Rev. Burton, Lou Mock, Rosett Wilsdorf, Addie Shively, Mrs. Shrader, Amy Smith, Mrs. Ormsby, Addia Day, Mamie Hawkins, Elsie Mock, Sadie O'Niel, Howard Woolf, Mrs. Woolf, Dora Hoyle, Charles Jewell, Mrs. Jewell, Mrs. Burton, and Miss Burton. Rev. W.W. Burton was minister at the church from 1908-1910.

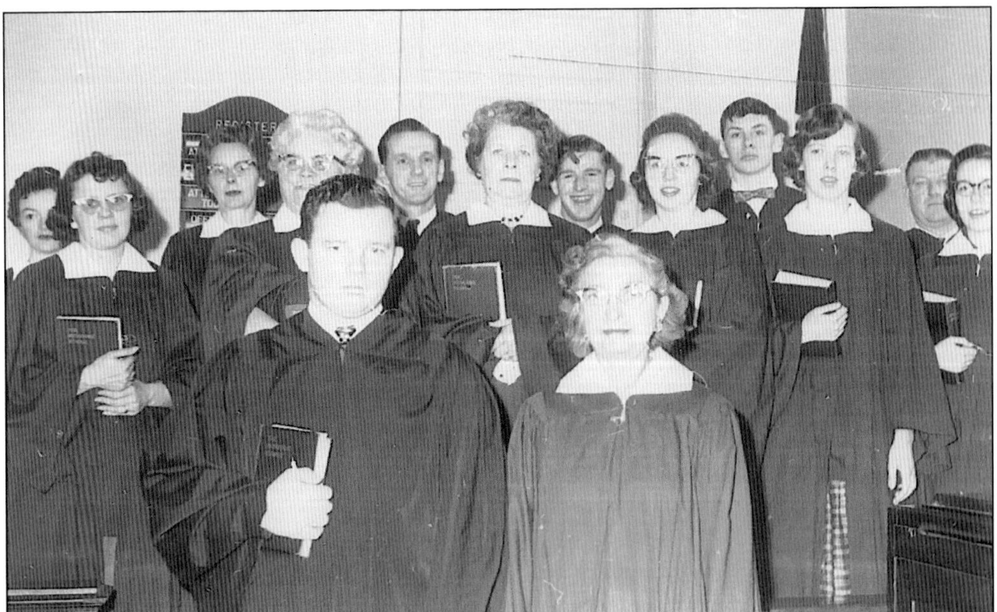

Pictured from left to right in this late 1950s photograph are members of the Methodist Church Senior Choir: (front row) Director Francis St. Clair and accompanist Dorothy Vickers; (middle row) Ruth Kurtz, Beulah Weidenmier, Hazel Cline, Linda Hilles, Nancy Newell, and Bonnie Hilles; (back row) Janet Carter, Maxine Hilles, Pat Harmon, Jeff Smith, Bob Myers, and Sandy Smith.

Five

SCHOOLS

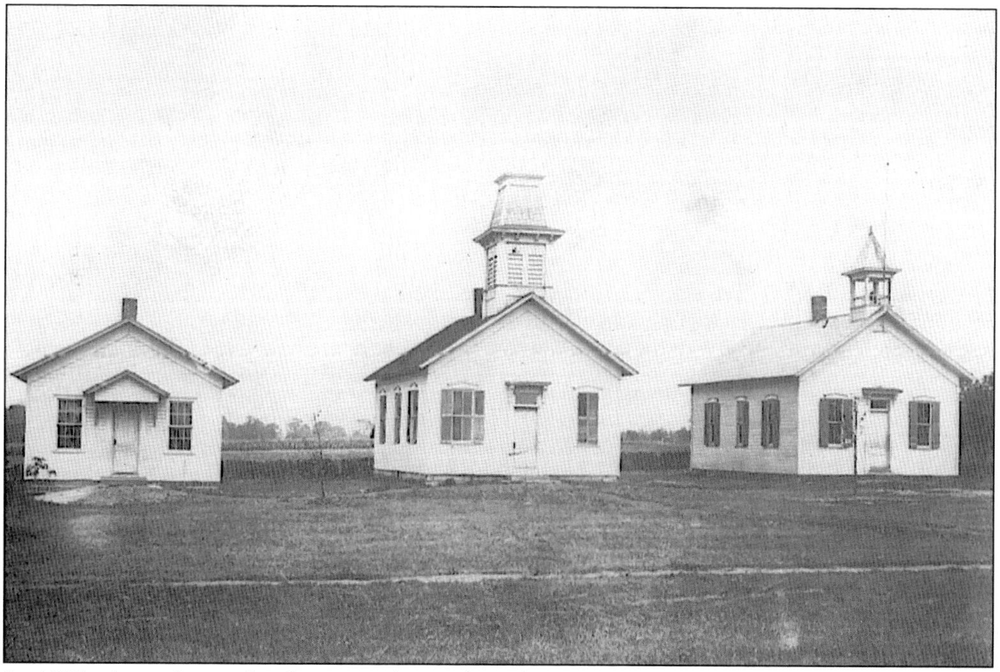

In 1905, these three schools were relocated to the center of the township. Four others were located in the township's corners. This reflects a vast change from 1874, when the area relied on nine one-room schools: Quiet Valley, east of the center near Weaver Road; Center School, located near the center; Fumbleton, west on route 224; Oak Hill or Shillings Mill, northwest on Mock Road; Dutch School, north on route 534; Shelltown School, northeast on Weaver Road; Hornets Nest, southeast at Cook Road and Leffingwell; Berlin Station School, south on Route 534; and Christytown School, southwest at Bedell Road and Leffingwell. Just 249 pupils (including 12 from Ellsworth and one from Smith Township) populated the schools in 1883.

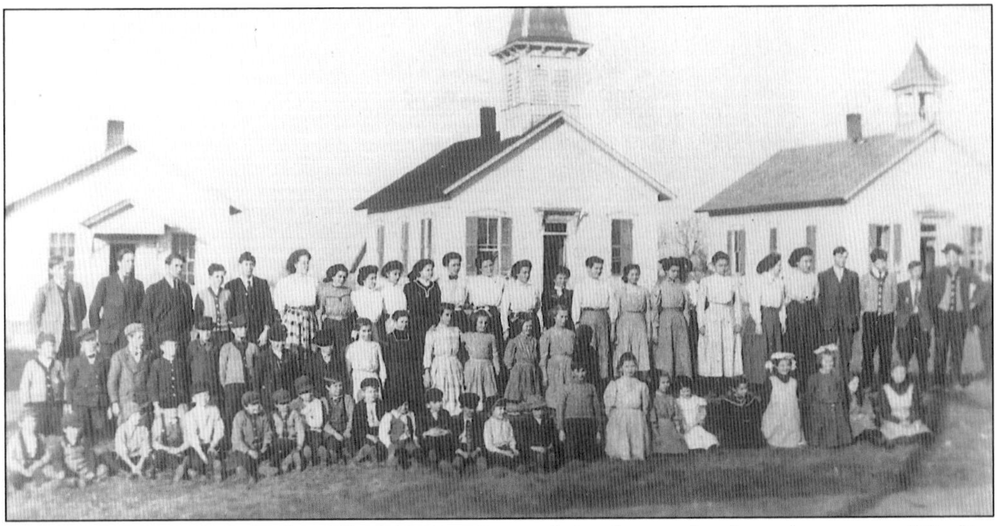

This picture was taken in the fall of 1909 in front of the three schools at the center of Berlin. Shown from left to right are, as follows: (front row) unidentified, Myron Renkenberger, Harold Kale, Richard Hawkins, Harold Slough, John Hawkins, Frank Cline, Carrie Jewell, Paul Kille, Tracy Slough, Frank Green, Wallace Heiser, Elmer Kale, Tressel Hawkins, Roy Booth, Irene Newell, Ione Renkenberger, Elma Hawkins, Dorothy Kline, Lena Diver, Leota Kline, Audalegne Belmont, and Jessie Harmon; (middle row) Earl Hawkins, Glenn Fifer, Charles Hoyle, Bryon Myers, Olin Hartzell, Fred Woolf, Harold Eckis, Lynn Hawkins, Clara Hartzell, Blanche Myers, Edna Hartzell, Bernice Eckis, Carol Hawkins, and Edna Painter; (back row) Wilbur Heiser, Robert Hilles, Professor Howard Kirchner, Farris Eckis, teacher Ward Myers, Pheobe Hoyle, Iva Burkey, Blanche Burton, Unity Stanley, Honor Carson, Mary Woolf, teacher Bertha Maxwell, Ethel Burkey, Theo Felnogle, LeeEtta Cline, Bertha Galbreath, Mary Hyitt, Charlotte Hoyle, Gladys Mock, Hazel Hoyle, Marie Johnson, Harry Wilson, Elgie Newell, Oscar Cover, Vernon Booth, and Lee Bardo.

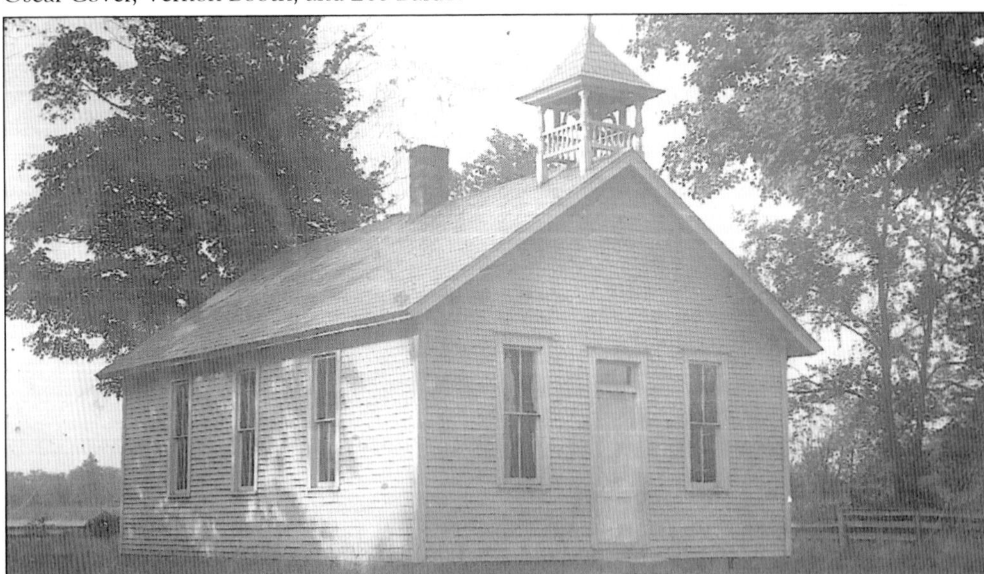

Christytown School was located on Leffingwell Road east of Bedell. It has since been remodeled into a house.

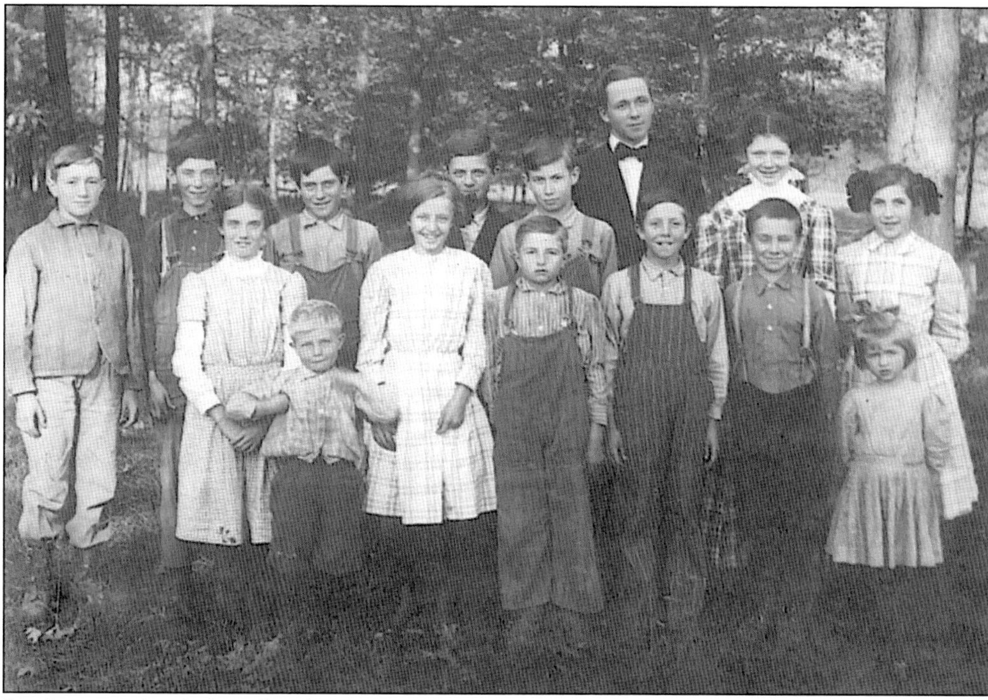

Students at the Oak Hill School pose for a photograph with their teacher, Robert Hilles, on October 19, 1911.

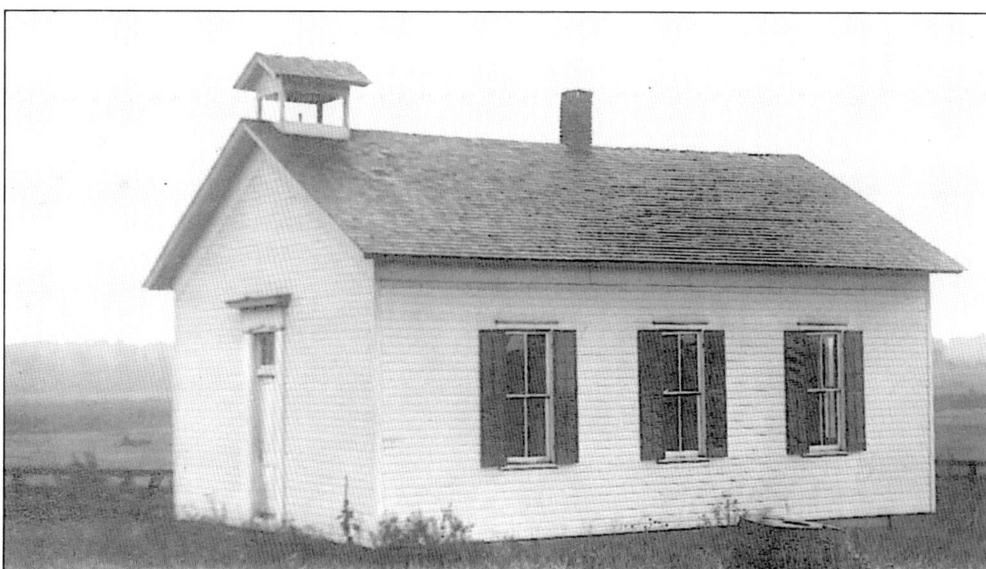

Oak Hill School, sometimes referred to as Shillings Mill School, was located on Mock Road east of Bedell Road on the property owned by Mr. and Mrs. Don Kille.

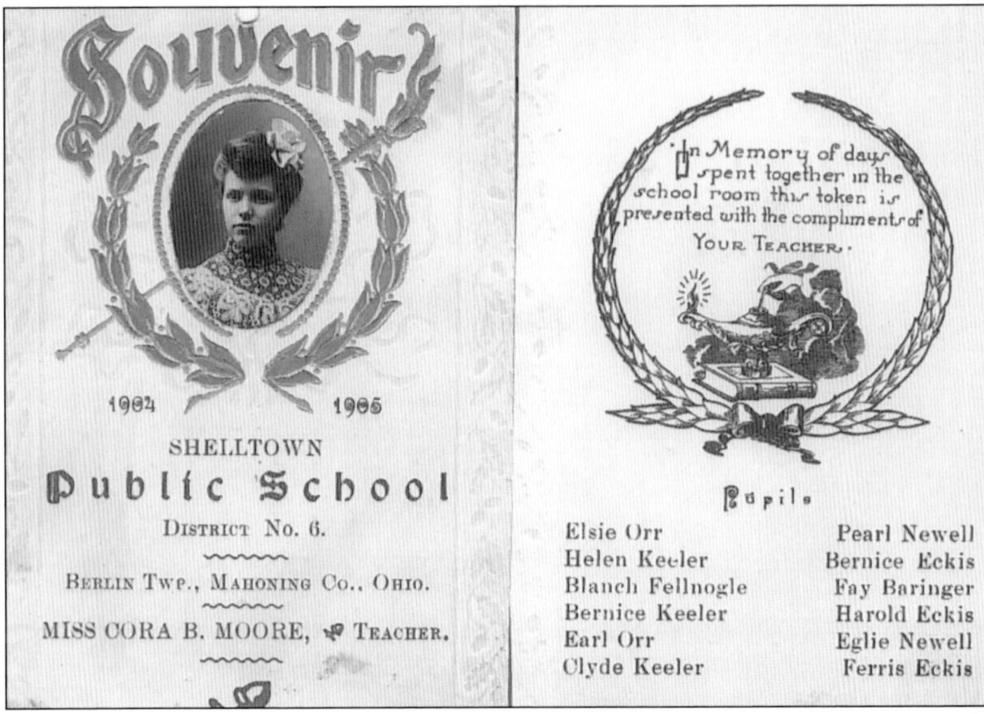

Teacher Miss Cora B. Moore offered this photographic remembrance, known as a Souvenir, for the 1904-05 academic year at Shelltown School, located on Weaver Road near Ellsworth Road.

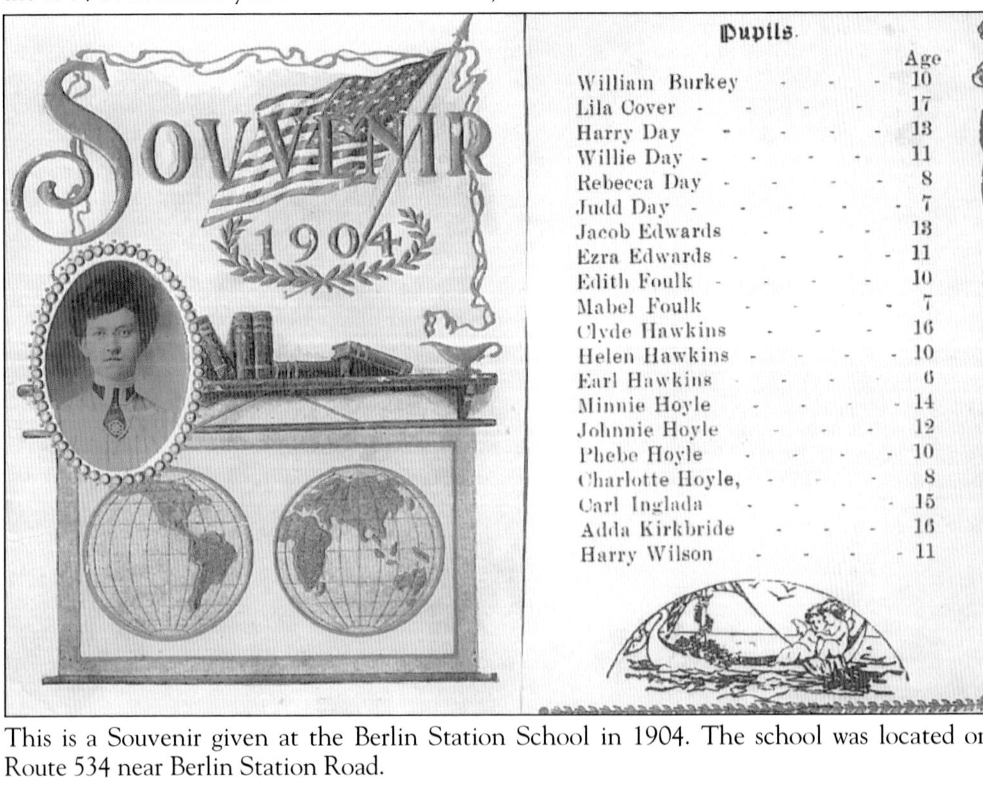

This is a Souvenir given at the Berlin Station School in 1904. The school was located on Route 534 near Berlin Station Road.

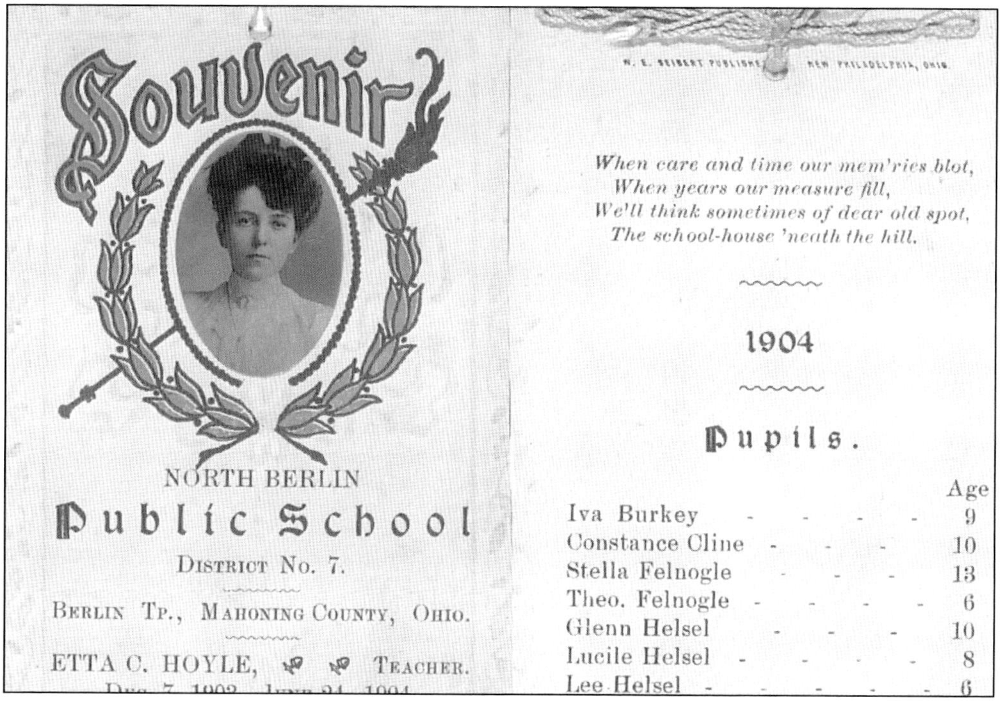

Souvenir

NORTH BERLIN

Public School

DISTRICT NO. 7.

BERLIN TP., MAHONING COUNTY, OHIO.

ETTA C. HOYLE, TEACHER.

W. E. SEIBERT PUBLISHER, NEW PHILADELPHIA, OHIO.

When care and time our mem'ries blot,
When years our measure fill,
We'll think sometimes of dear old spot,
The school-house 'neath the hill.

1904

Pupils.

	Age
Iva Burkey	9
Constance Cline	10
Stella Felnogle	13
Theo. Felnogle	6
Glenn Helsel	10
Lucile Helsel	8
Lee Helsel	6

Etta Hoyle is featured in this 1904 Souvenir at the North School, located on Route 534 near Mock Road.

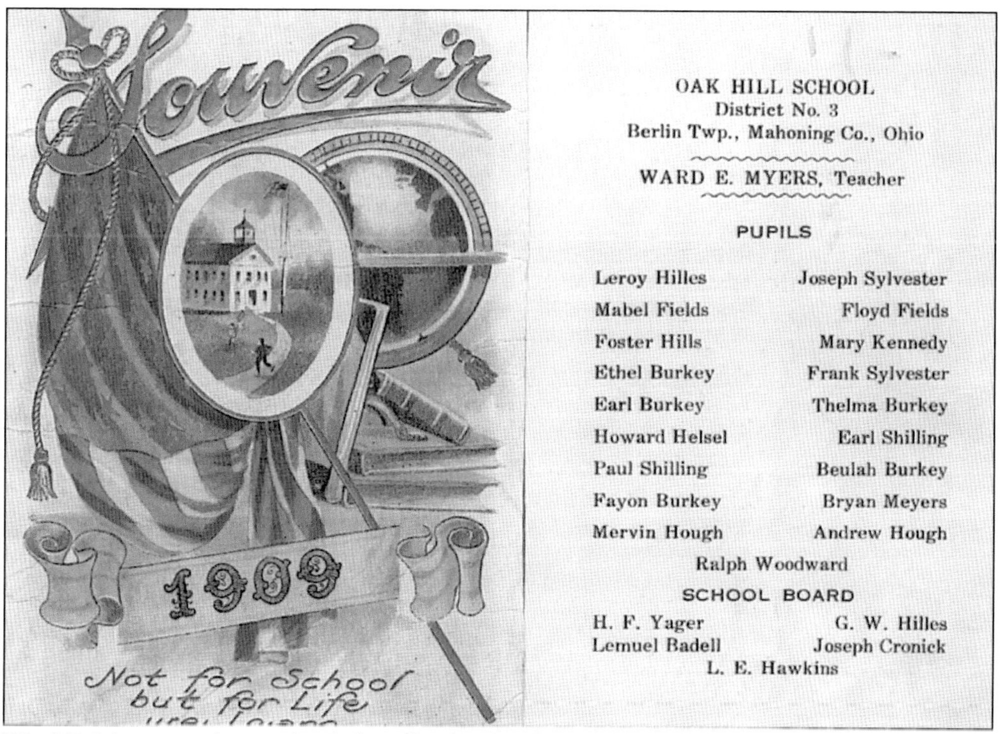

Souvenir

1909

Not for School but for Life

OAK HILL SCHOOL
District No. 3
Berlin Twp., Mahoning Co., Ohio

WARD E. MYERS, Teacher

PUPILS

Leroy Hilles	Joseph Sylvester
Mabel Fields	Floyd Fields
Foster Hills	Mary Kennedy
Ethel Burkey	Frank Sylvester
Earl Burkey	Thelma Burkey
Howard Helsel	Earl Shilling
Paul Shilling	Beulah Burkey
Fayon Burkey	Bryan Meyers
Mervin Hough	Andrew Hough

Ralph Woodward

SCHOOL BOARD

H. F. Yager	G. W. Hilles
Lemuel Badell	Joseph Cronick

L. E. Hawkins

Ward E. Myers, teacher at the Oak Hill School, offered this Souvenir in 1909. The school was located on Mock Road near Bedell Road.

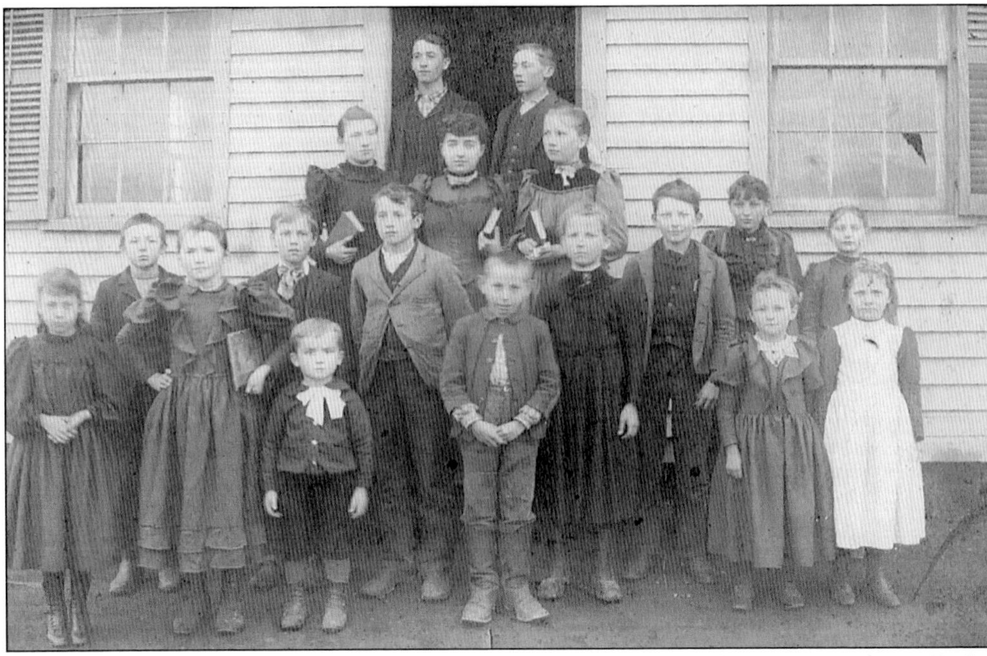

This picture was taken in 1894 at the Berlin Station School, located on Route 534 near Berlin Station Road. Pictured from left to right are, as follows: (first row) Pearl Culler, Ruby Inglad, Carl Inglad, John Hushour, Madge Kirkbride, Clarence King, May Inglad, and Etta Hoyle; (second row) Charles Flickinger, Robert Kirkbride, Tod Inglad, Lizzie Hushour, and Rose Hushour; (third row) Lulu Porter, Rose Walker, and Mabel Kirkbride; (fourth row) Joseph Hardy and Chauncey Inglad. The picture was printed in the August 17, 1935, edition of *The Telegram* newspaper as part of the old classmate picture series.

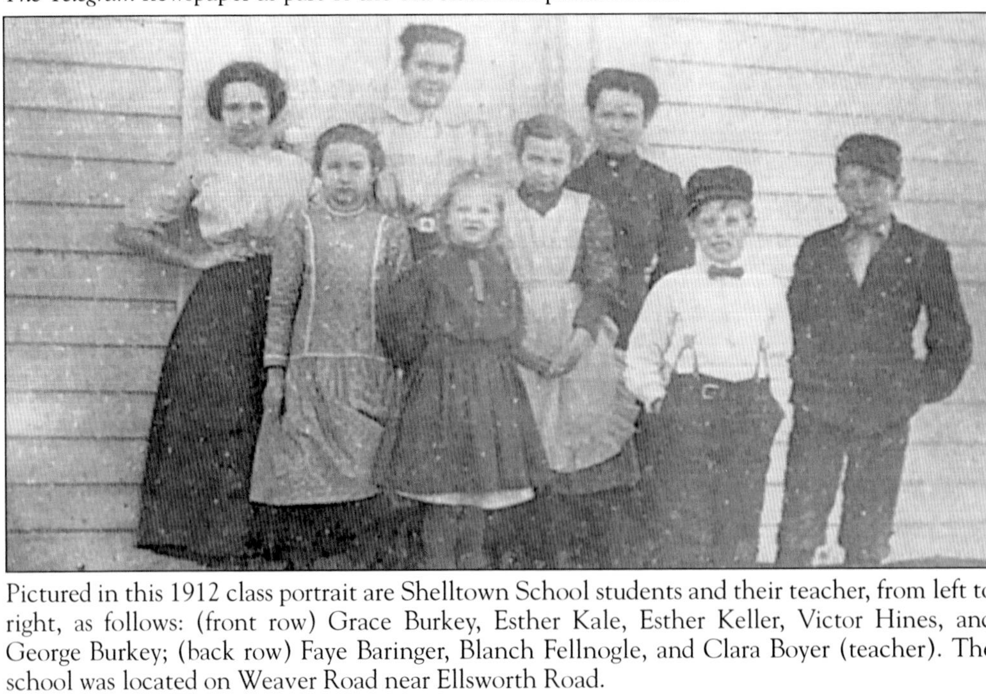

Pictured in this 1912 class portrait are Shelltown School students and their teacher, from left to right, as follows: (front row) Grace Burkey, Esther Kale, Esther Keller, Victor Hines, and George Burkey; (back row) Faye Baringer, Blanch Fellnogle, and Clara Boyer (teacher). The school was located on Weaver Road near Ellsworth Road.

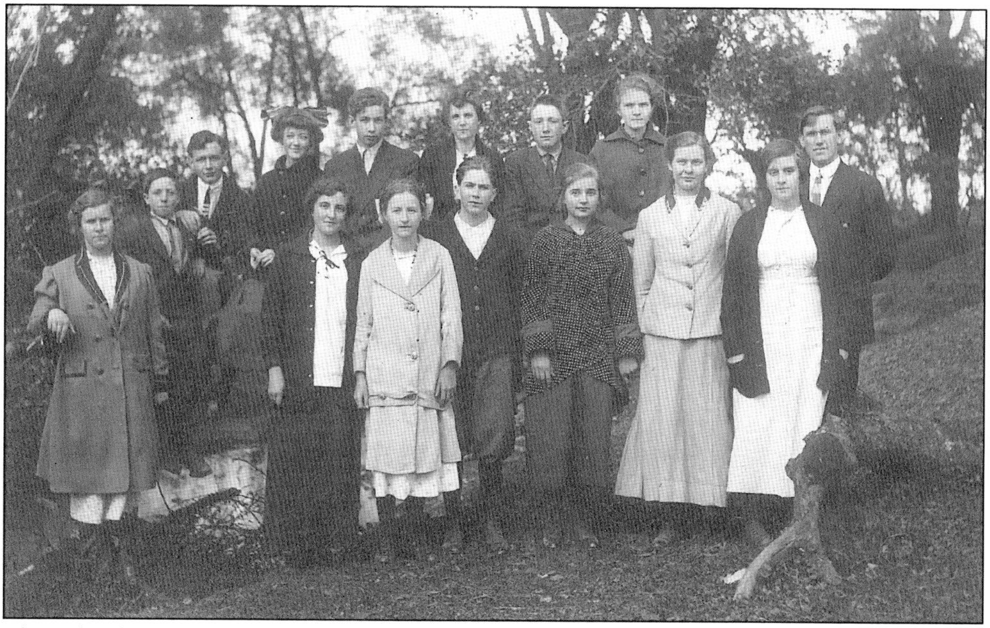

This school picture was taken in 1915 alongside Turkey Broth Creek near the schools at the center. Shown from left to right are, as follows: (front row) Bernice Eckis, Grace Burkey, Dewey Middleton, Hazel Siddal, Blanch Fellnogle, Clara Hartzell, and Professor Evan Dressel; (back row) Leota Cline, Foster Hilles, Theo Nichols, Carol Hawkins, Ralph Woodward, Audalegne Smith, Bryan Myers, and Theo Fellnogle. Seniors were A. Smith, B. Fellnogle, T. Nichols, and F. Hilles. Post-graduates were B. Eckis and C. Hawkins.

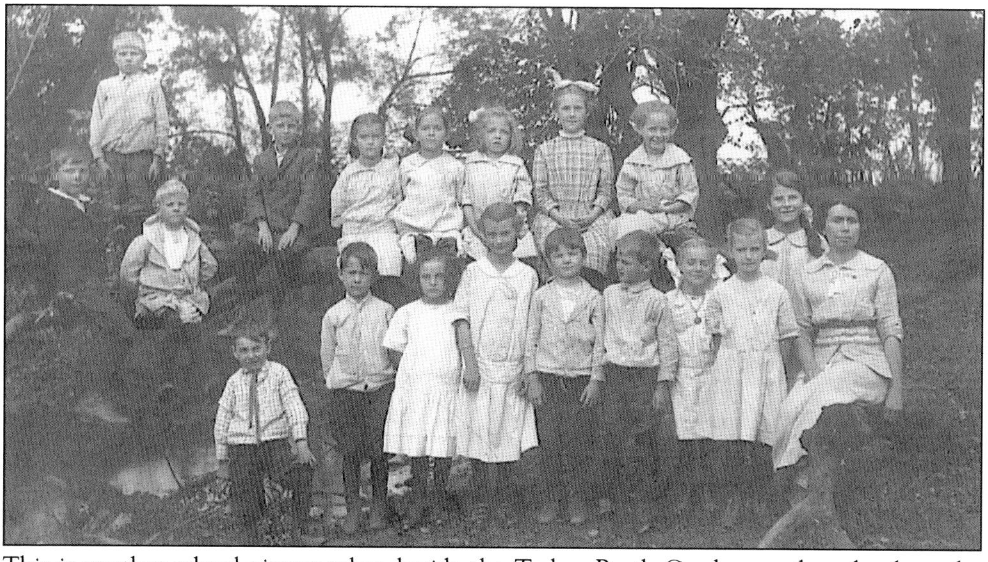

This is another school picture taken beside the Turkey Broth Creek near the schools at the center around 1914-1915. From left to right are: (front row) Bennie Kille, Myron Renkenberger, Leona Cline, Mae Hartzell, Forest Newell, Raymond Hartzell, Leta Lewis, Violet Kime, Alice Hartzell, and teacher Miss Lovelock; (back row) Myron Hawn, Stewart Burkey, Charles Rakestraw, Howard Rakestraw, Lucy Diver, Mary Cover, Sarah Shively, Dorothy Felnogle, and Alene Cline.

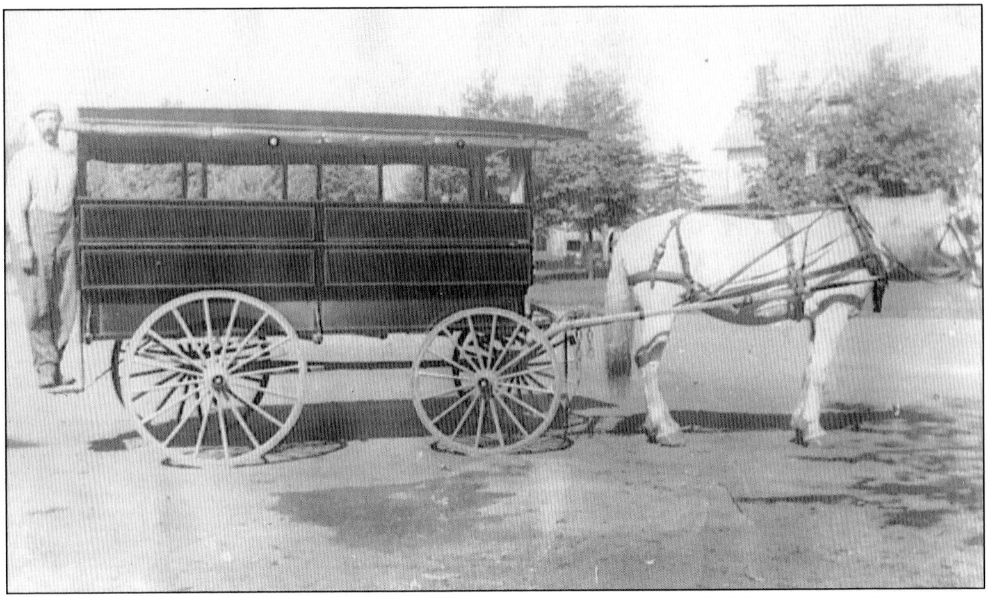

This "Kid Wagon" was used at the turn of the century to transport children to school.

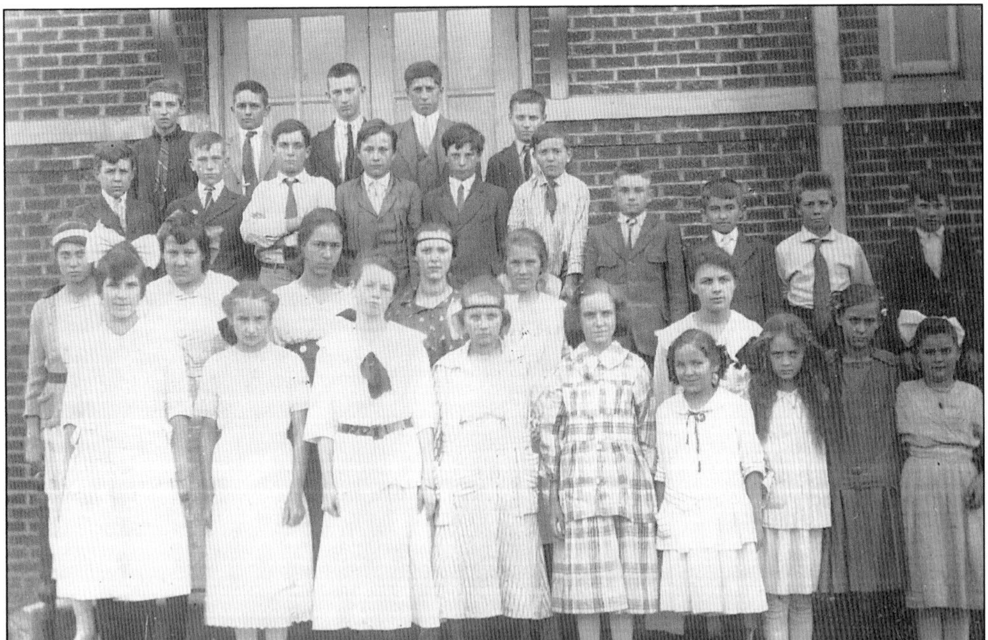

Grades six, seven, and eight pose for a 1917-18 class photograph at the Berlin Center building. Pictured from left to right are, as follows: (front row) Alice Hartzel, Irene Teeters, Helen Brown, Leora Rakestraw, Grace Wilson, Mary Cover, Alene Cline, Rilda Leyman, and Lucy Diver; (second row) Beatrice Brown, Pearl Bowman, Ione Renkenberger, Maggie Leyman, Dorothy Felnogle, and teacher Miss Chysler; (third row) Tracy Slough, Richard Hawkins, Philip Wack, Floyd Teeters, William Slusher, Herbert Roberts, Earl Eshler, Orrie Diver, Stewart Burkey, and Ralph Helsel; (fourth row) Glen Burkey, John Hawkins, Howard Best, Lawrence Hoyle, and Clifford Cassiday.

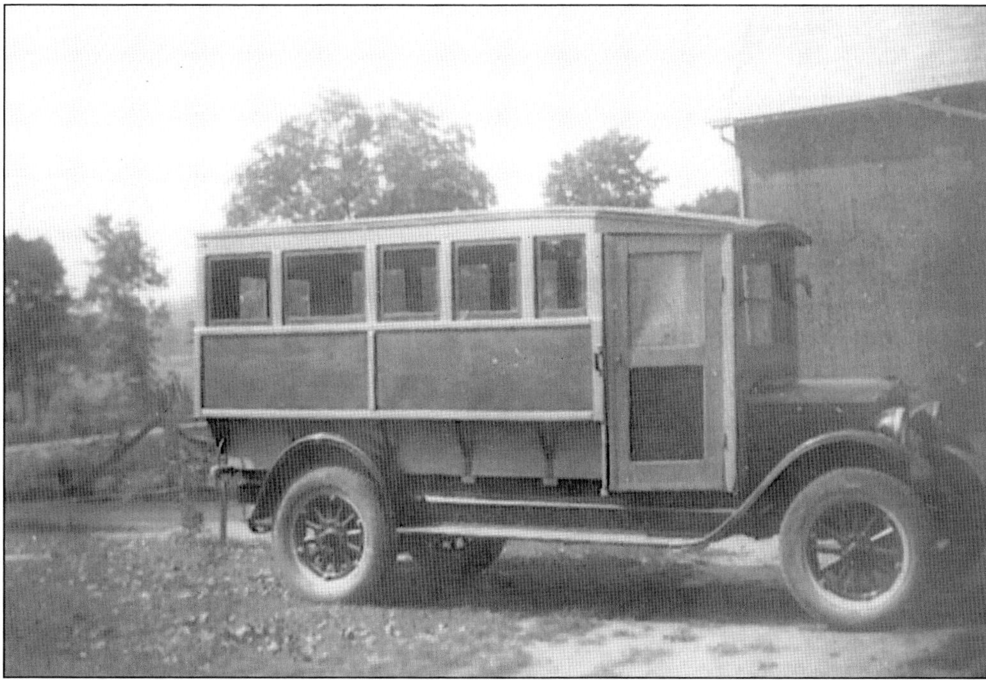

This motorized school bus was owned by its driver, Tilden Harmon. Buses like this one, used in the 1920s and 1930s, were fitted with wooden benches attached lengthwise along the interior sidewalls.

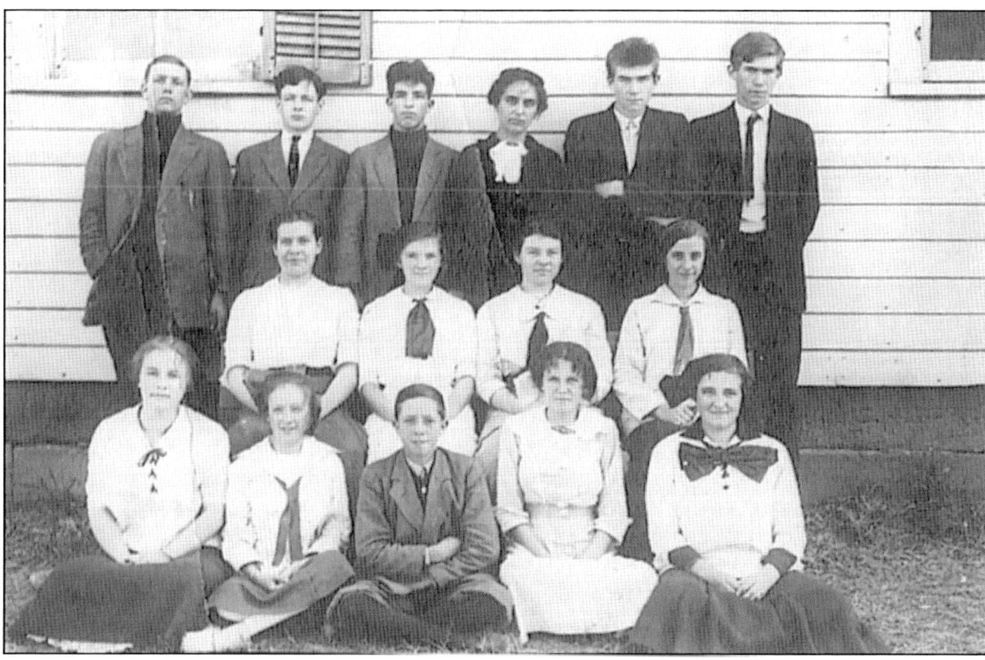

This school picture was taken in 1913-14, and includes the following students (not in order): Earl Bedell, Foster Hilles, Bernice Eckis, Carol Hawkins, Theo Fellnogle, Amy Smith, Blanch Fellnogle, and Theo Nichols. The others were not identified.

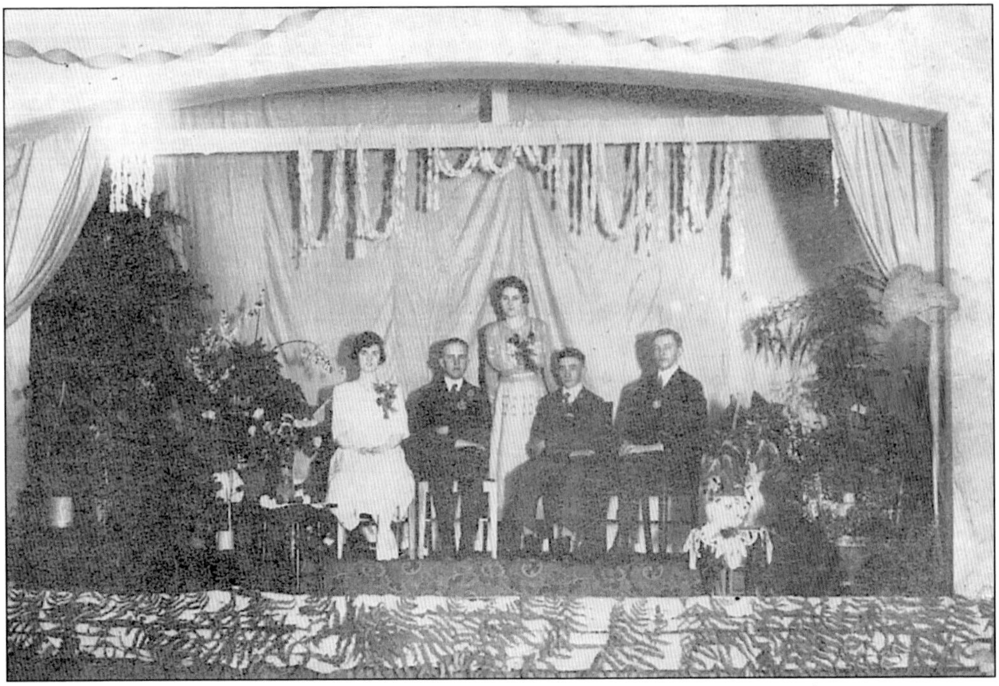

This top picture shows the graduating class of 1919, and the bottom image the accompanying commencement program. The graduation ceremony took place in the original Berlin Center auditorium with Rev. William Caven offering the invocation. The graduates, along with their speech titles, appear from left to right as follows: Thelma Burky, "Past and Present Opportunities;" Marion Diehl, "Conservation of Forests;" unidentified teacher; Harley Eshler, "Immigration Problems;" and Wallace Heiser, "The New Era."

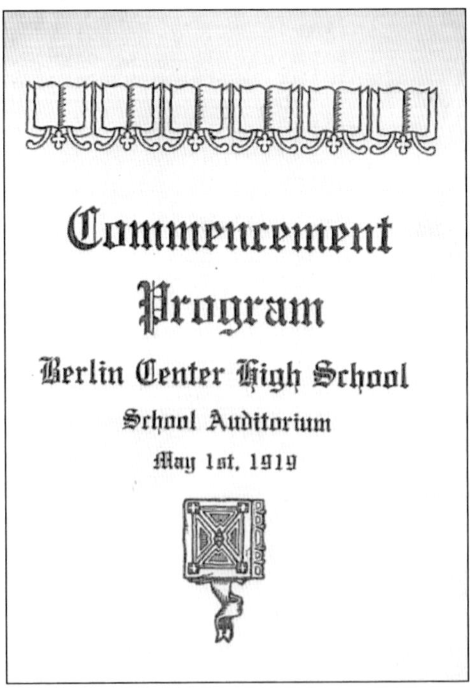

Commencement Program

Berlin Center High School

School Auditorium

May 1st, 1919

This is a school picture taken in 1924 at the Berlin Center School. Pictured are, from left to right, as follows: (first row) Marion Newman, Maurice Dickson, Ernest Harmon, Ralph Kaley, Joe Johnson, and Harold Hartzell; (second row) Carol Gudgel, Gladys Newman, Bernice Williams, Paul Stallsmith, Cecelia Goodman, Charles London, Don Shrader, Gladys Kuhns, and Paul Spell; (third row) Twila Baringer, Martha Kale, Anna Moenich, Mildred Eshler, Dorothy Flickinger, Elizabeth Velicky, Darrell Renkenberger, and teacher Dorothy Hartzell; (fourth row) Laura London, Catherine Czik, and Joe Moenich; (fifth row) Helen Schiben, Billy Paxson, Woodrow Harmon, Steve Goginsky, Marion Helsel, Donald Kaley, Charles Hilles, Paul Vodhandel, Dale Shively, and Maurice Rakestraw; (back row) Nellie Kaley, Myra Shilling, and Mary Kaley.

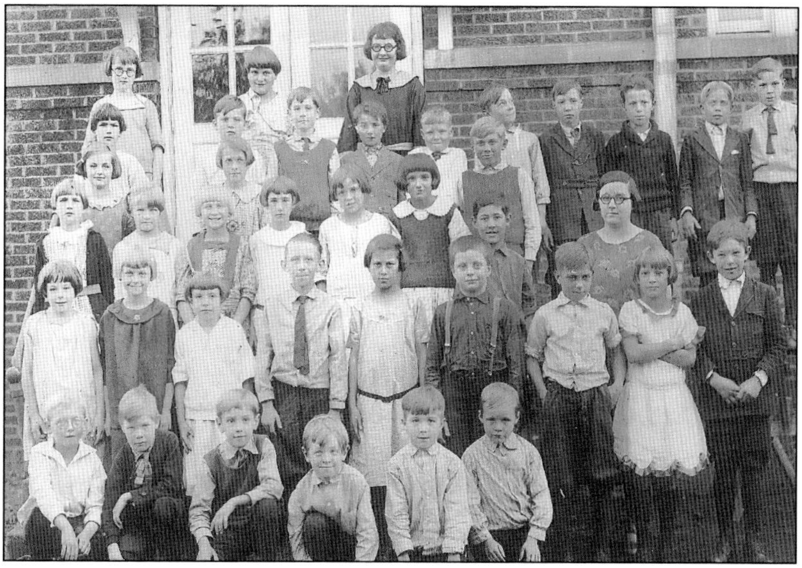

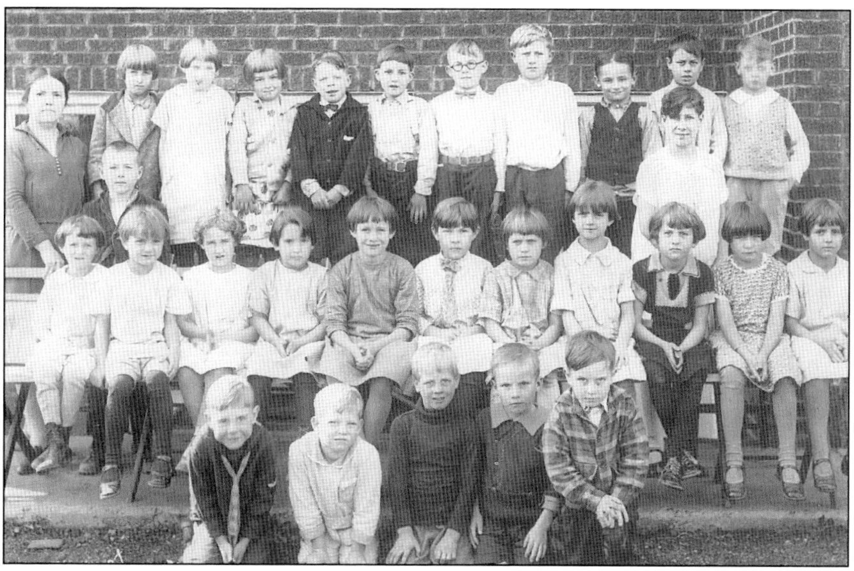

This is a group picture of the first and second grade classes of the Berlin Center School in 1927-28. From left to right are, as follows: (first row) Orville Berry, Carl Edwards, Lohr Kuhns, Delbert Helsel, and Fred Williams; (second row) Theresa Hilles, Bertha Czink, Mary Cline, Mildred Kale, Elsie Edwards, Audalagine Allen, Julia Kovach, Margaret Czink, Mildred Paxson, Grace Hartzell, and Dora Fields; (third row) Howard Brown and Leona Fingel; (fourth row) Teacher Miss Boyer, Nellie Simnick, Mildred Keller, Annie Johnson, Kenneth Barnett, two unidentified boys, Steve Kovach, John Halzchak, Robert Goodman, and Kenneth Cronick.

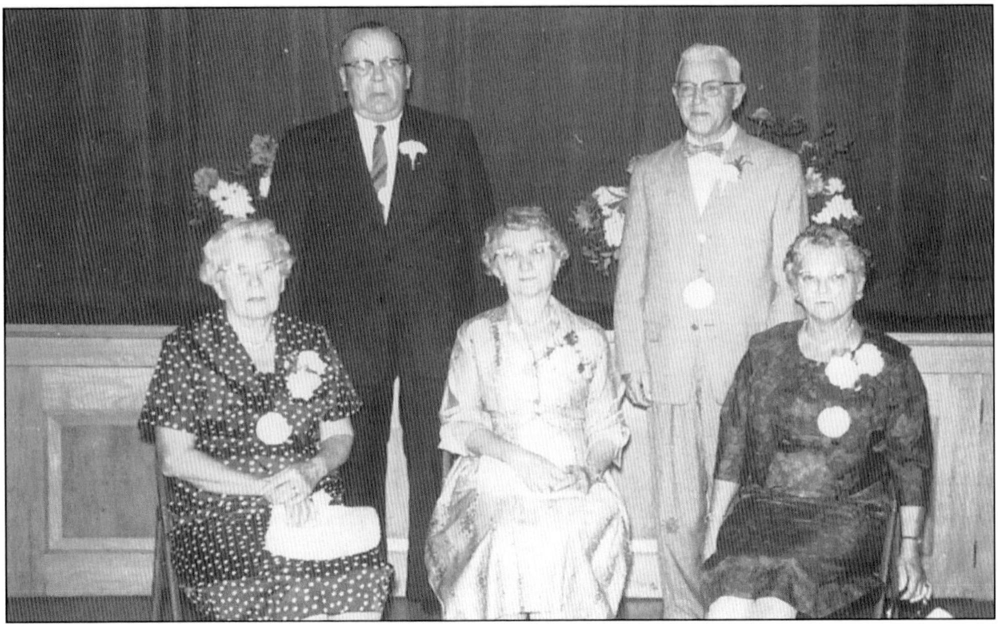

The Berlin Center High School graduating class of 1910 reconvenes for their 50th reunion at the Ellsworth School alumni banquet of 1960. Pictured from left to right are, (front row) Hazel Hoyle Ripley, Mary Woolf Rakestraw, and Unity Stanley Shreve; (back row) Robert Hilles and Wilbur Heiser. There were eight in their graduating class.

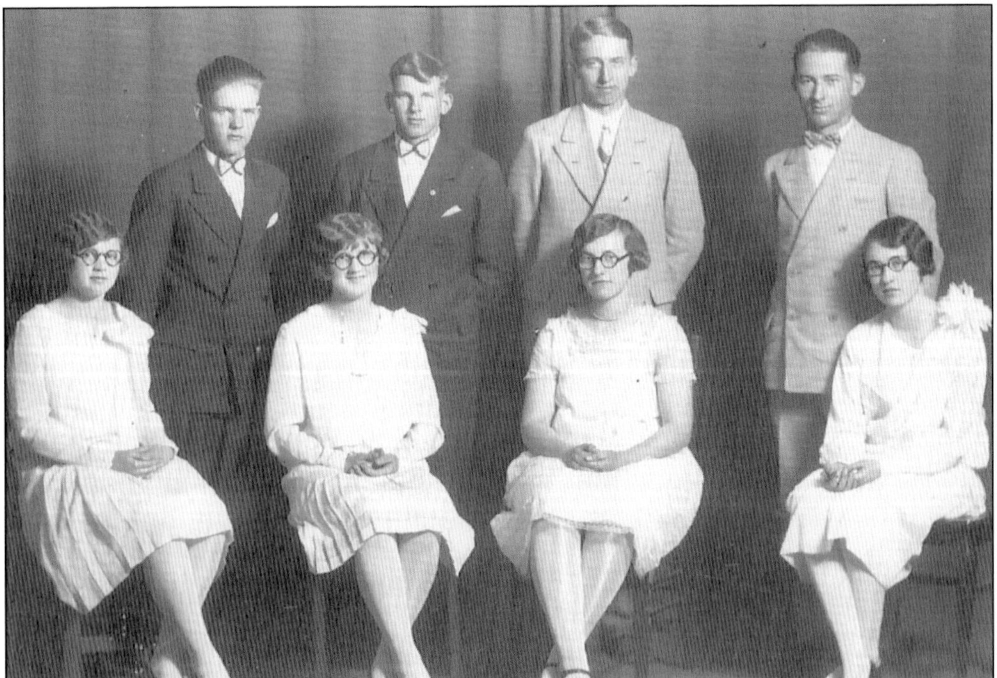

Pictured from the Berlin Center High School graduating class of 1927 are, from left to right, (front row) Lois Summers, Laura Janseski, Wahneta Allen, and Odessa Jones; (back row) Charlie Rakestraw, Howard Rakestraw, Bob Ruggles, and Mike Renkenberger.

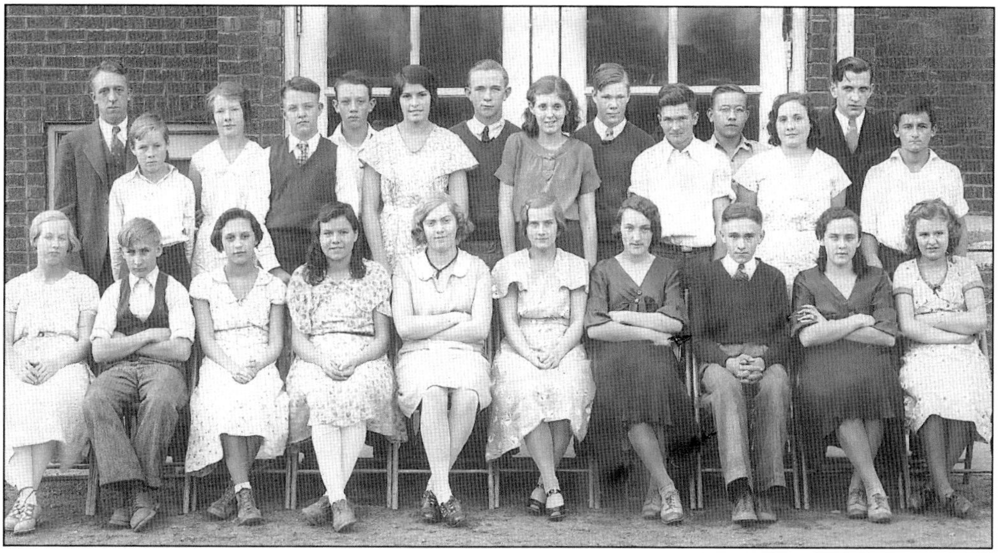

This photograph of the Freshmen and Sophomore Class of 1932-33 was taken at the Berlin School building. Pictured from left to right are, as follows: (front row) Velma Kuhns, Carl Sczysmak, Genevieve Florence, Helen Kurta, Gwendolyn Edwards, Naomi Hawkins, Mildred Keller, Jacob Eshler, Viola Keller, and Helen Boyle; (middle row) Harold Hartzell, Gordon Wilson, Rose Kale, Erma Pettit, Irvin Snyder, Eleanor Hilles, and Pete Halczysack; (back row) Professor Ward, Margaret Dickson, Burton Hilles, Richard Cover, Maurice Dickson, Harold Smith, and teacher Willard Barker.

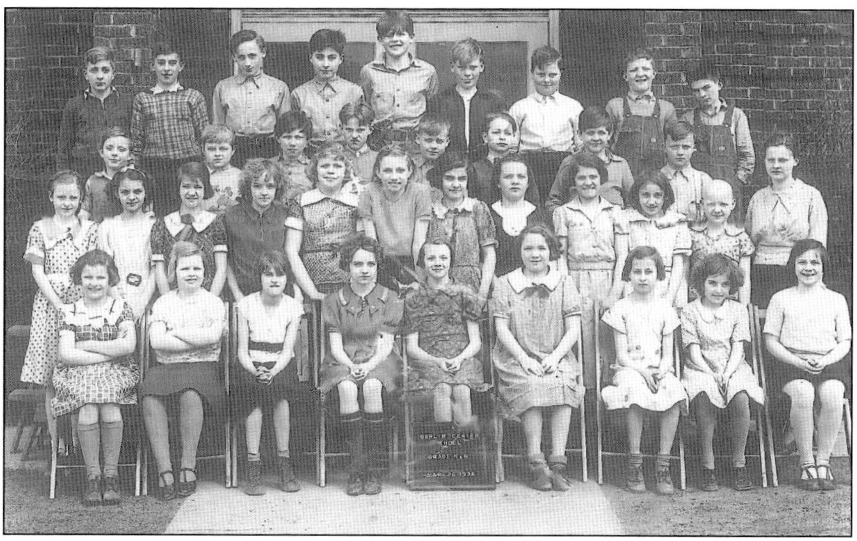

Berlin Center School grades five and six are featured in this 1936 photograph. Pictured from left to right are, as follows: (first row) Roene Woolman, Virginia Bardo, Audrey Miller, Bonnie Miller, Ruth Hilles, Mary Esther Cain, Sophie Syzazmack, Lolly Coman, and Joanne Conkle; (second row) Jean Kurtz, Gloria Cover, Thalia Bedell, Frances Coman, Katythn Fladding, Doris Shrader, Evelyn Noble, Opal Smith, Elma Young, Betty Serensky, Margret Cain, and teacher Ardis Jones; (third row) Charles Brooks, Bennard Burky, Leroy Hull, Glen Needham, Dick Noble, Randall Baringer, Richard Craig, and Joe Ondreko; (fourth row) Malcolm Obenauf, Robert Shumaker, George Serensky, Raymond Anderson, James Craig, James Kurtz, Harvey Goodman, Wilbur Kale, and Forest Kale.

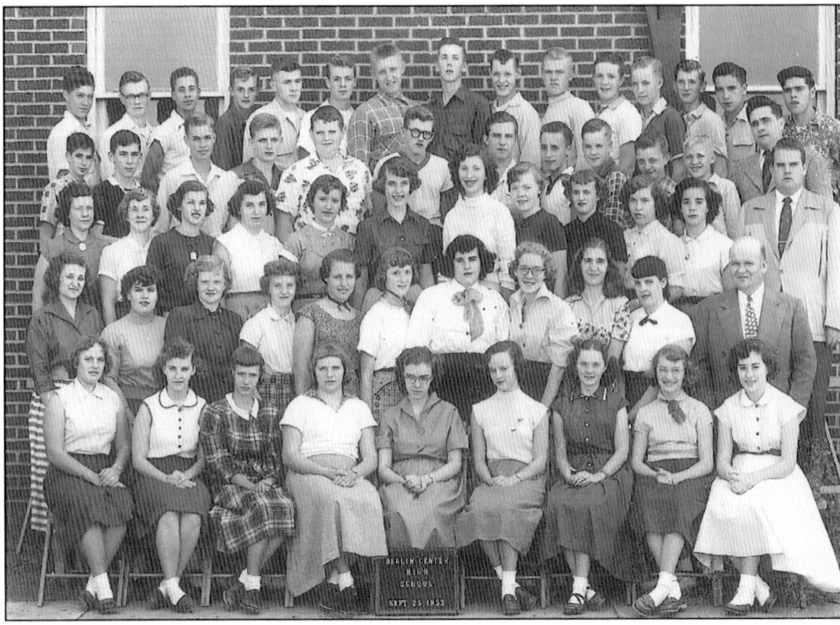

Left to right are 1953 high school students: (first row) Alice Walters, Lucille Wilson, Judy Keller, Janet Grim, Eileen Parks, Irene Johns, Elaine Snyder, Carol Green, and unidentified; (second row) teacher Miss Dometrovick, Elaine Goodman, Darthella Yeager, Lucille Oesch, Darlene Engle, Marguerite Vickers, Ann Evanoff, Evelyn Covington, Beverly Vasbinder, Rosemarie Van Kirk, and principal Mr. Dressel; (third row) unidentified, Rosemary Gasper, Lucille Grondeski, Hermine Streber, Betty Smith, Joanne Burkey, Kathryn Slough, Janet Coleman, Darlene Miller, Helen Davis, Gail Smith, and teacher Mr. Scott; (fourth row) Richard Van Kirk, James Hawkins, Harold Wilson, Jerry Sallaz, Larry Schisler, David Keller, Louis Carnesalli, Bob Bieshelt, Wayne Wilson, Frank Mills, John Vasbinder, and teacher Mr. Anderson; (fifth row) Lonnie Johnson, Carl Weidenmier, Jack Dickerson, Jim Coman, John Dudley, Oral Bates, Arthur Lovitz, Denver Gatrell, John Hartzell, Ronnie Goodman, Darryl Hilles, Paul Wilson, Carl Yeager, Delbert Briet, and unidentified.

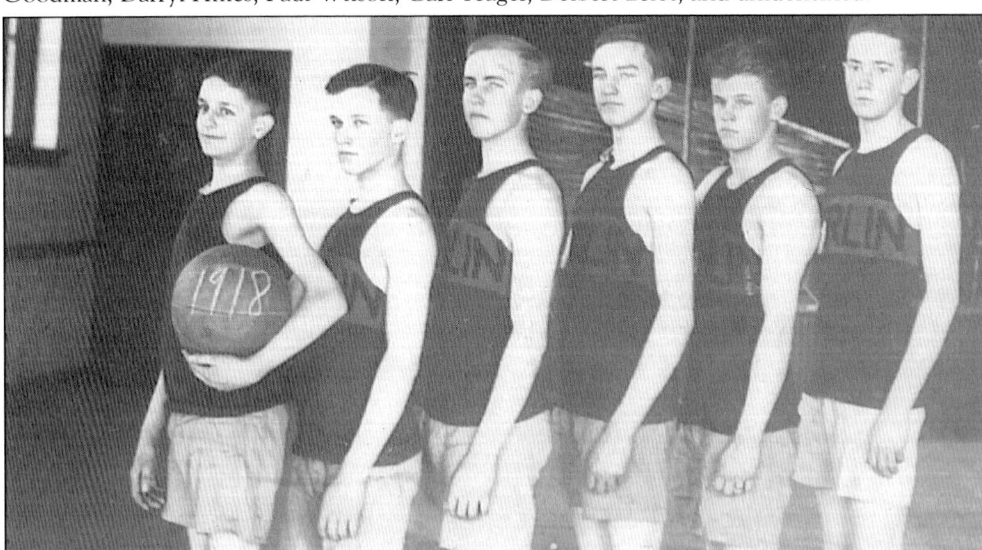

The junior high school basketball team in 1918 featured, from left to right, John Hawkins, Lynn Hawkins, Marion Diehl, Wallace Heiser, Charles Miller, and Frank Cline.

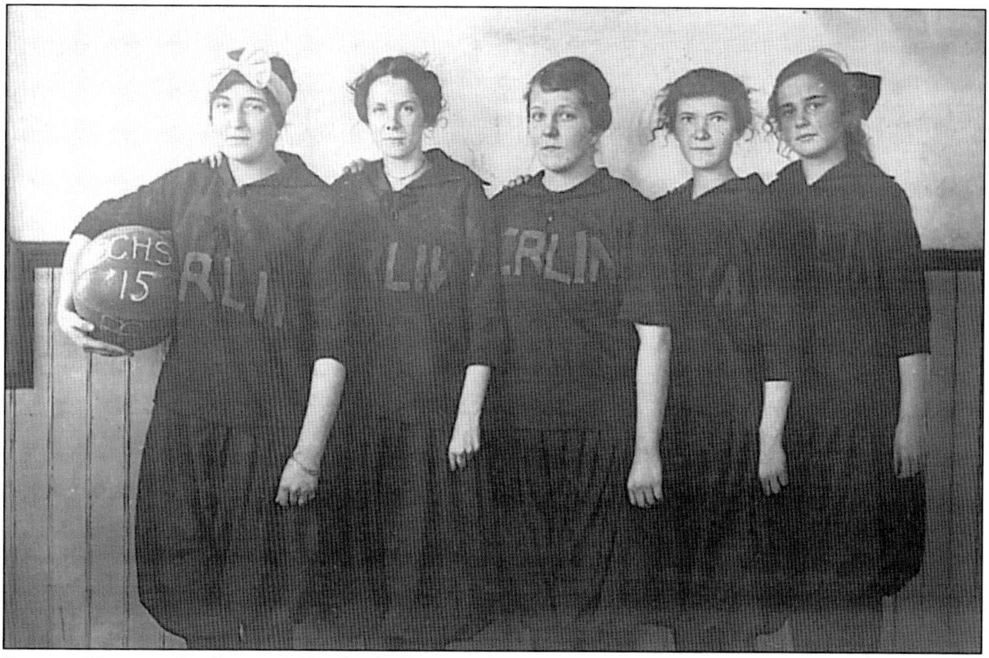

Featured here is the first girls' basketball team, dressed in the long bloomers and black stockings that distinguished their uniforms. The gymnasium was part of the new school built in 1915.

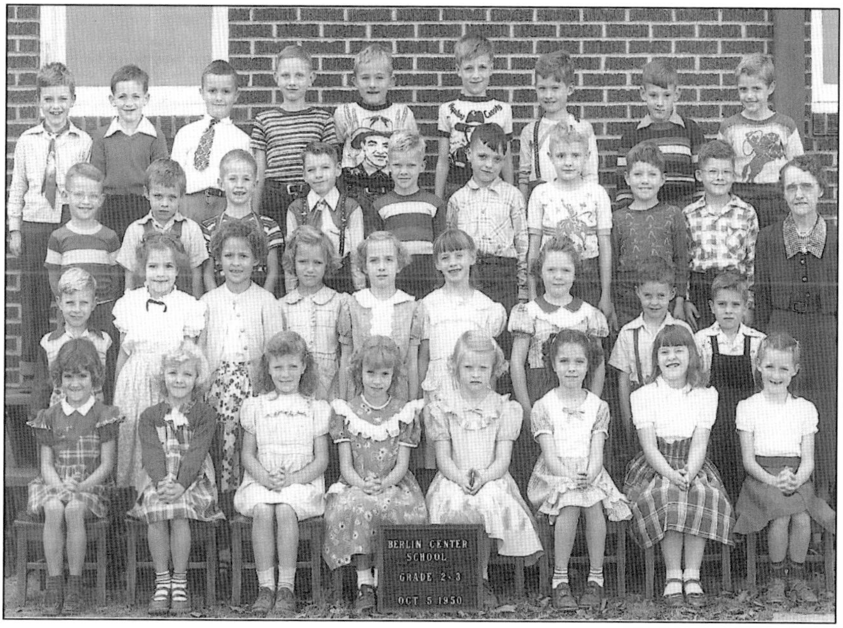

Grades two and three are photographed at the Berlin Center School on October 5, 1950. From left to right are, as follows: (first row) Cecelia Snyder, Lonna Baird, Eleanor Swank, Marie Zimmerman, Shirley Miller, Connie Spade, Jerry Ann Pickelsimer, and Jessie Jean Hodge; (second row) Charles Swank, Naomi Vasbinder, Betty Engle, Nancy Confoey, Carol Shaeffer, Rachael ?, Florence Baer, Glenn Hartzell, Pat Ross, and teacher Miss Alta Pershing; (third row) Dick Engle, Patrick ?, Harry Walters, Gerald Woods, Jerry Harmon, John Cain, Jay Pettit, Donnie Johnson, and Gary Westfall; (fourth row) Roger Crites, Jack Craig, Billy Knutti, Don Shaeffer, Teddy Paxson, David Burkey, Jim Cain, Ronnie Truitt, and Charles Cole.

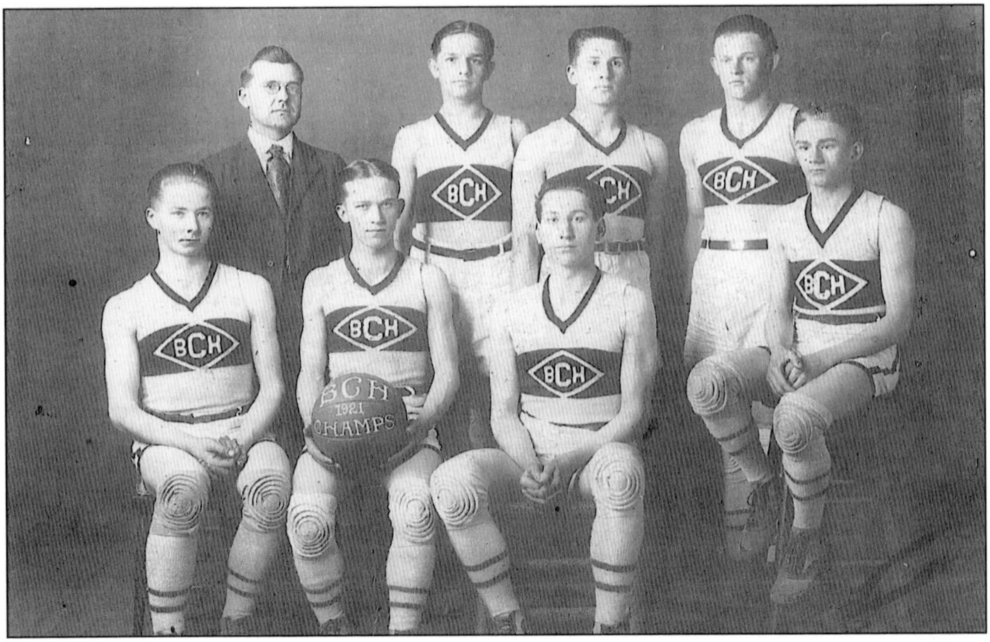

Pictured from left to right in this 1921 photograph are the Mahoning County champs: (front row) Howard Stitle, Dick Hawkins, Clyde Helsel, and Earl Eshler; (back row) Coach B.T. Myers, John Hawkins, Theodore Helsel, and Charles Miller. The team won the league championship for three consecutive years from 1920 through 1922.

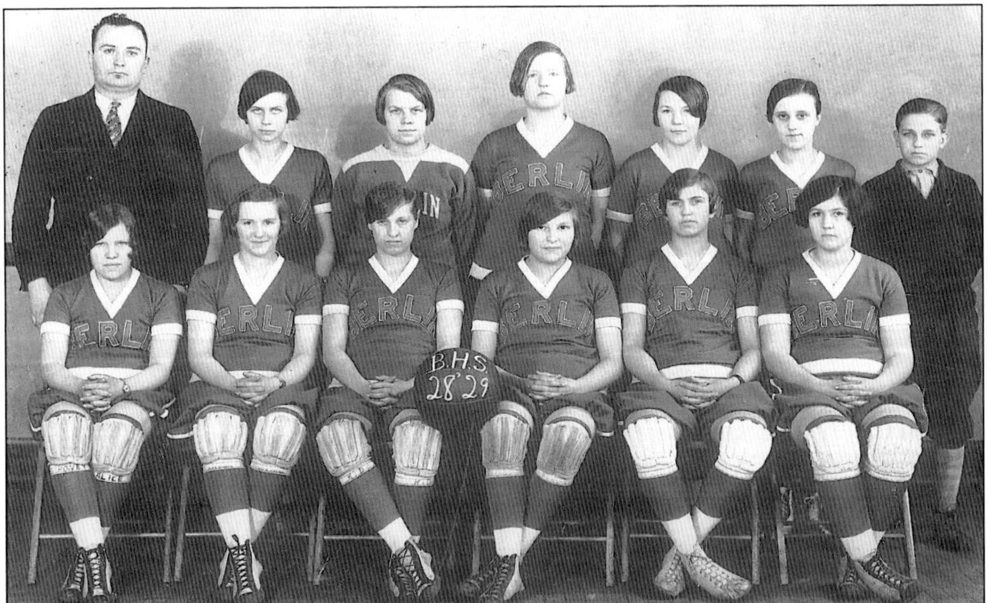

The 1928-29 Berlin Center Girl's Basketball team are pictured from left to right, as follows: (front row) Alice Dustman, Elsie Harmon, Dorothy Kuhns, Emogene Creed, Sarah Shrader, and Olga Allen; (back row) Coach Miller, Dorothy Stallsmith, Ethel Stallsmith, Elinor Currier, Bernice Hartzell, Virginia Shively, and mascot Don Shrader.

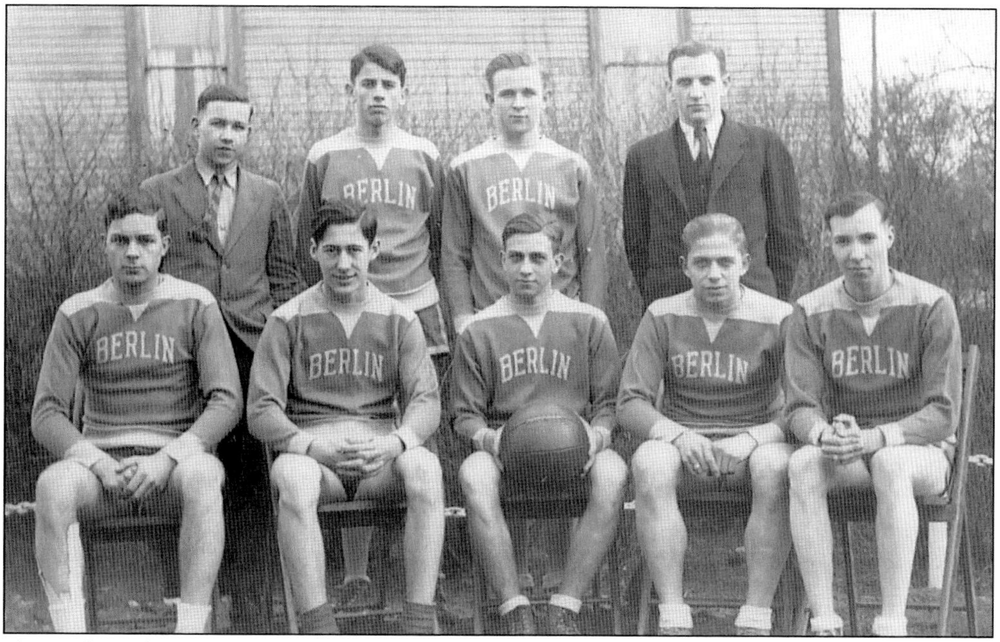

Shown here from left to right are members of the 1933 Berlin High School boys' basketball team: (front row) Maurice Rakestraw, Darrell Renkenberger, Don Shrader, Dale Shively, and Charles Hilles; (back row) manager Harold Smith, Joe Vargo, Dick Cover, and Coach Willard Barker.

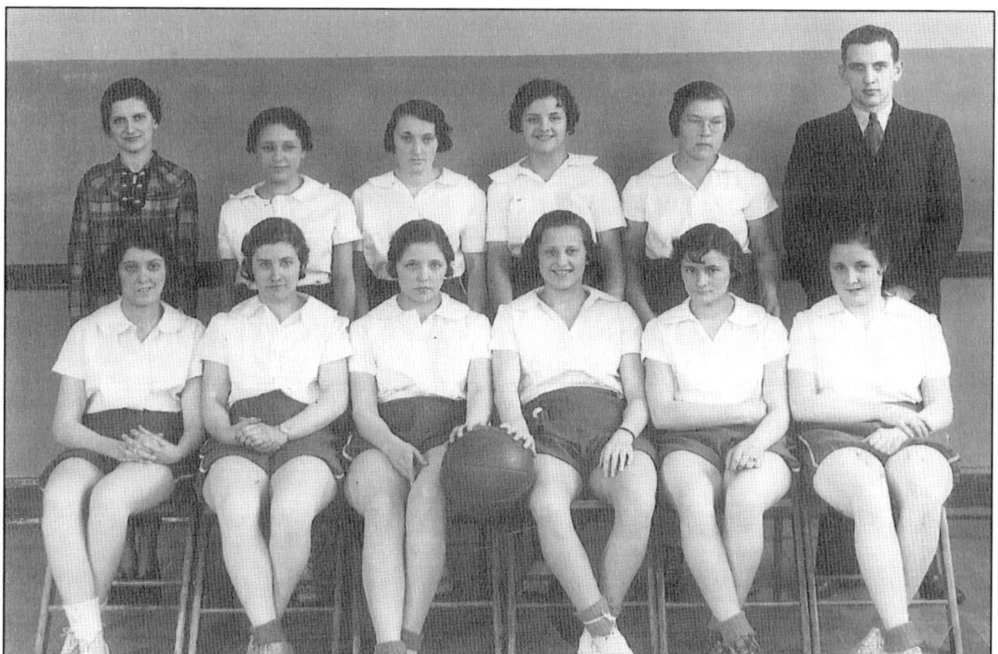

Pictured from left to right are members of the 1933-34 Berlin High School girls' basketball team: (front row) Erma Pettit, Dorothy Young, Marie Shively, Mildred Paxon, Rosie Halcyszak, and Eleanor Hilles; (back row) Miss Schnurrenberger, Genevieve Florence, Mildred Keeler, Dora Fields, Audaline Allen, and teacher Willard Barker.

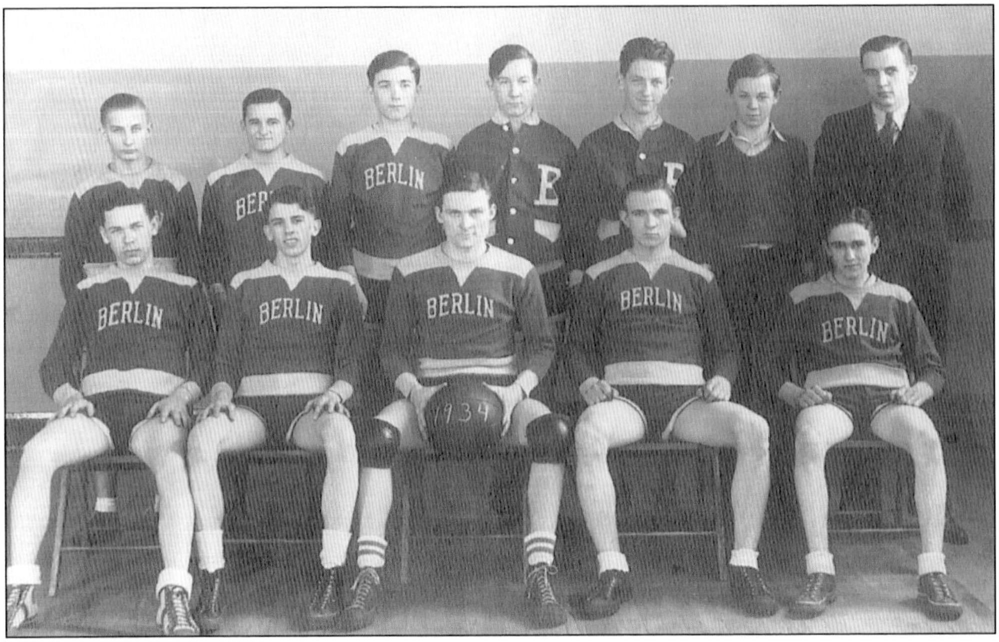

The boys' basketball team in 1934 are shown from left to right as follows: (front row) John Liana, Joe Vargo, Bill Paxson, Dick Cover, and Jacob Eshler; (back row) Carl Simscik, Pete Halcyszak, Joe Johnson, Clarence Cline, Ralph Kaley, Willard Kaley, and Coach William Barker.

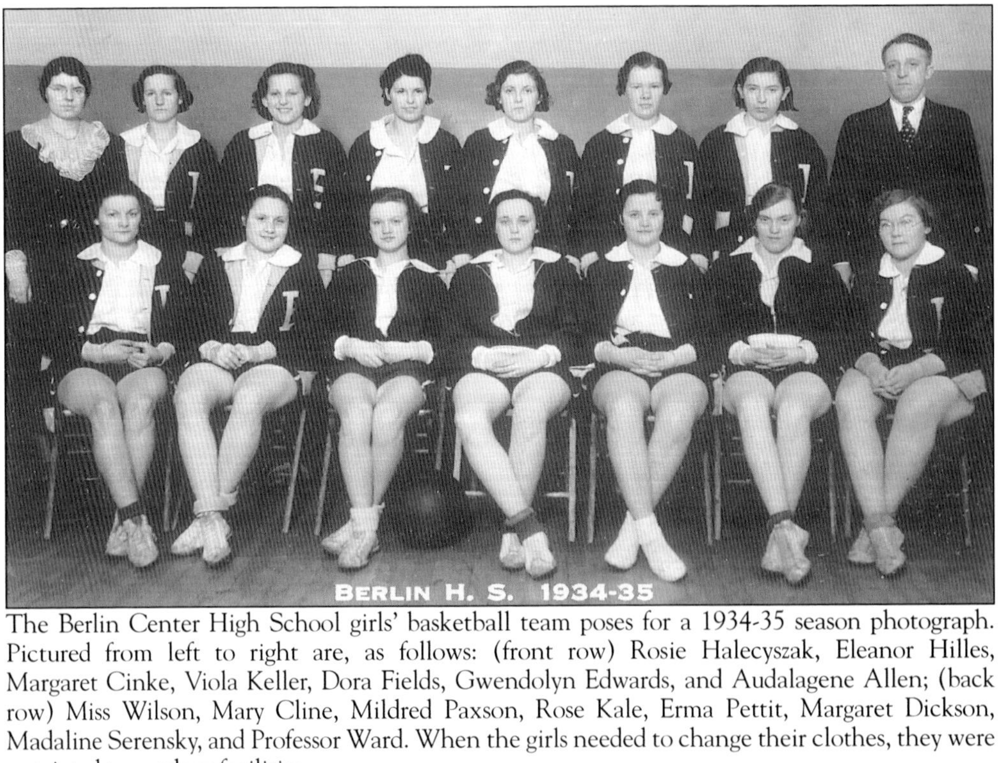

The Berlin Center High School girls' basketball team poses for a 1934-35 season photograph. Pictured from left to right are, as follows: (front row) Rosie Halecyszak, Eleanor Hilles, Margaret Cinke, Viola Keller, Dora Fields, Gwendolyn Edwards, and Audalagene Allen; (back row) Miss Wilson, Mary Cline, Mildred Paxson, Rose Kale, Erma Pettit, Margaret Dickson, Madaline Serensky, and Professor Ward. When the girls needed to change their clothes, they were restricted to outdoor facilities.

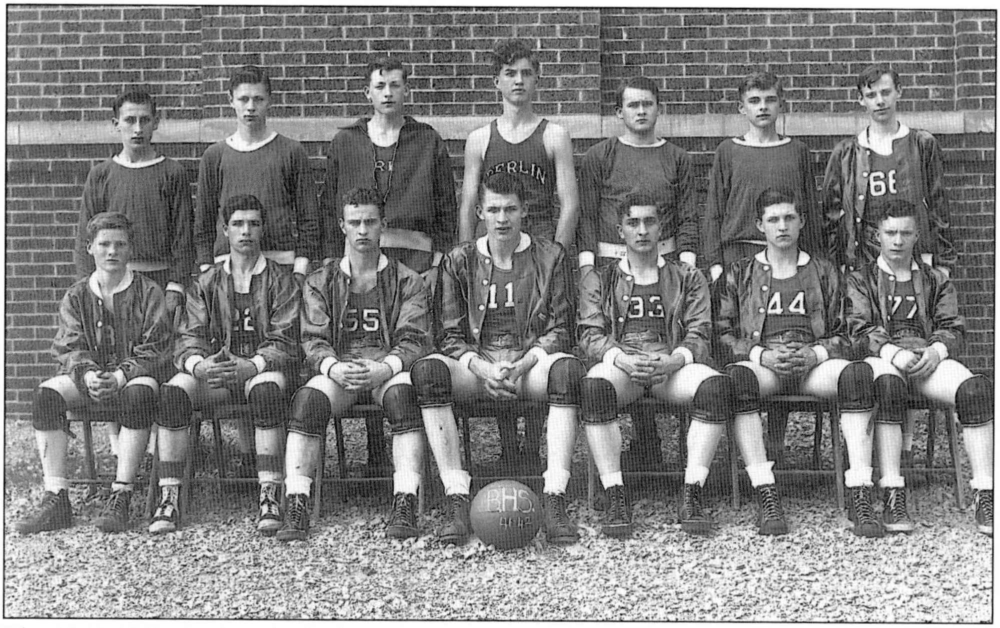

The 1941-42 Berlin boys basketball team are shown here from left to right: (front row, varsity team) Bobby Kurtz, Clyde Woolman Jr., Glen Needham, James Craig, Malcomb Obenauf, Richard Craig, and Donald Eckenrode; (back row, junior varsity team) Max Simix, Virgil Hoyle, Bill Kenride, Millard Keslar, Howard Manypenny, Bennie Burky, and Frank Dessel. Their coach was Dave Hatcher.

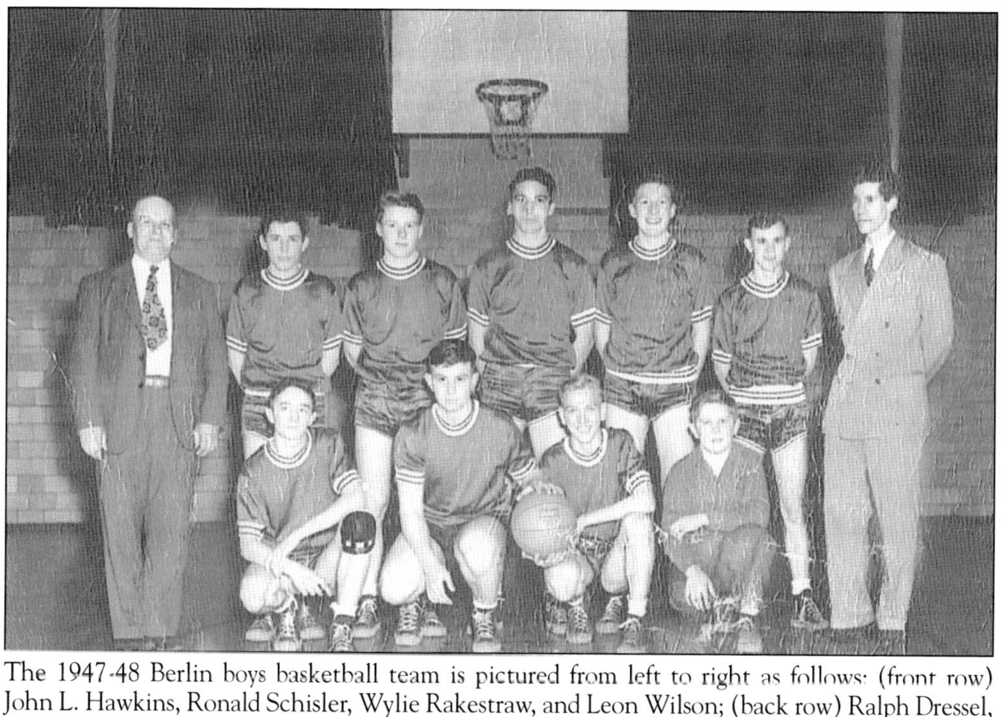

The 1947-48 Berlin boys basketball team is pictured from left to right as follows: (front row) John L. Hawkins, Ronald Schisler, Wylie Rakestraw, and Leon Wilson; (back row) Ralph Dressel, Charles Makar, Dick Ward, Leonard Mace, Bob Woolman, Dick Miller, and Mr. Giesy.

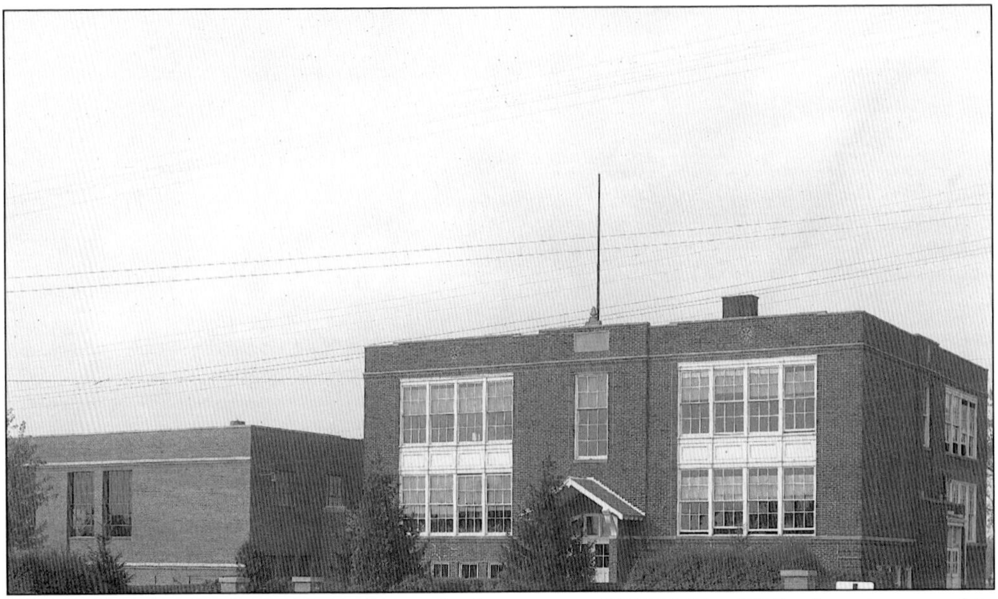

The three story structure on the right was built at a cost of $22,000 in 1915, when the township schools were centralized. The addition on the left of the new gymnasium was dedicated in 1940. The building, with changes and additions, is now used as a middle school for the Western Reserve school system.

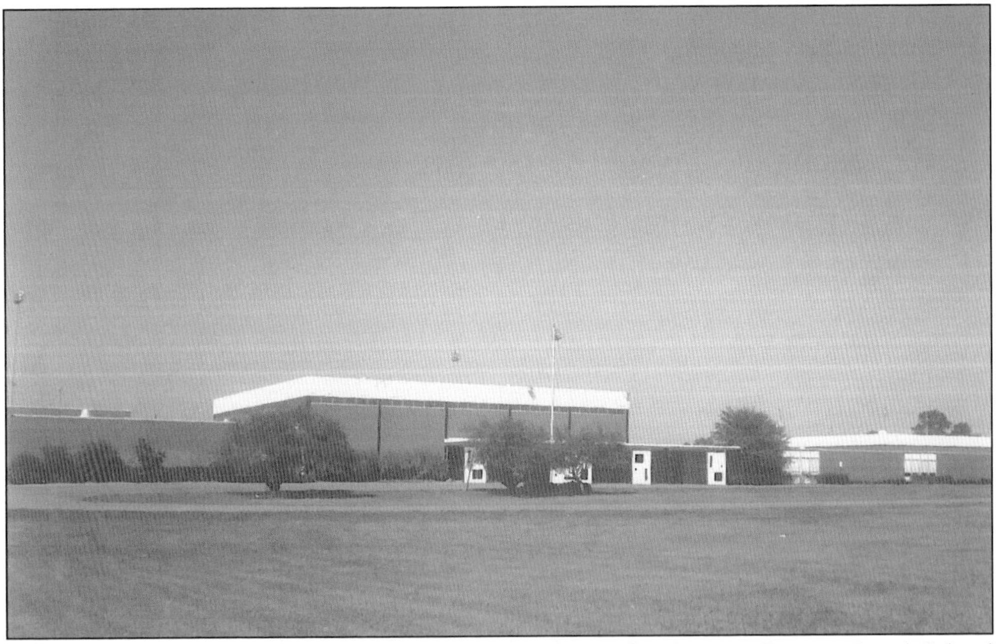

In 1957, Ellsworth and Berlin Schools consolidated into the Western Reserve Local School District. Planning for the new high school began in 1963 with an approved bond issue for $590,000 at 3.25% interest. The Serensky Farm, consisting of 109 acres located on Route 224 just west of Duck Creek Road, was purchased for this purpose. Pictured is the high school as it appears today.

Six

People and Personalities

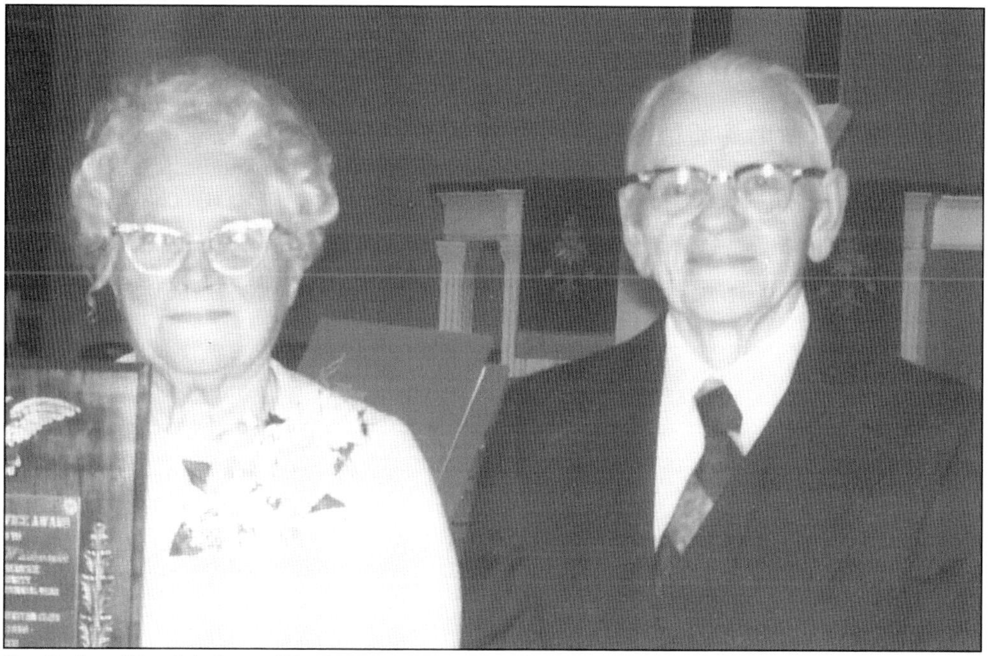

Dr. Carl and Beulah Pettit Weidenmier are pictured receiving an award. Dr. Weidenmier served the Berlin area for 40 years, retiring in 1969. The Weidenmier House, now occupied by the Berlin Center Historical Society as well as the township offices and meeting room, is named in honor of the Weidenmiers. The doctor maintained his office in the front of the house while the family residence filled the remainder of the home. Their son, Dr. Carl Henry Weidenmier, now resides in Florida.

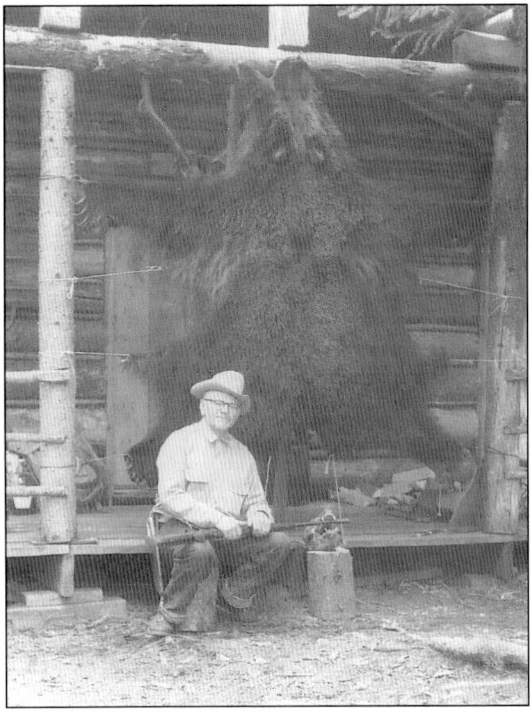

Dr. Carl Weidenmier's hobbies were big game hunting and marksmanship. Here, he poses in front of a bear skin hunted in the mountains of British Columbia. Dr. Weidenmier maintained a den in his home to display his collection of guns, game mountings, and furs.

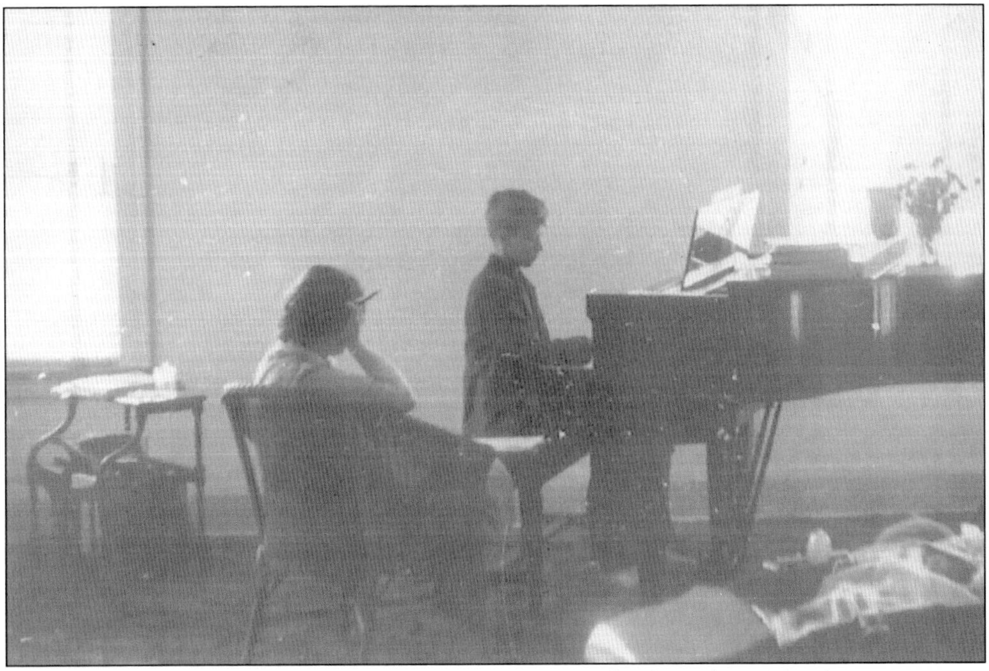

Beulah Pettit Weidenmier came to Berlin Center as a school teacher. After her marriage to Dr. Weidenmier, she offered piano lessons, served on the school board, directed the choir at the Methodist Church, participated in church women's groups, headed the festival to buy school band uniforms, and served as chairperson of the bicentennial celebration in 1976. Pictured here with Beulah is Virgil Hoyle, one of her many piano students.

Pictured in front of Dr. W.T. Gudgel's office in Berlin Center are Dr. Gudgel, Myrtle Burnett Gudgel, and son Byron Gudgel. Dr. Gudgel practiced medicine in Berlin Center from 1910 to 1928, charging $5 to deliver babies. Mrs. Gudgel was a registered nurse, and the couple's four children were delivered at home.

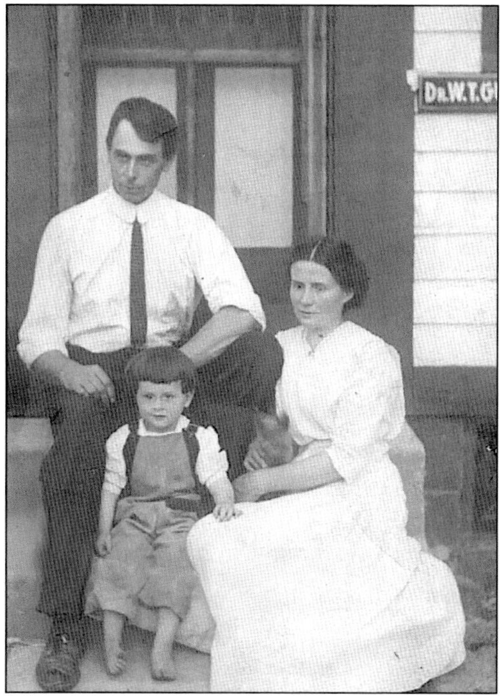

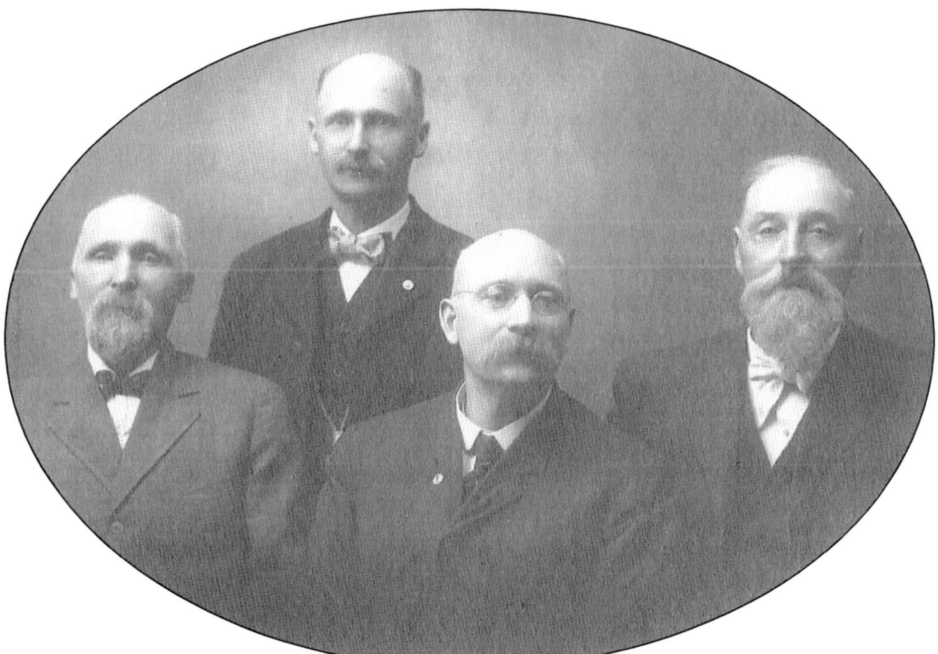

The Carson brothers, sons of George and Catherine Gross Carson, appear from left to right as follows: Uriah, Dr. William Frank, Elmer, and David. There were eleven children in the family. Uriah served in the Civil War at the battle of Shiloh; Dr. W.F. worked as a doctor in Berlin for 30 years; Elmer moved to Alliance, Ohio; and David was a schoolteacher and justice of the peace in Deerfield, joining the firm of Carson and Diver along the way.

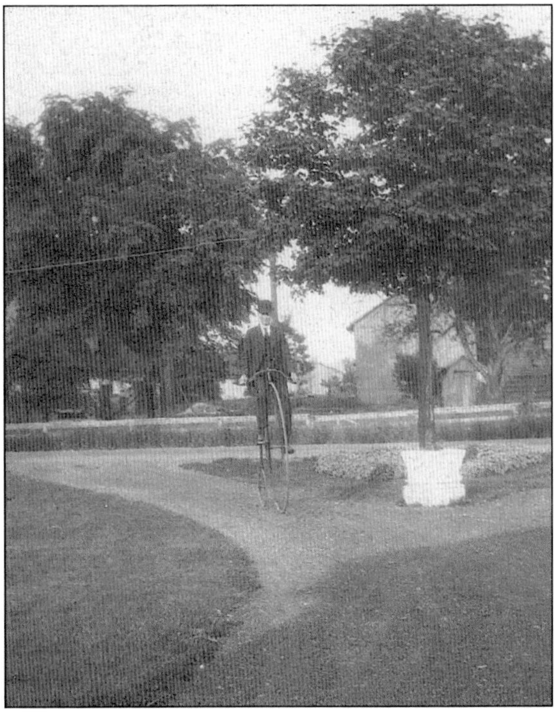

Carey Shively rides his high wheeled bicycle on his 65th birthday in 1923. He rode only twice a year, to mark his own and his mother's birthday. As a young man, Shively was one of the best high wheel bike riders around, purchasing the bicycle at 17 in Youngstown, then riding it home to Berlin Center. On his 67th birthday, Shively rode the bicycle around the square in downtown Youngstown. He considered the bike inadequate for city traffic, especially as it lacked brakes.

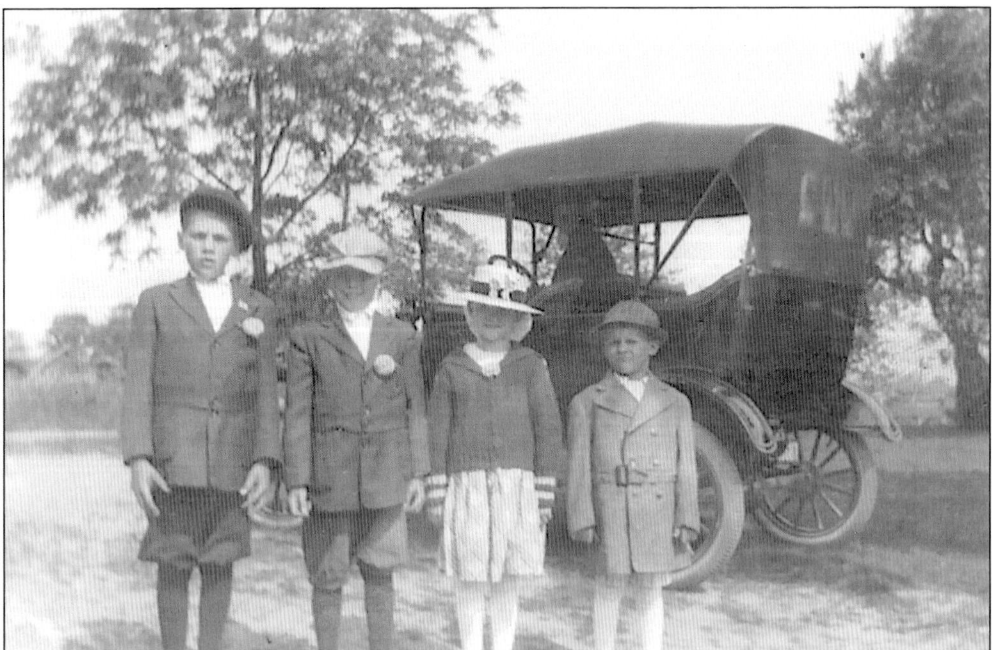

Shown here are Melvin, Richard, Kathleen, and Ivan, the children of Clyde and Etta Hoyle Baringer, all dressed up for a ride in the car.

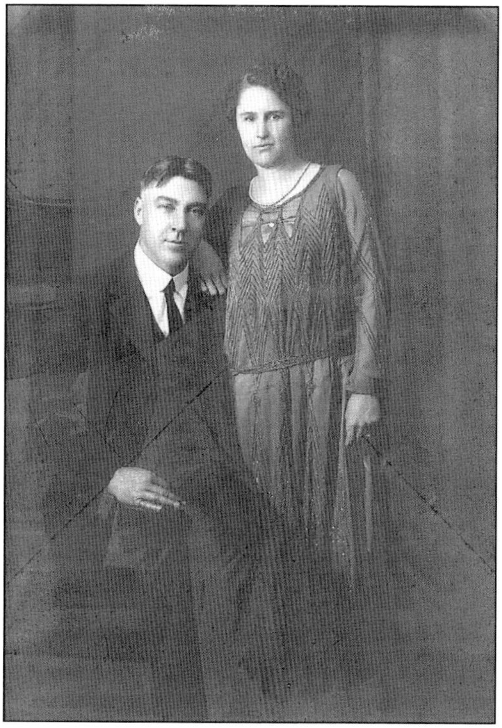

This is the wedding picture of Frank and Addie Forney (date unknown). The dress, which was donated to the Historical Society by Ralph and Phoebe Davis for display, is a dark brown color embellished with many beads.

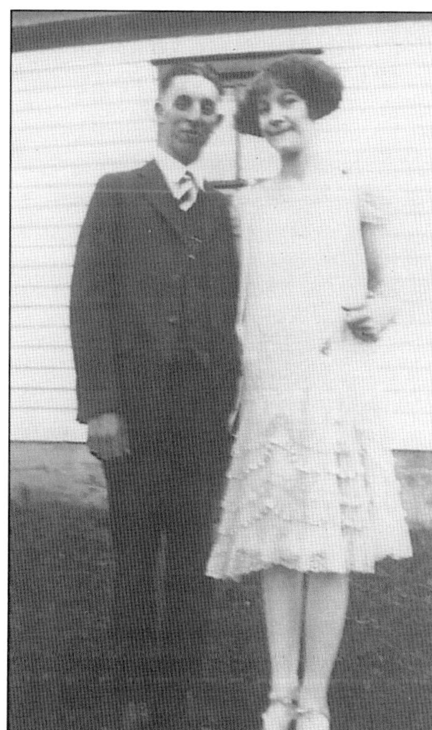

The wedding picture of Hugh and Helen Shively Taylor is dated June 30, 1927. Helen appears in a sheer pale green dress with a scalloped hem and rows of small ruffles around the skirt. This dress was donated by Kathleen and Hugh Taylor Jr., and may be viewed at the historical society's museum.

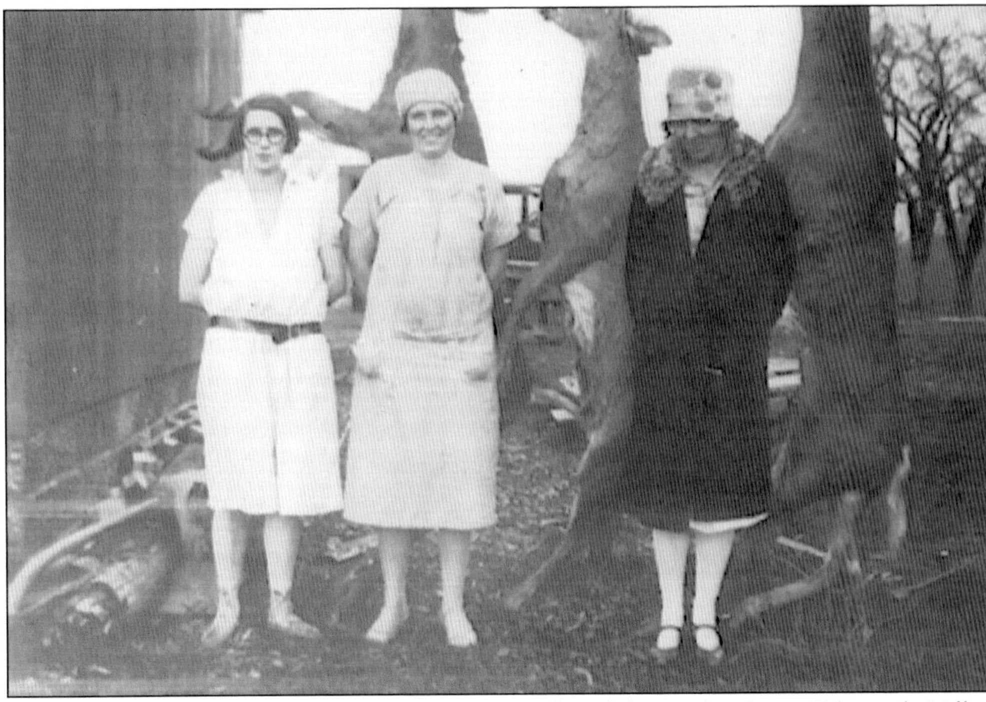

The three local ladies in front of the large deer are, from left to right, Grace Eckenrode Hilles, Pearl Jenkins Kale, and Etta Hoyle Baringer.

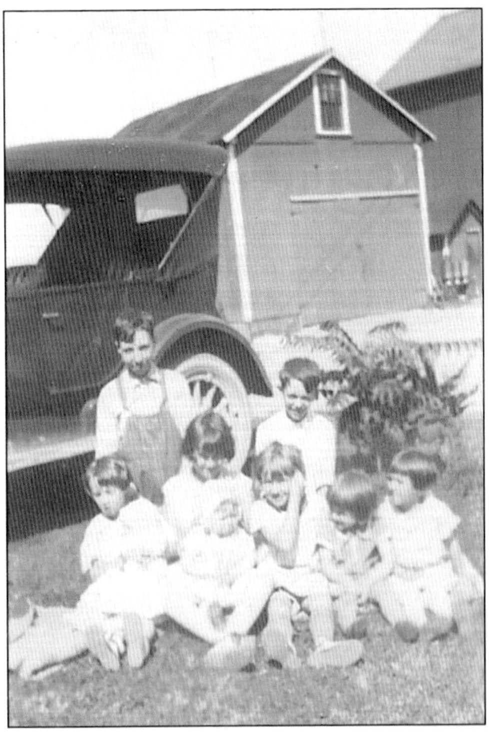

Pictured here are the grandchildren of George and Olive Crutchley Hilles. The nine Hilles children, from left to right, are as follows: (front row) Theresa (holding Evelyn), Eleanor (holding Marjorie), Viola, Ruth, and Alice; (back row) Charles and Burton. The picture was taken around 1927 on what is now known as the Miller farm at 17440 Mock Road.

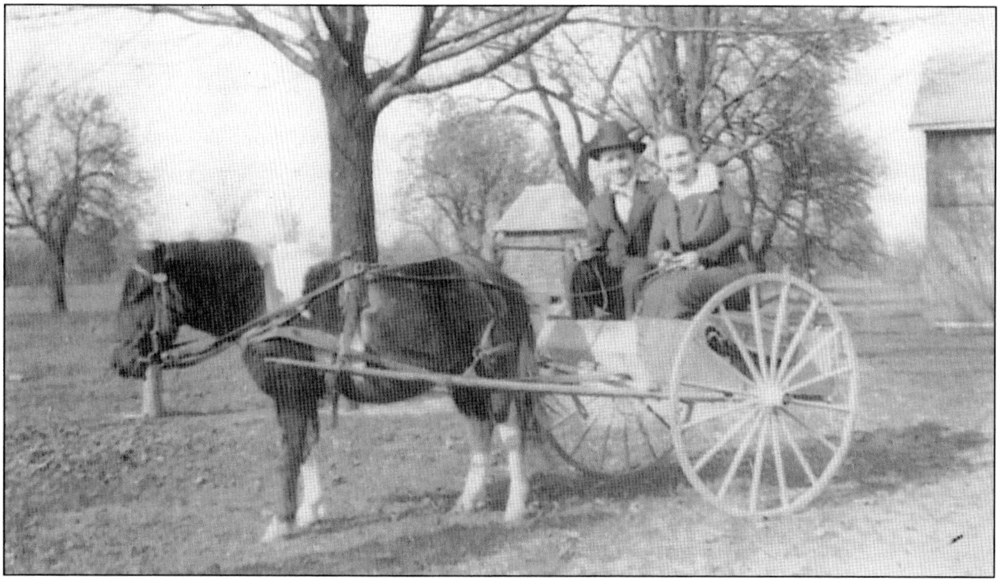

Burt and Madge Kirkbride Shively drive their pony cart in the 1920s. Burt served as a rural route mailman for many years. The couple lived at 17370 Berlin Station Road, where great granddaughter Tina Taylor Smith and her husband Lee Smith live today.

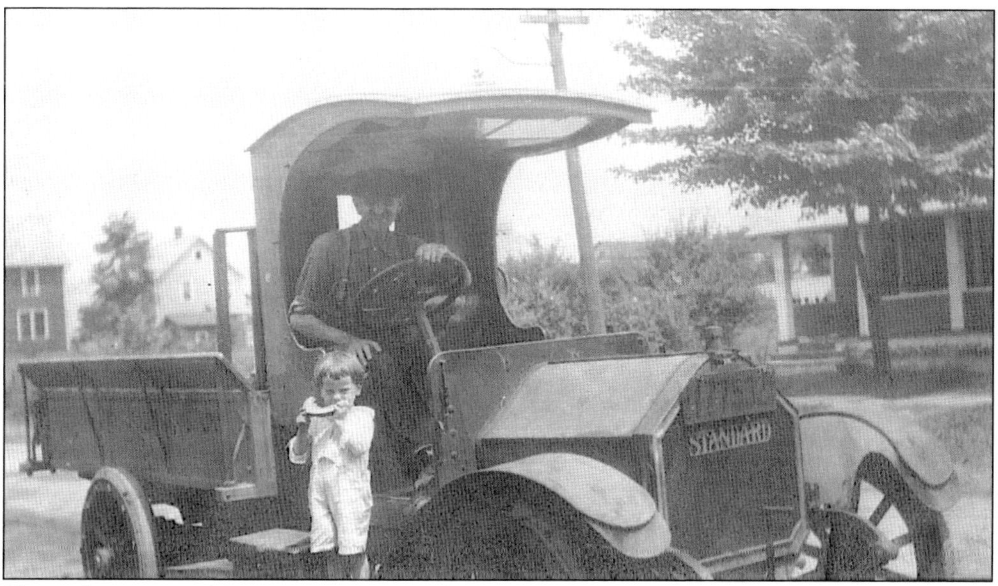

Shown here is an old time "Standard" pickup truck with the steering wheel on the right side. Melvin Hawn sits in the driver's seat as Byron Gudgel enjoys a slice of watermelon.

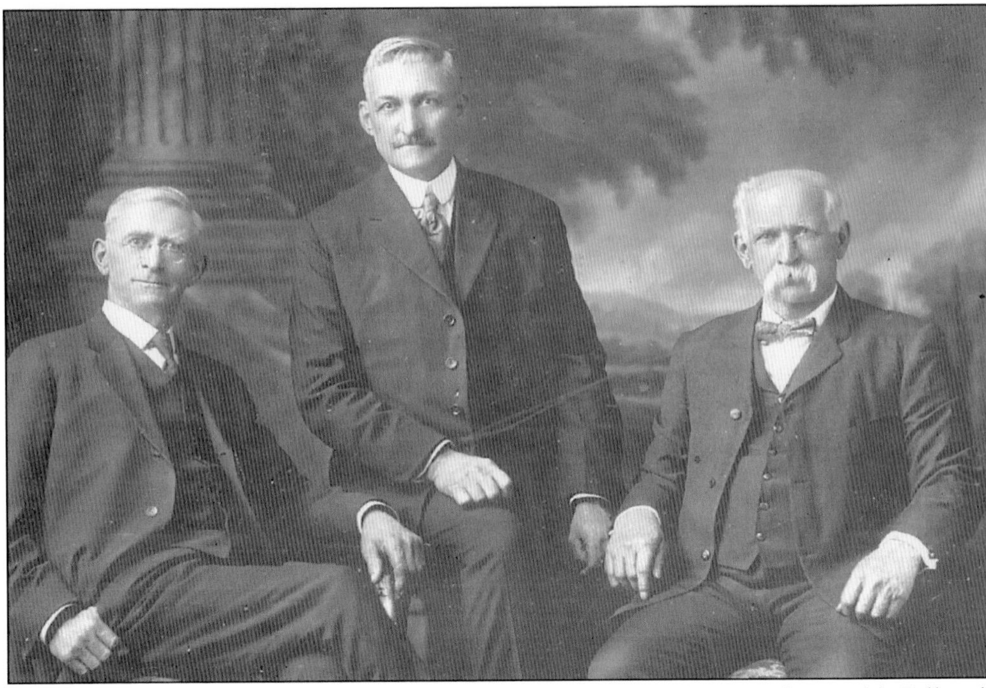

These handsome brothers were three of Lewis (Ludwig) and Susan (Susanah) Fellnogle Renkenberger's seven children. Pictured from left to right are, as follows: Steven, born in 1860; William, born in 1865; and Theodore, born in 1852. Their grandfather, Christopher Renkenberger, came to Columbiana from Germany in 1826.

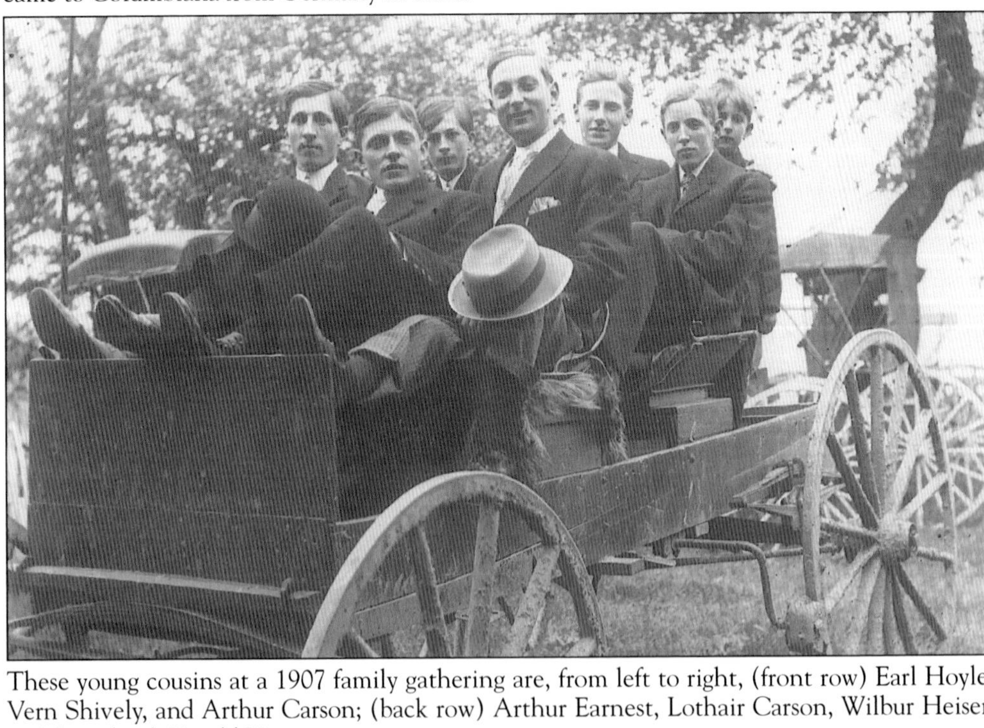

These young cousins at a 1907 family gathering are, from left to right, (front row) Earl Hoyle, Vern Shively, and Arthur Carson; (back row) Arthur Earnest, Lothair Carson, Wilbur Heiser, and (standing) Harold Heiser.

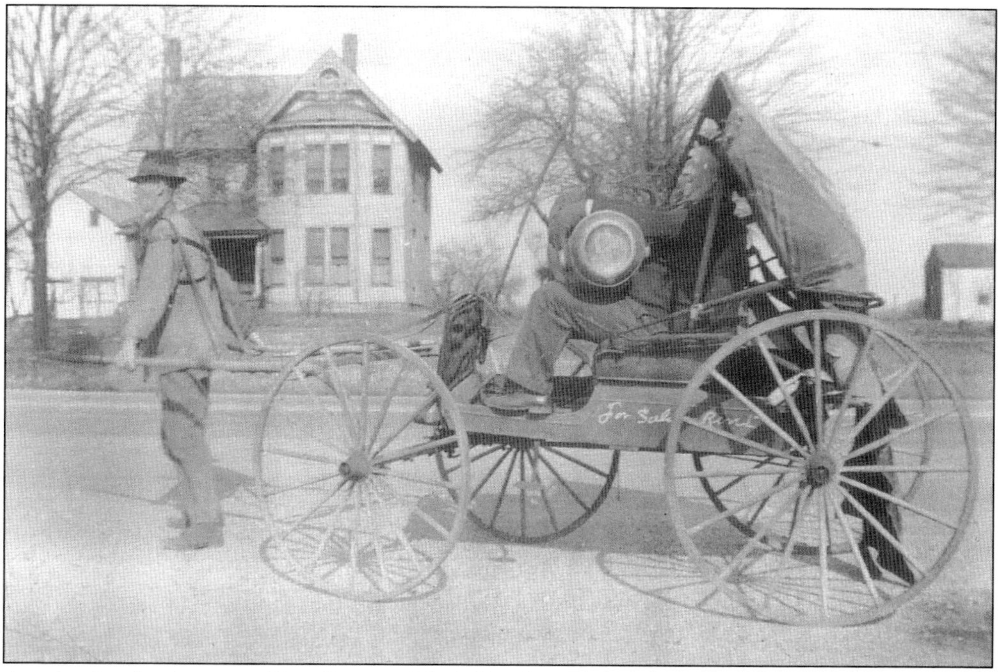

An election bet between Burt Durr and Jack Smith ended with Durr pulling Smith in a wagon down the main street in Berlin Center.

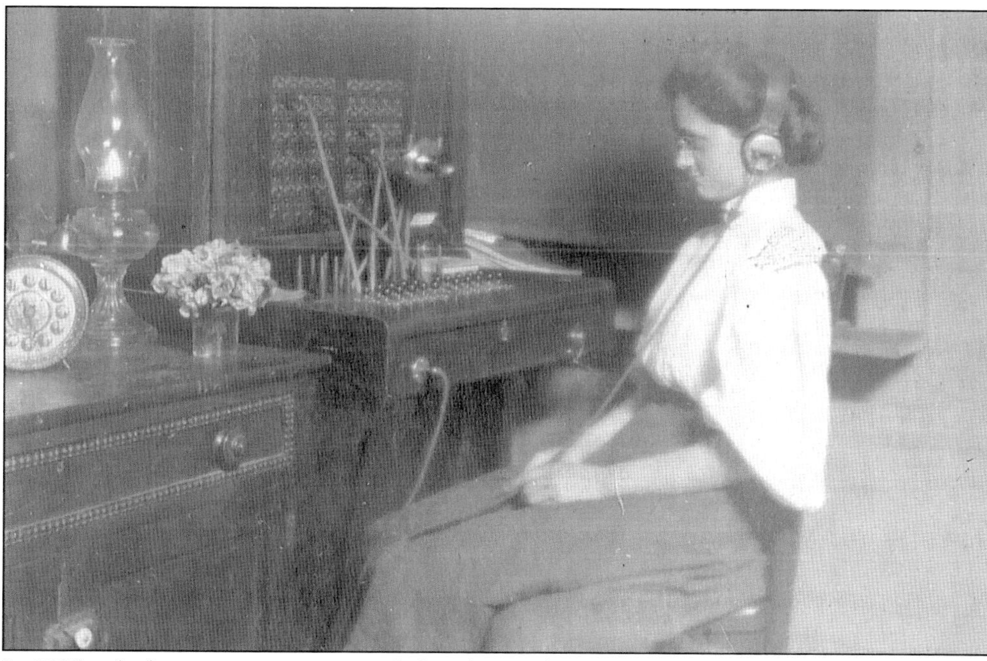

In 1905, telephone service was provided to the residents near the Center, and Martha Hoover was one of the early operators. In 1910, the Berlin Center Telephone Company was formed by Fifer, Mascury, and Shrader. The phones were the ‘hand crank” style, requiring callers to dial the operator for connection to their desired party. The company was sold to Ohio Central in 1932. In later years, ownership passed to United Telephone, and eventually to Sprint.

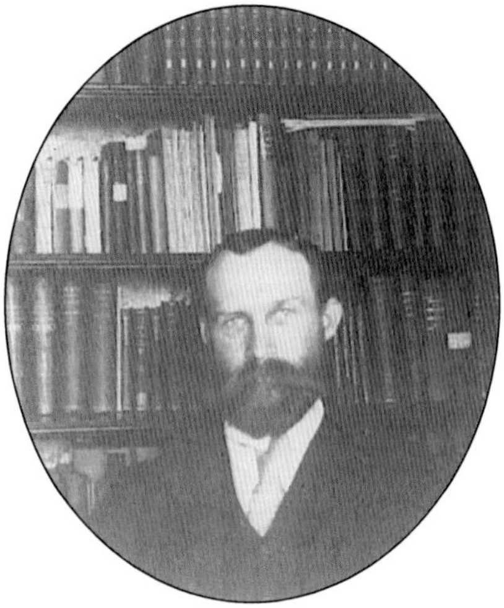

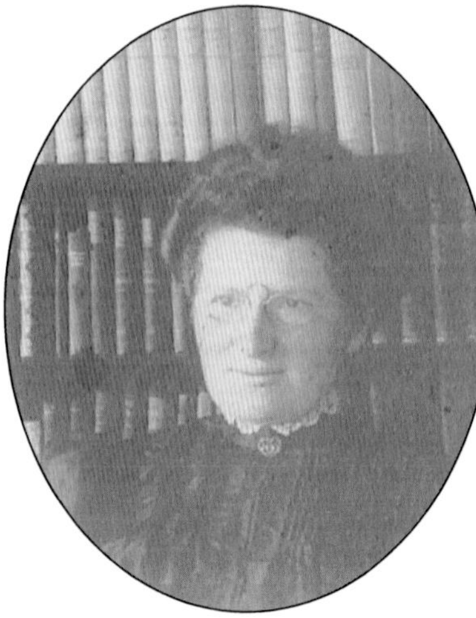

E.W. (Earnest Waters) Vickers and Lottie Spauling Vickers are pictured here in their home. Earnest was the first park naturalist at Mill Creek Park in Youngstown, Ohio. Lottie was seamstress for many local ladies. They moved to Berlin Center in 1912, and called their home "Bird Acre".

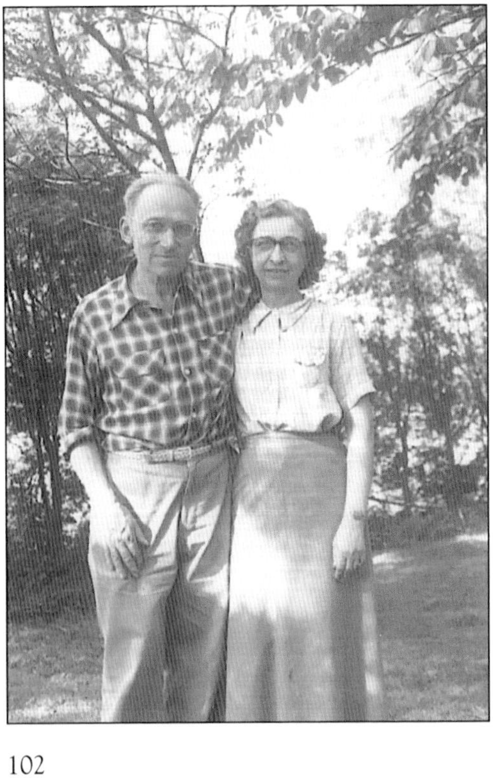

(Horace) Lindley Vickers, son of E.W. and Lottie S. Vickers, was Youngstown's Mill Creek Park naturalist for 40 years. He married Dorothy Winch and together they had four children. Dorothy played the piano and organ for the Methodist Church for many years. It is estimated that Lindley took 500,000 children on nature hikes and walked 32,000 miles in the park during his employment. He retired in 1970.

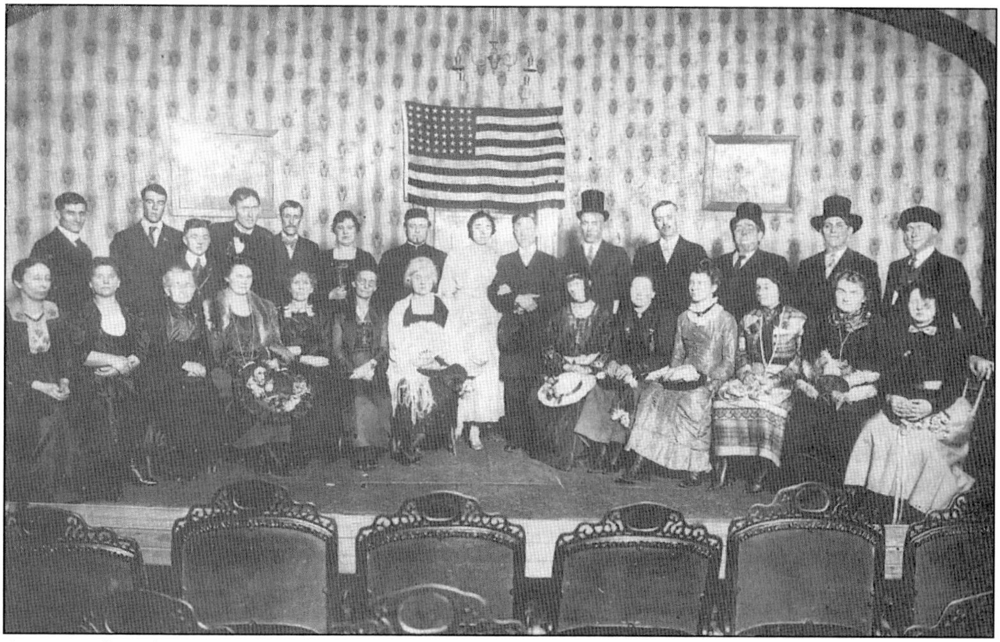

A musical, "The New Minister" was presented by the Berlin Center and Deerfield Methodist Episcopal Church choirs in 1920. Scott McConnell played the part of the new minister. Others in the musical were listed as I.J. Smith, Wm. Caven, L.G. Kime, Fred Williams, Harold Phillips, L.L. Allen, Mrs. Robinson, Miss Williams, Miss DeLong, L.E. Hawkins, Miss Myers, Mrs. Mary Hawkins, and Wm. Lane. The group went to College Chapel in Canfield to have this portrait taken.

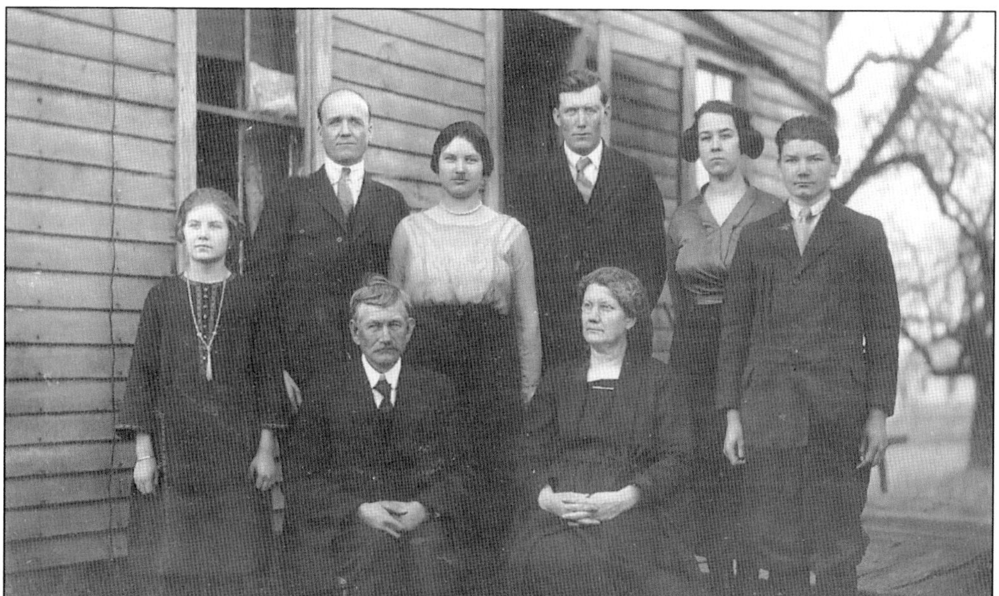

The family home on Pricetown Road became the site of the Newell family reunion around 1922. Pictured from left to right are, as follows: (front row) Mary Newell Parks, Frank Newell, Emma Newell, and Forrest (Bud) Newell; (back row) Clyde Keslar, Irene Newell Keslar, Elgie Newell, and Ruth Shefleton Newell.

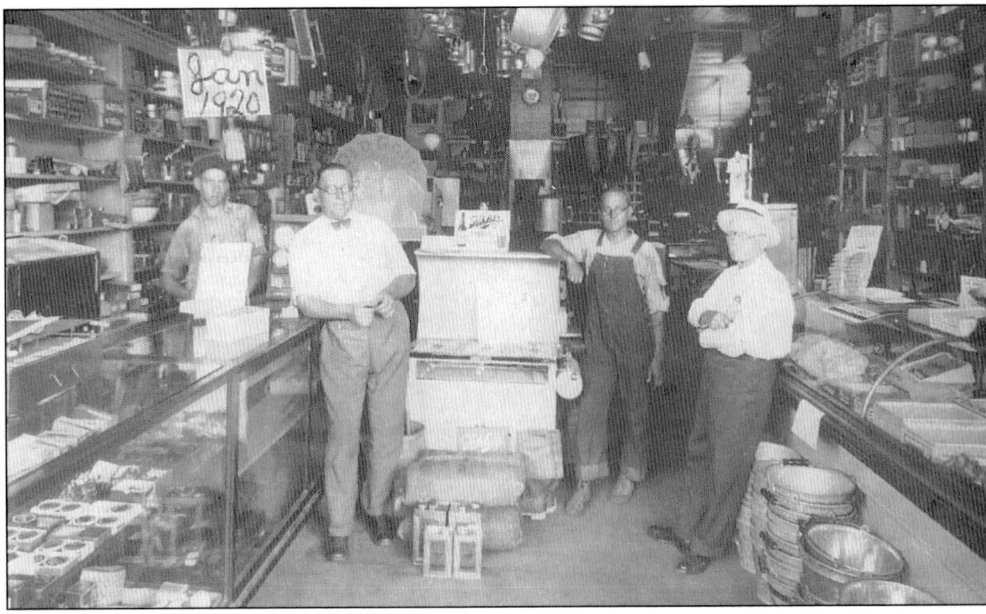

Here is a glimpse inside the Galbreath and Shively Hardware Store in 1920. The Hardware was located on Akron-Canfield Road beside the home now owned by the Brobst family. Appearing are, from left to right, unidentified, Bernard Bell (oil salesman), Henry Shively (co-owner), and Delormi Rose. The building burned in the 1933 fire.

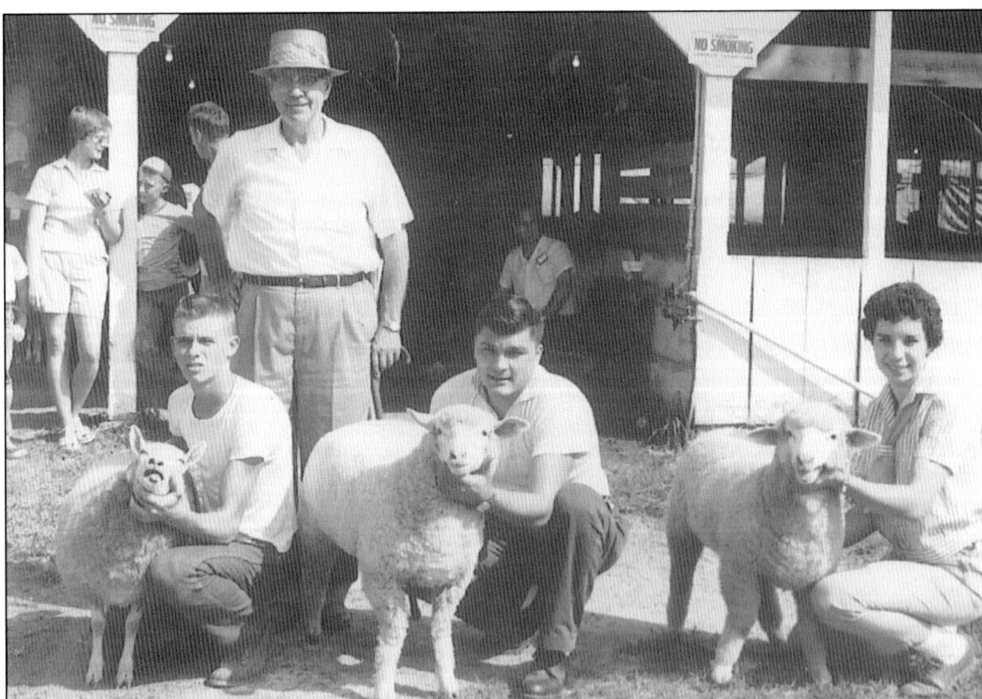

Champions at the 1957 Canfield Fair display their prize-winning sheep. Pictured from left to right are Don Taylor with the Champion Cheviot Sheep, Gene Baringer with the Champion Columbia Sheep, and Carolyn Zambar with the Champion Corriedale Sheep.

Seven

GOVERNMENT

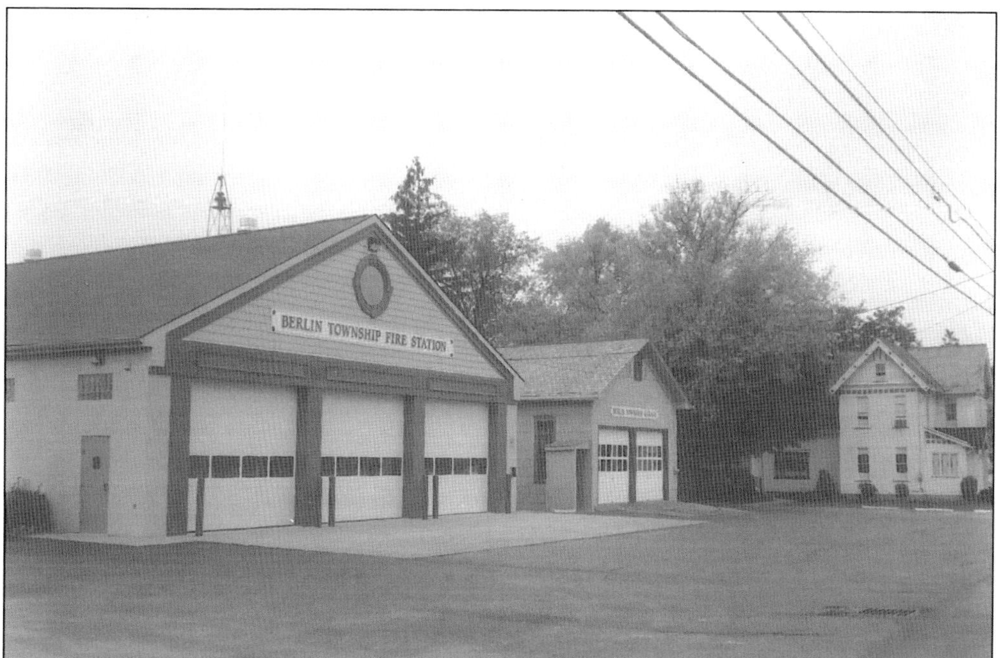

The Berlin Township government buildings are located on Akron-Canfield Road (Route 224) approximately 500 feet west of Route 534. The fire station is located on the left, the road garage in the center, and the Weidenmier House (town hall) on the right.

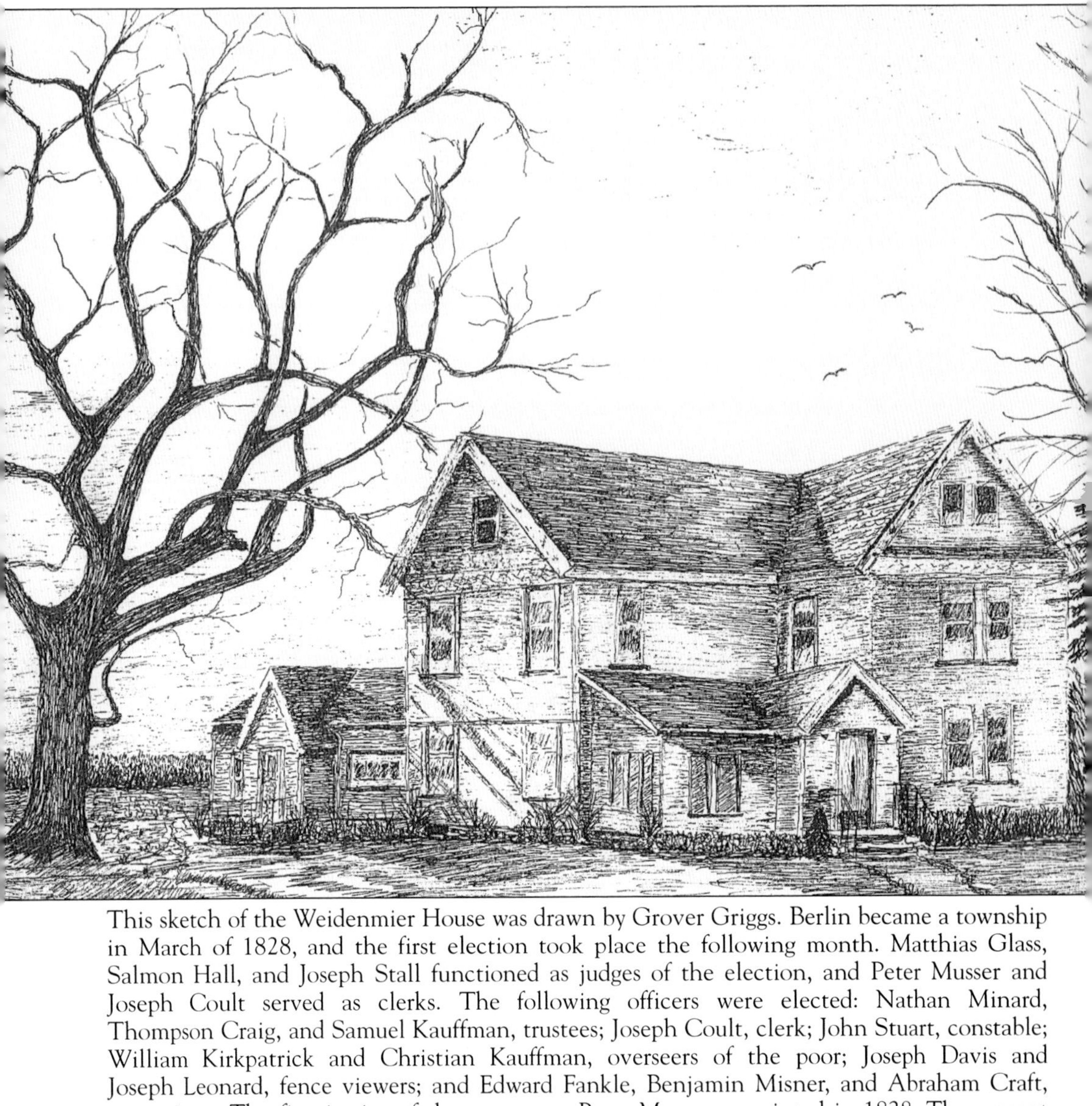

This sketch of the Weidenmier House was drawn by Grover Griggs. Berlin became a township in March of 1828, and the first election took place the following month. Matthias Glass, Salmon Hall, and Joseph Stall functioned as judges of the election, and Peter Musser and Joseph Coult served as clerks. The following officers were elected: Nathan Minard, Thompson Craig, and Samuel Kauffman, trustees; Joseph Coult, clerk; John Stuart, constable; William Kirkpatrick and Christian Kauffman, overseers of the poor; Joseph Davis and Joseph Leonard, fence viewers; and Edward Fankle, Benjamin Misner, and Abraham Craft, supervisors. The first justice of the peace was Peter Musser, appointed in 1828. The present officers of the township are Sandie Engle, Jim Brown Jr., and Ivan Hoyle (trustees), and Dolly Bennett (clerk).

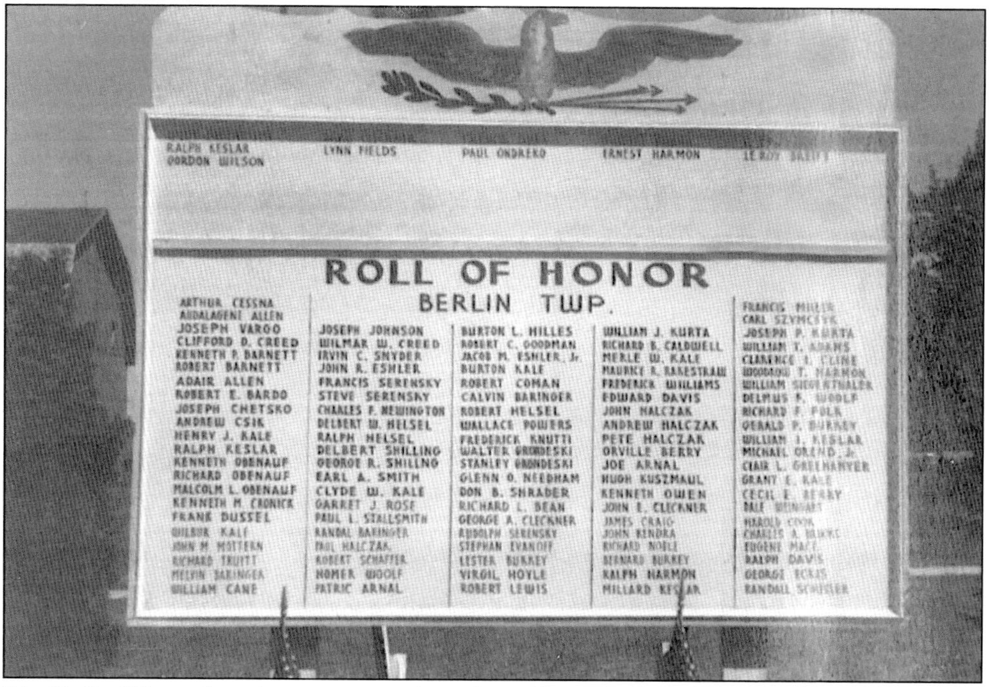

The Roll of Honor board, now mounted on the wall inside the road garage, lists the men and women who served our country in the armed forces during World War II. The residents of Berlin Township take pride in the many young men and women who served.

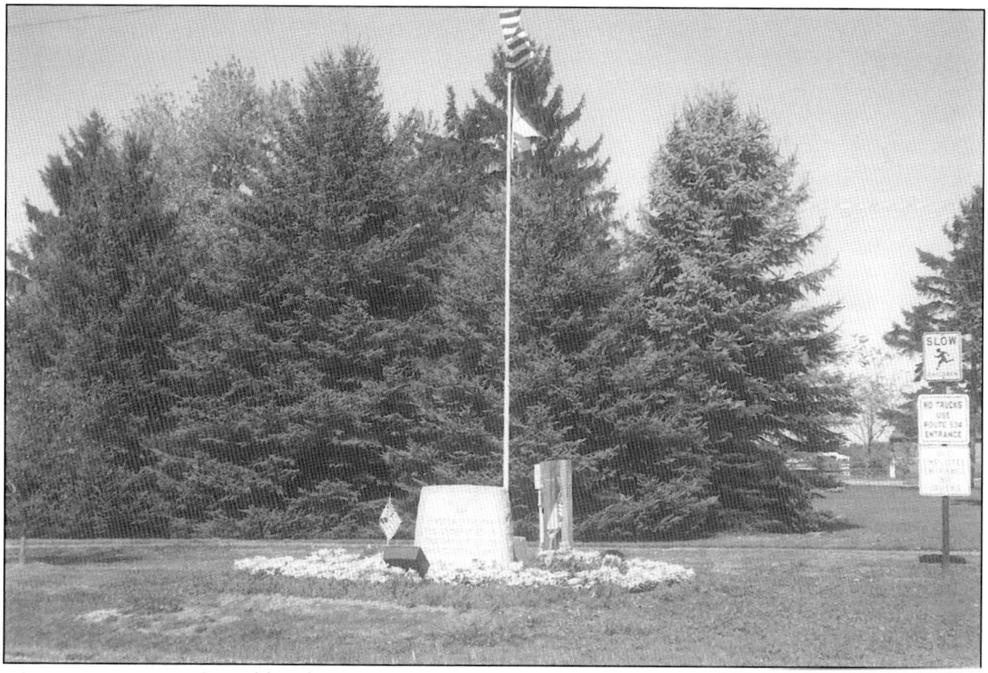

The Roll of Honor board has been replaced with this monument honoring all who have served in the armed forces. The memorial and flagpole are located across the road from the fire station. Flowers are planted at the memorial each spring by a local 4-H club.

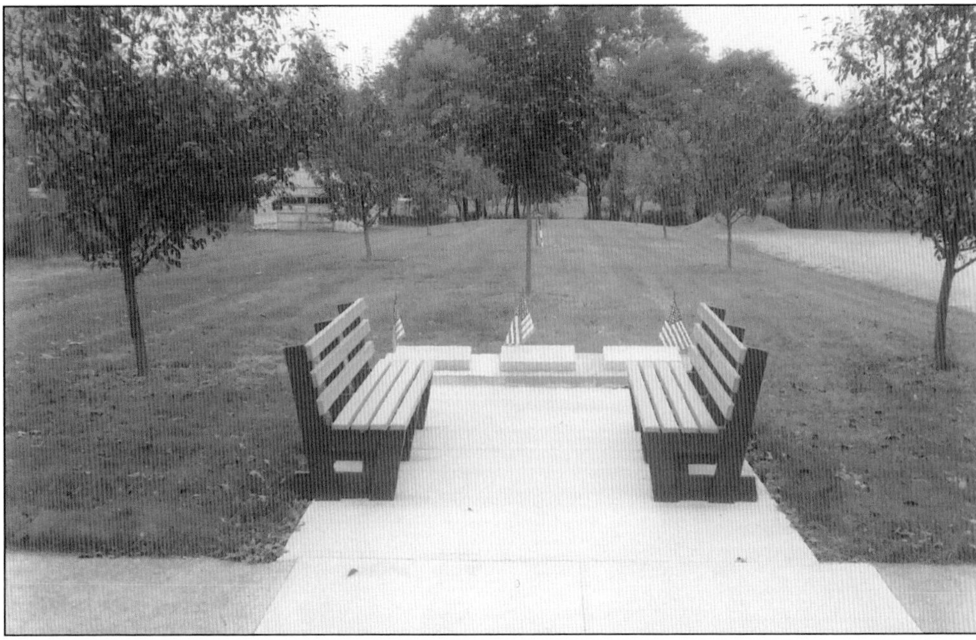

Trees may be purchased in memory of loved ones for the Berlin Township Memorial Tree Garden. The garden was established in 1994, providing an area for trees to be planted beside and behind the government buildings. Names of those with trees planted in their honor are engraved on the memorial stone.

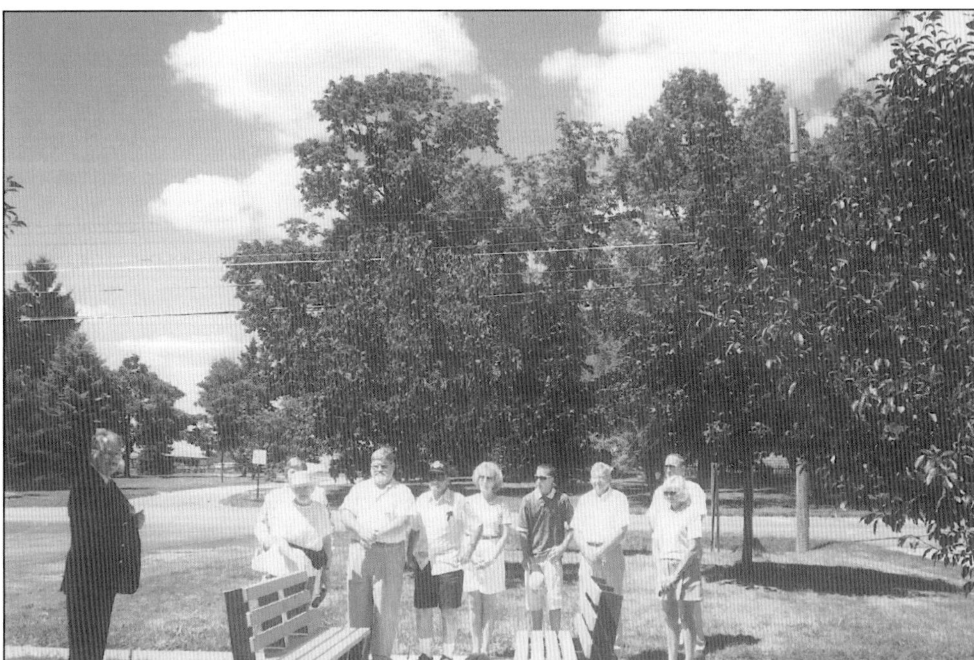

After the memorial trees are planted in May, a local minister conducts an on-site memorial service for families and friends of those honored.

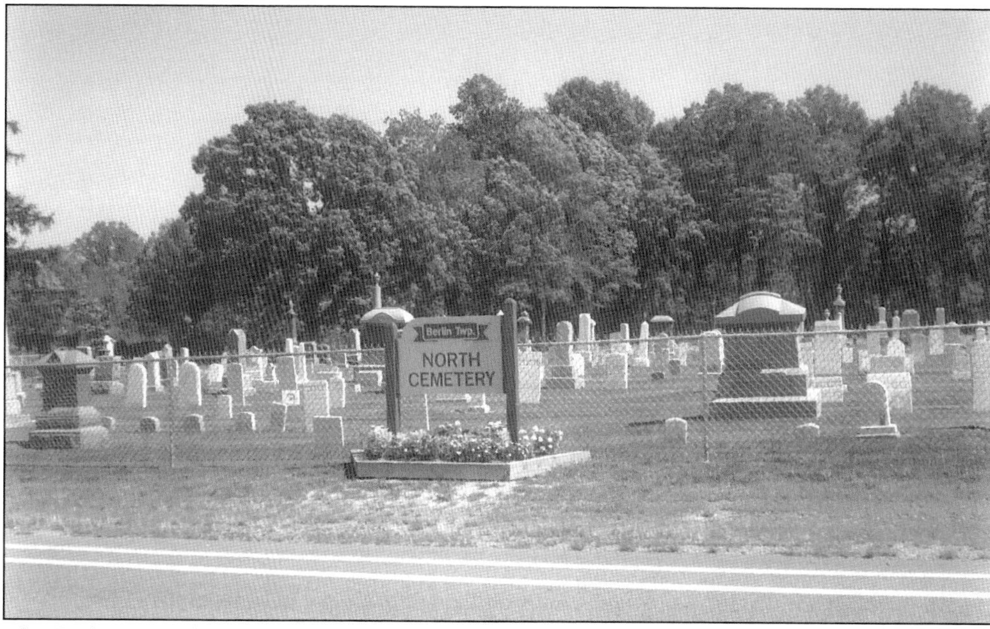

The Berlin Township North Cemetery is located two miles north of town on Route 534. From 1828 until 1836, a log church was situated at the northwest corner of the cemetery. In 1836, a new frame building was constructed across the road where the Mt. Moriah Lutheran Church is now located. Recent improvements to the cemetery include a blacktop drive, improved drainage, and clearing, grading, and seeding of the back acreage.

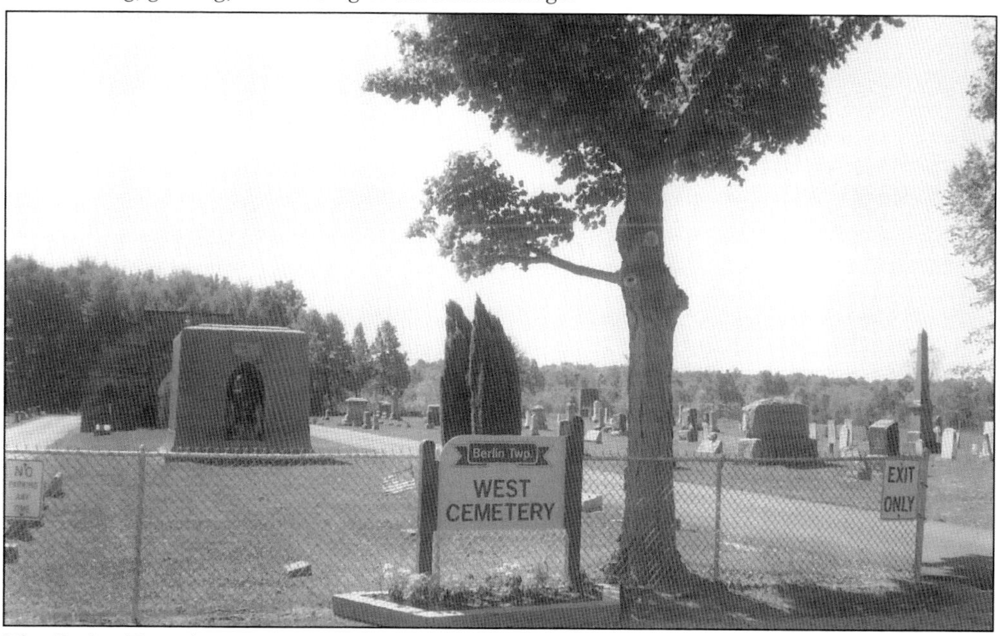

The Berlin Township West Cemetery is located one mile west of the center on Route 224. The private Carey Shively Mausoleum can be seen near the public mausoleum to the rear. Recent improvements to the cemetery include a blacktop drive, a row of flowering trees, and a new driveway at the back of the cemetery. The township purchased six additional acres around the existing land for future expansion.

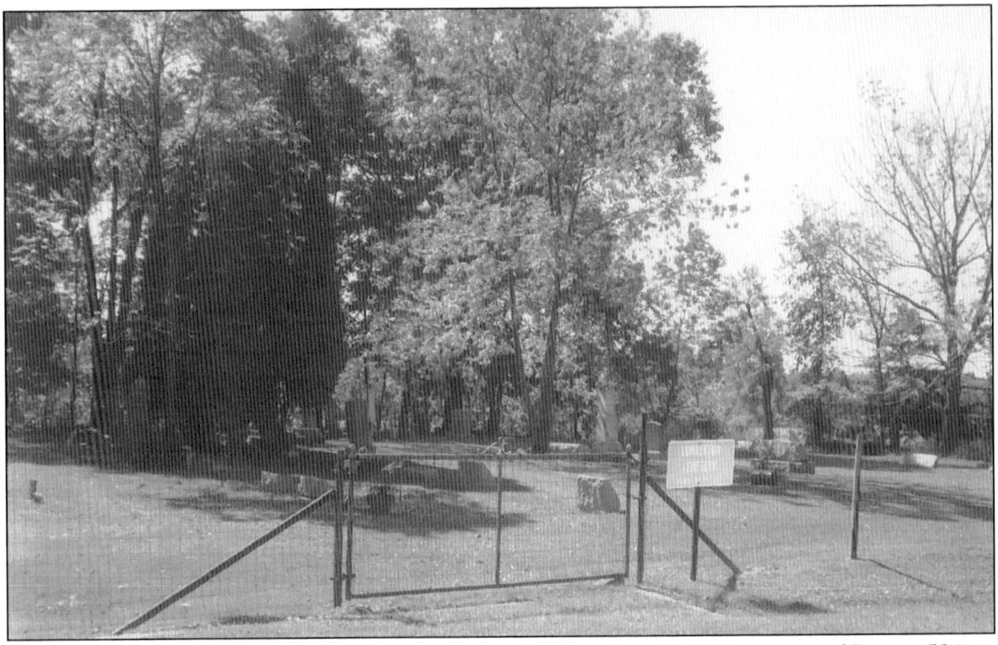

The Lumberton Cemetery, located on Western Reserve Road 200 feet east of Route 534, is jointly owned by Berlin and Goshen Townships. Both townships share equal responsibility for its maintenance. At one time, a church was located across the road in Berlin Township.

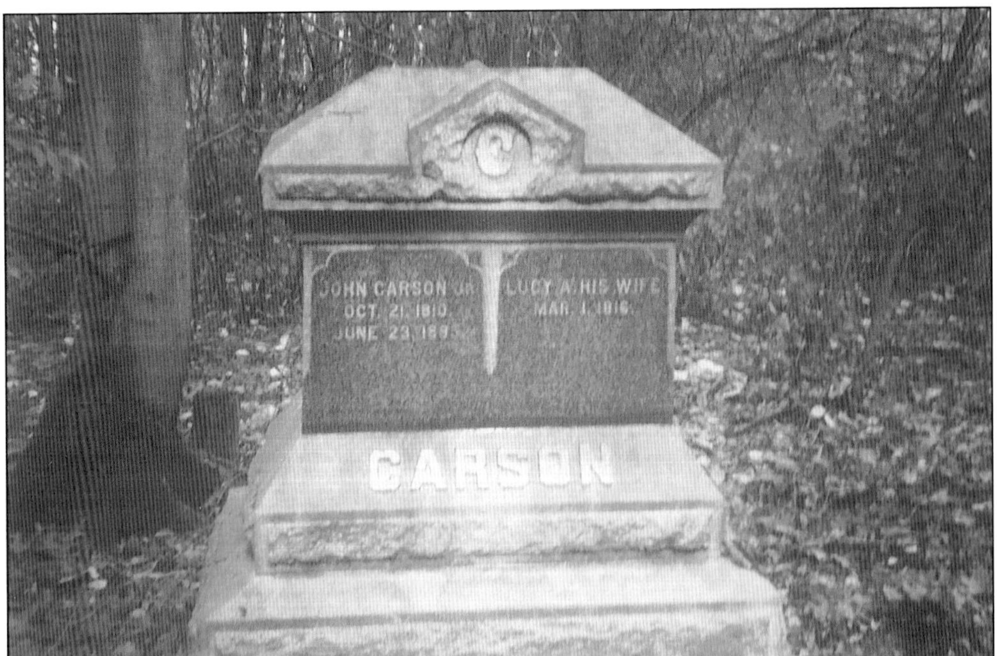

The Carson Cemetery is located near Shillings Mill on private property owned by Mr. and Mrs. Gus Olson. Because the last burial took place around 1900, only a few grave markers remain legible. John Carson Sr. served in the War of 1812.

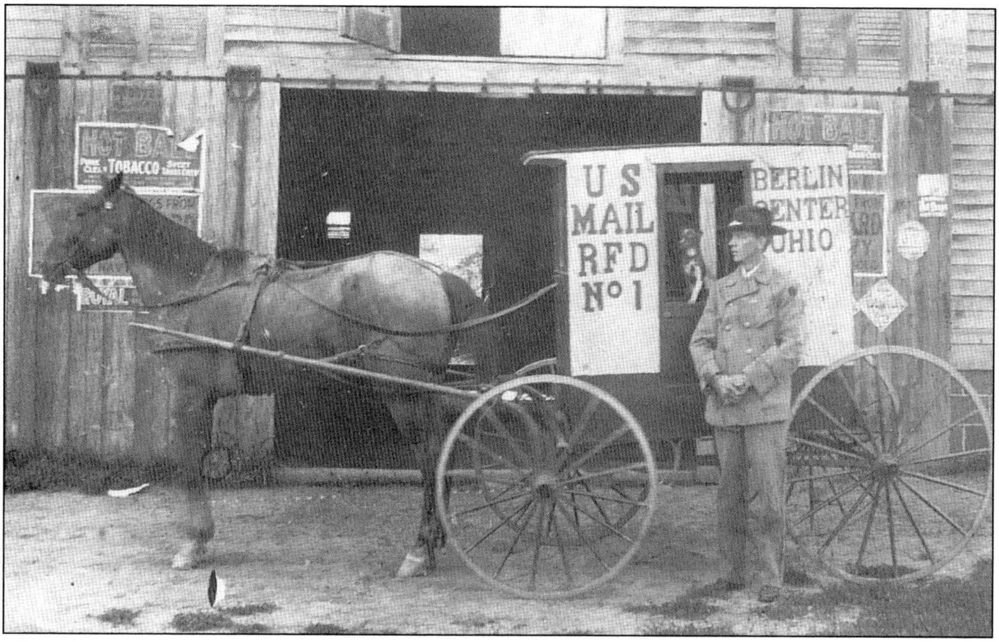

Eli Rakestraw was appointed one of two rural letter carriers in Berlin Center in 1900. He maintained his post until 1933 when retiring at the age of 65. It is estimated he traveled 234,748 miles during this time using the following three methods: on foot, with horse and buggy, and by car.

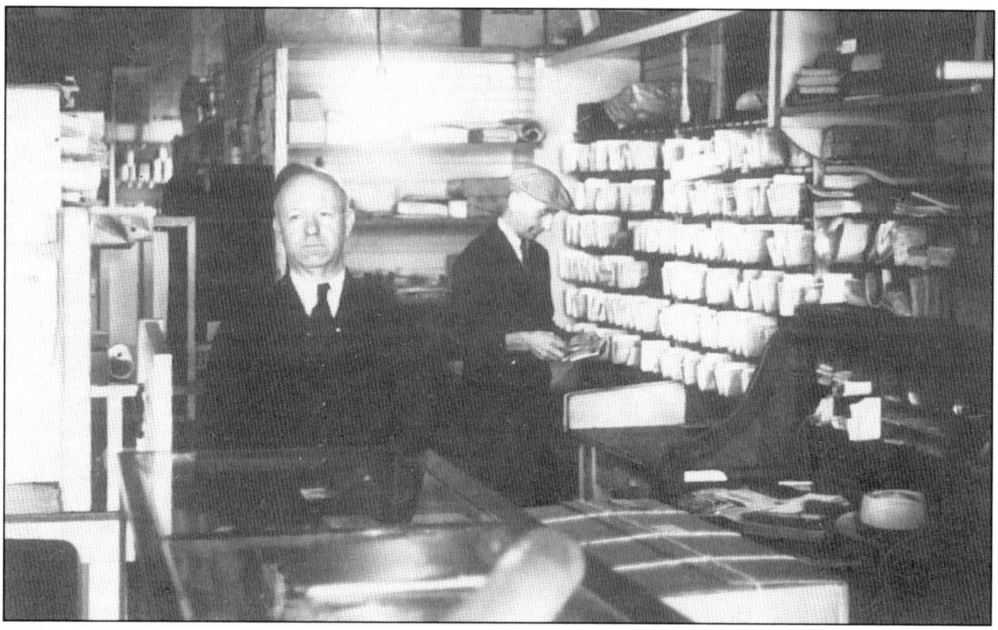

Berlin Center Post Office was located in Hawkins Store before moving to the K of P Lodge Building. Scott McConnell (left) served as postmaster from 1920 to 1953. Burt Shively (right) was rural mail carrier from 1923 to December of 1951. The mail in 1883 arrived once a week, alternating between Atwater and Canfield. The first postmaster was Joseph Edwards. In 1900, Eli Rakestraw and Chester Harmon served as the first rural letter carriers.

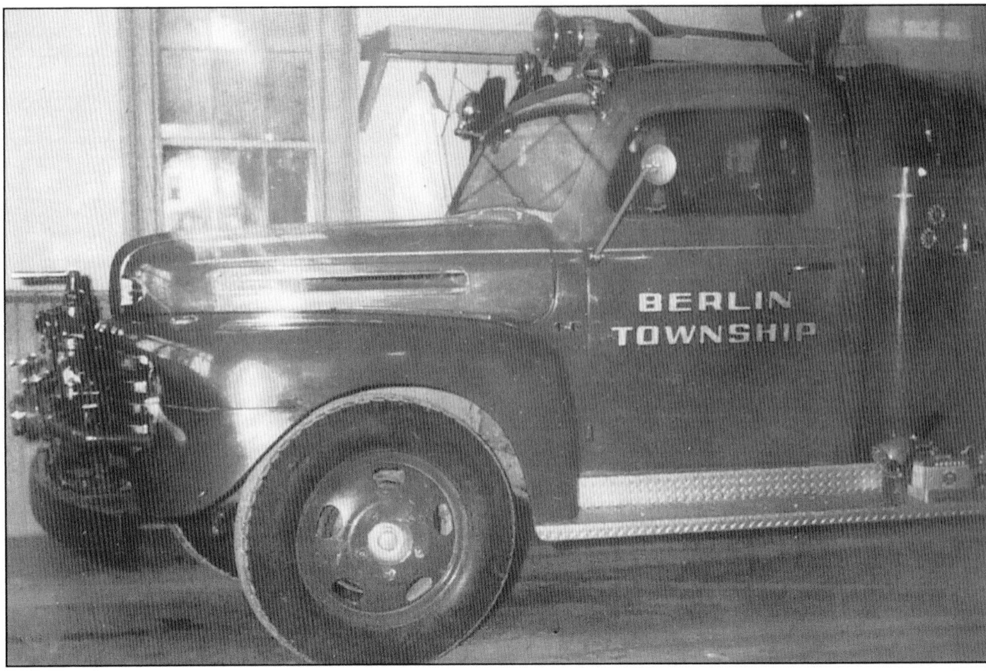

In the spring of 1947, Berlin Township suffered the loss of two houses due to the township's lack of fire protection. On July 16, 1947, forty-six men attended a meeting to organize the Berlin Township Volunteer Fire Department. This new fire truck arrived in September of 1948. The truck was retired in 1972 and sold to a local resident. In 1997, the vehicle was reclaimed by the township and historical society for restoration.

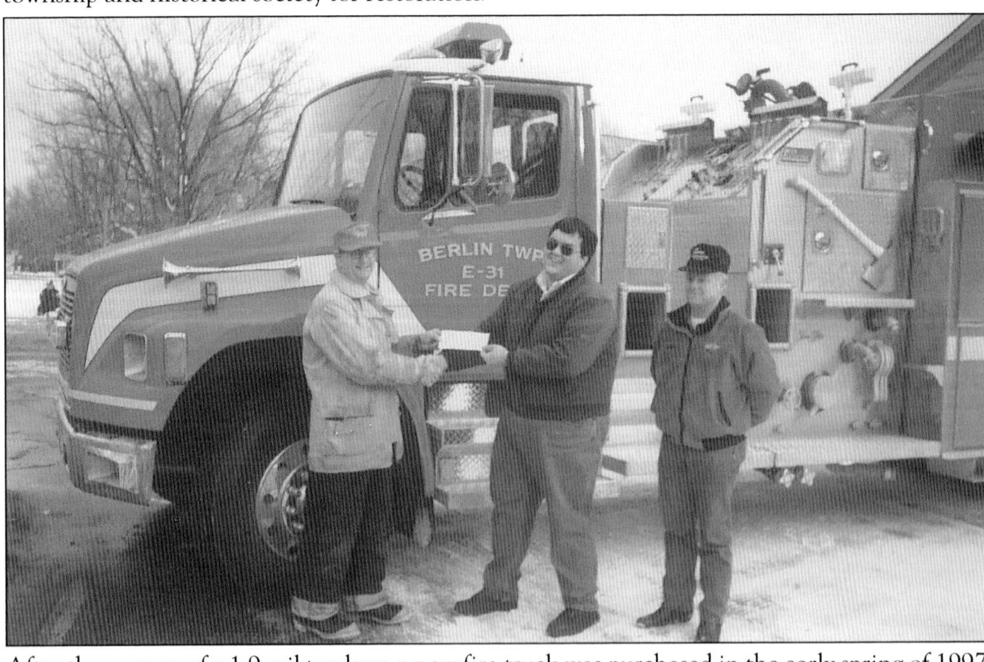

After the passage of a 1.9 mil tax levy, a new fire truck was purchased in the early spring of 1997. Pictured here is Chief John Morris accepting ownership of the truck, the cost of which was $165,000, from the manufacturer.

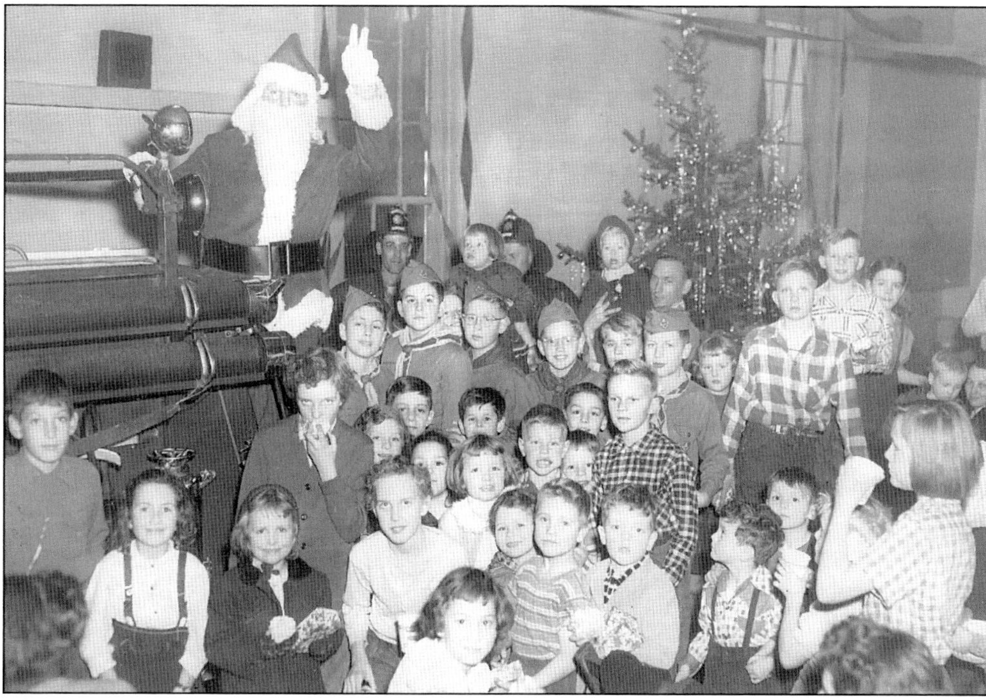

The Berlin Township Volunteer Fire Department are shown holding a Christmas party for the children of the community in 1953. Pictured from left to right are, as follows: (first row) Carol Truitt, Raymond Confoey, Nancy Confoey, and Erma Renkenberger; (second row) Ron Truitt, Darlene Batman, Jane Pettit, Carol Schaeffer, Susan Gillespie, Bobby Confoey, Dennis Cook, John Truitt, and Dennis Truitt; (third row) Judy Schaeffer, Sandra Eckis, Coleen Ross, Joann Pettit, Dale Baringer, and Jerry Harmon; (fourth row) Don Baringer, Joe Anthony, and Charley Ross; (fifth row) Jeff Renkenberger, Joe Craig, John Cole, Richard Burkey, and Don Schaeffer; (sixth row) Nancy Newell, Jay Pettit, and unidentified; (seventh row) Sandy Smith as Santa Claus, Ralph Newell, Edith Smith, Virgil Hoyle, Mary Lou Dunbar, Evert Dunbar, Jim Harmon, Beverly Kale, Raymond Kale, and Edith Kale.

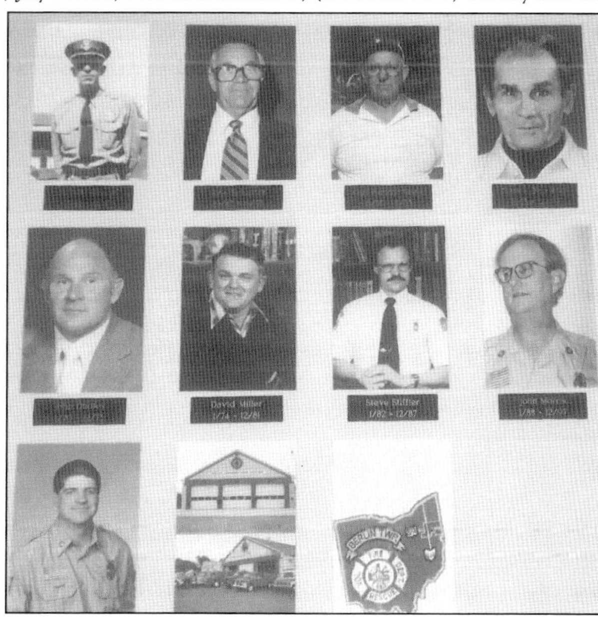

Pictured from left to right are Berlin Township Volunteer Fire Chiefs: (top row) Harold Slough (7/47-9/47), John Schaffer (10/47-6/53), Earl Smith (6/53-11/53), and Patrick Ross (11/53-12/69); (middle row) John Dudley (1/70-12/73), David Miller (1/74-12/81), Steve Stiffler (1/82-12/87), and John Morris (1/88-12/97); (bottom row) Kevin Windham (1/98-present).

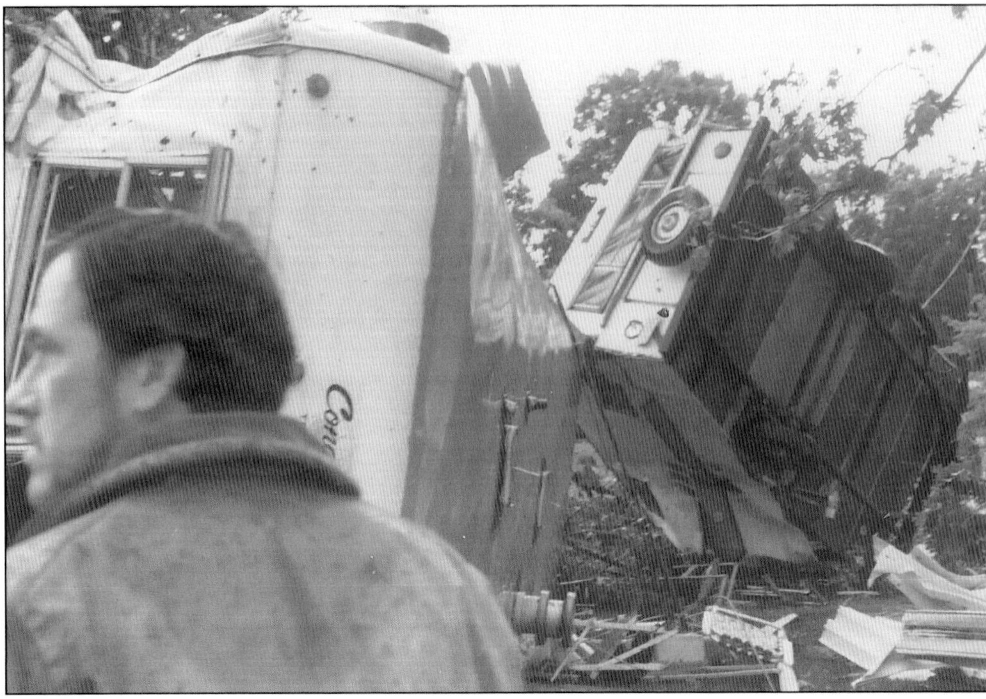

In case of a tornado or other emergency, the Berlin Township Volunteer Fire Department is well trained and equipped to handle the challenge. Firefighter Ken Bennett is pictured doing his part to help after the June 22, 1981 tornado that touched down at Lakeside Campgrounds.

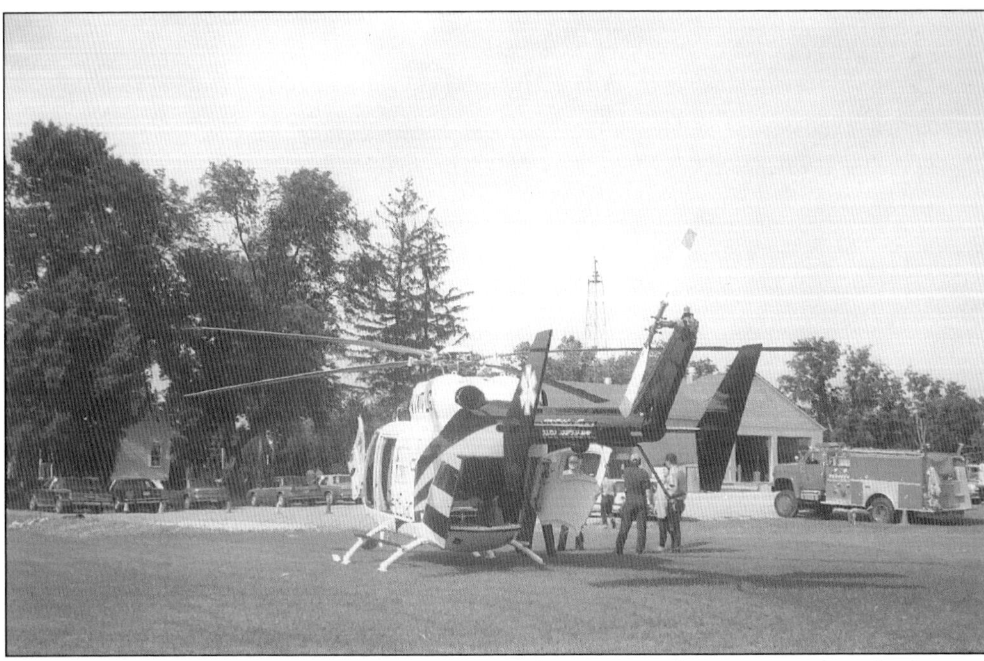

In case of an accident in the township, an injured person can be transported to the hospital from this helicopter pad located behind the government buildings.

Each year the Berlin Township trustees and clerk mount a display in the Government Building at the Canfield Fair. The current elected officials are, from left to right, Trustee Jim Brown Jr., Clerk Dolly Bennett, Trustee Ivan Hoyle, and Trustee Sandie Engle.

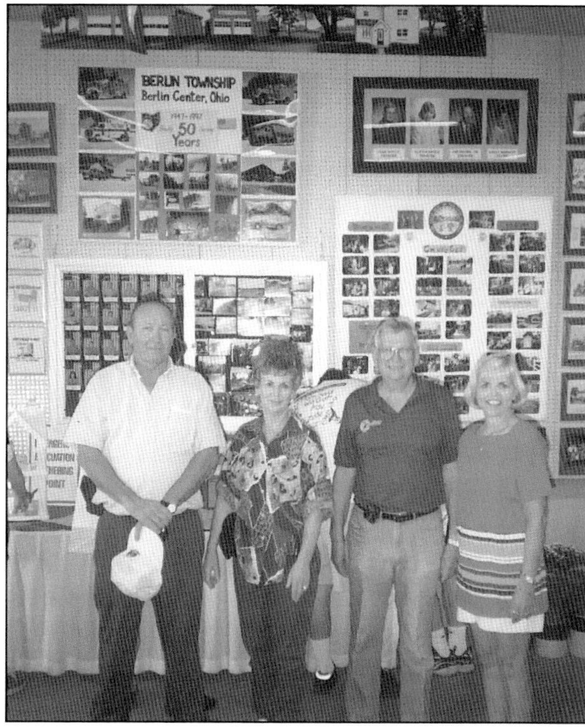

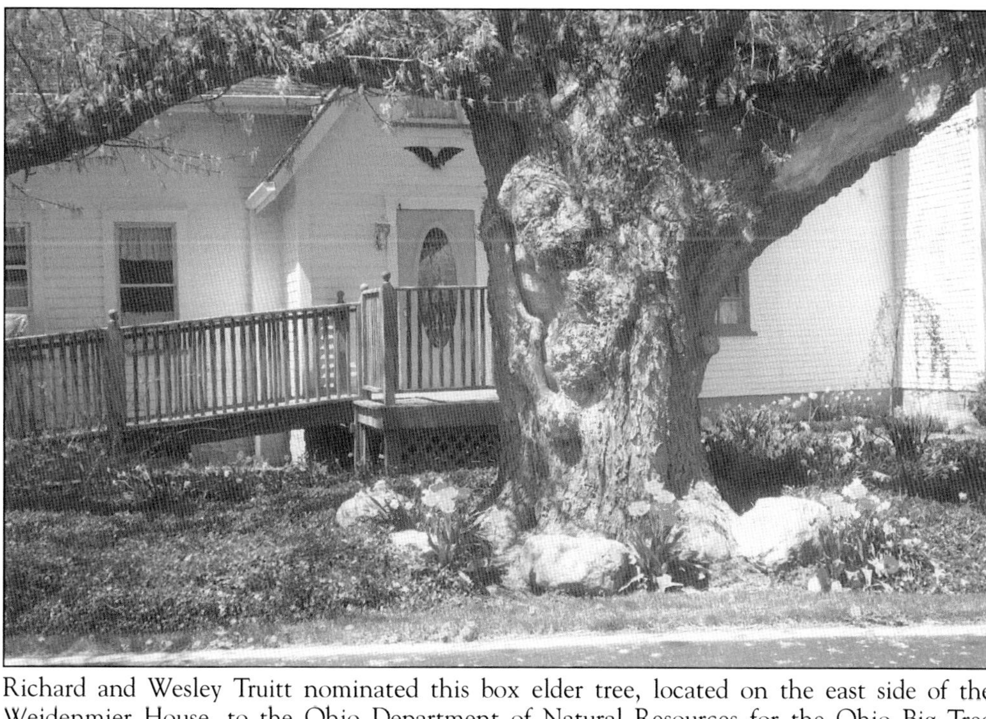

Richard and Wesley Truitt nominated this box elder tree, located on the east side of the Weidenmier House, to the Ohio Department of Natural Resources for the Ohio Big Tree contest. In 1990, the tree was determined to be the largest of its kind in Ohio, with a circumference of 159 inches, a height of 60 feet, and a crown spread of 83 feet.

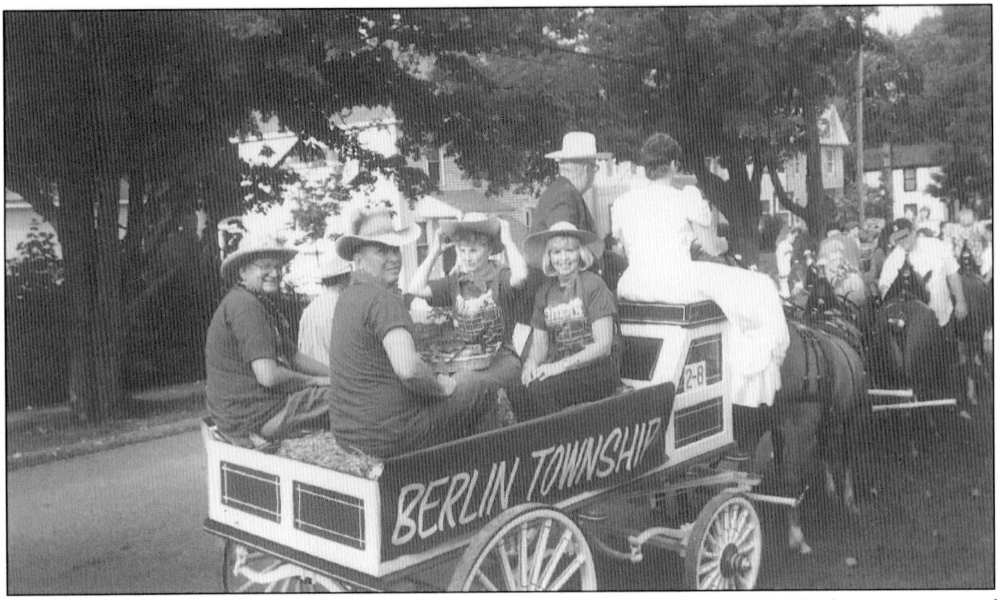

In the fall of 1996, Berlin Township took part in a parade to celebrate the 150th anniversary of Mahoning County and the Mahoning County Fair. The four-pony hitch-and-wagon is being driven by owner Richard Noble and his daughter Barbara. In the wagon, from left to right, are Ivan Hoyle, Jim Brown Jr., Dolly Bennett, and Sandie Engle.

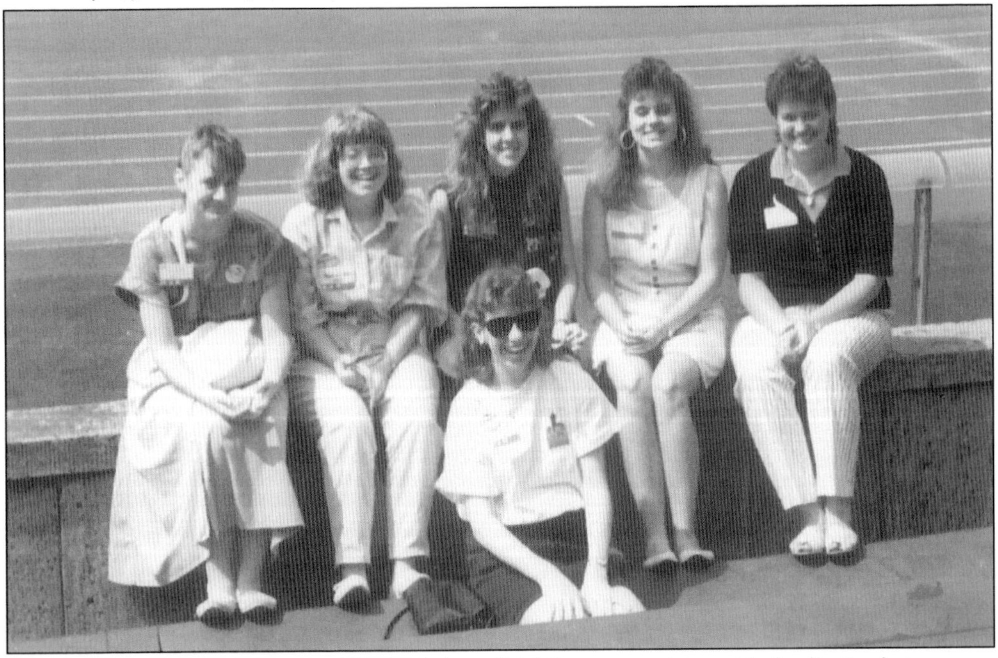
To celebrate Berlin, Germany's 750 birthday, all U.S. communities with Berlin in their names were invited to participate in a unique program. Young people from these areas were provided air transportation and family lodging in order to visit Germany's Berlin. The six young Berlin Center travelers were, from left to right, Tracie Diver, Melanie Moser, Laura Williams, Laura Hughes, Patty Marsh, and (front) Kay Taylor. They were able to visit both sides of the Berlin Wall, as well as sight-see in the city.

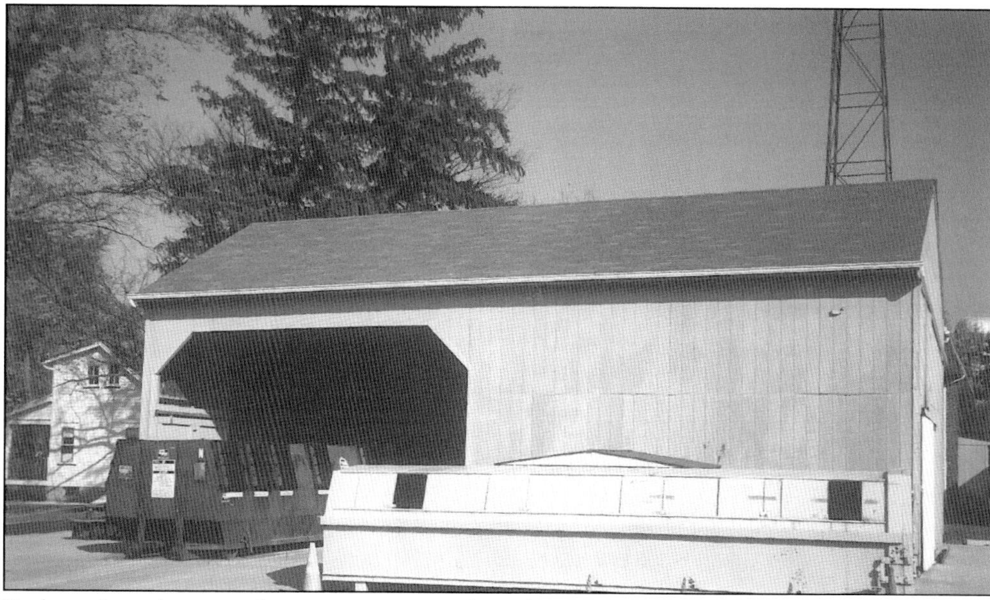

Each spring, the township sponsors a trash pickup, encouraging Berlin residents to place unwanted items at the roadside for removal. Trucks then transport the debris to a parking lot behind the fire station for reloading into large trailers. In 1999, thirteen trailer loads were recycled and twelve went to the landfill.

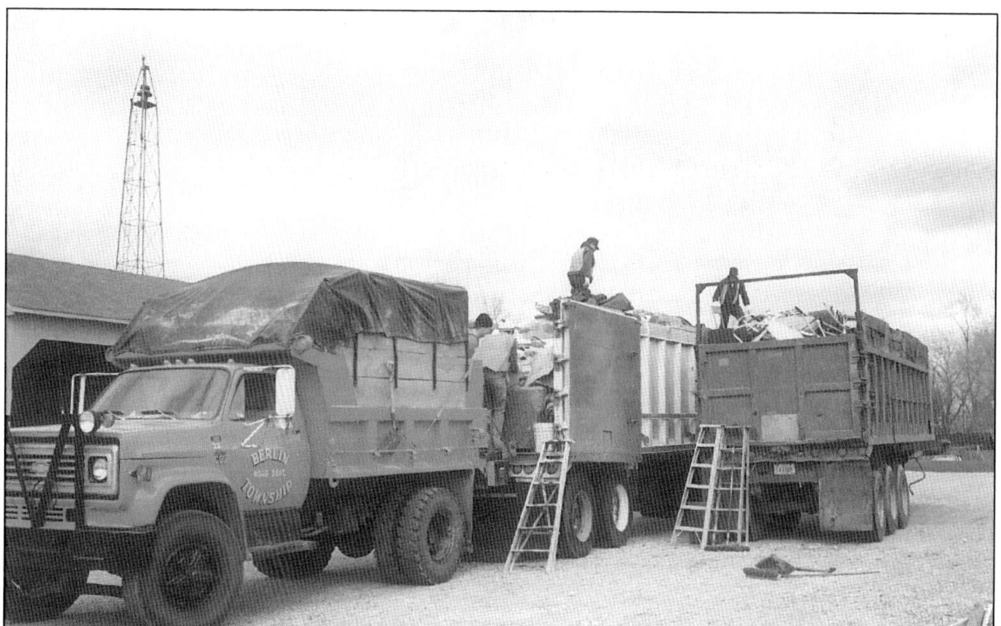

The Berlin Township Recycling center is located behind the fire station and road garage. The bin to the right holds magazines, the bin to the left all other recyclables.

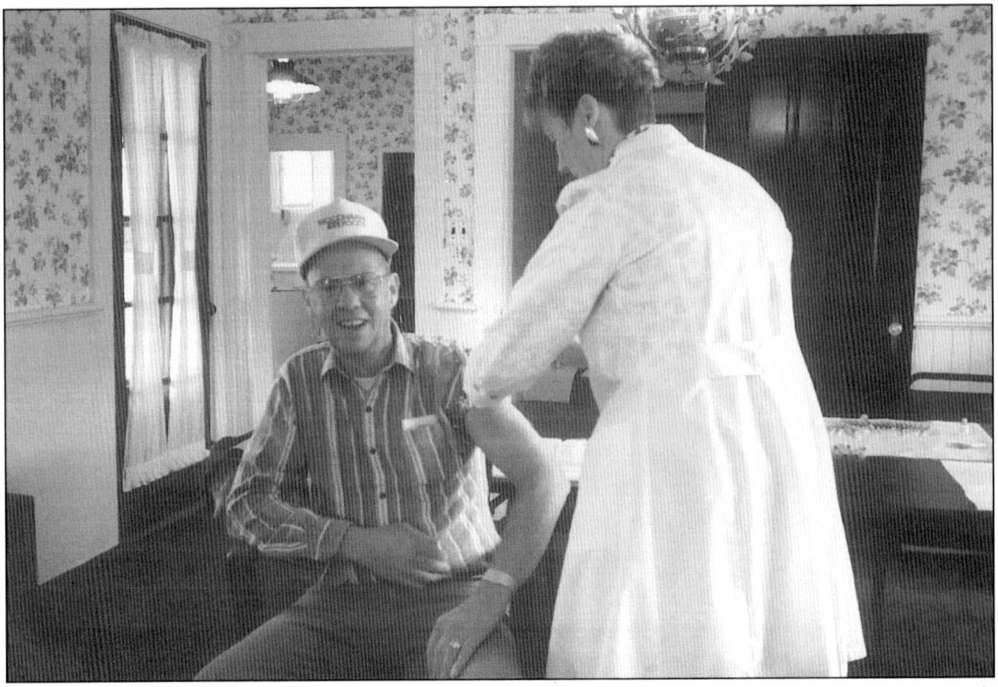

The Mahoning County Health Department holds a flu clinic at the Weidenmier House each year. Pictured is Lynn Fields receiving his shot.

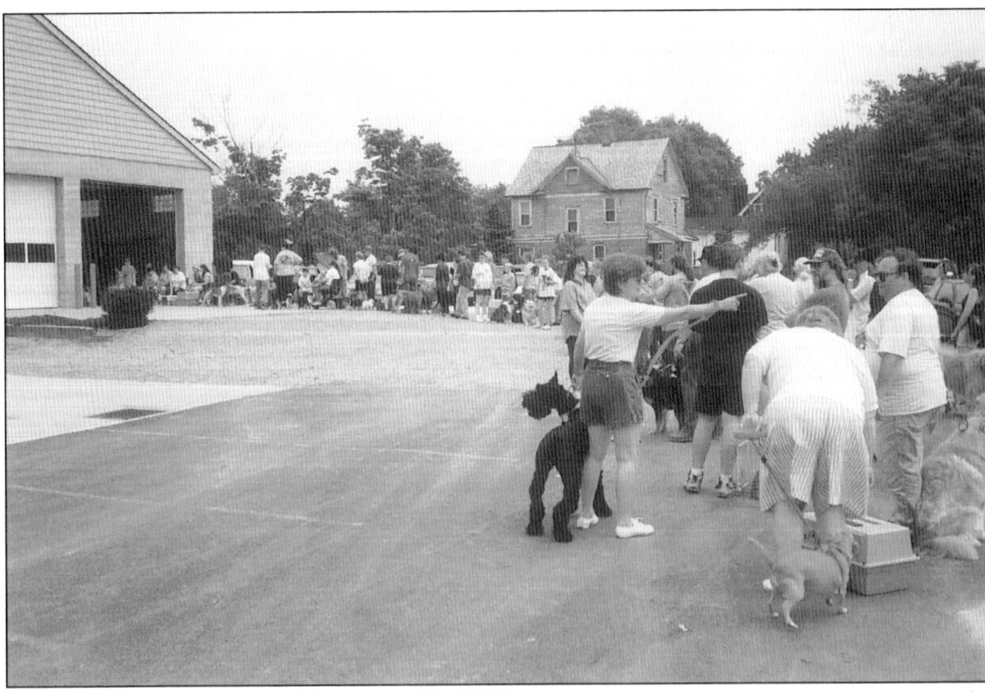

Every two years, the Mahoning County Health Department commonly holds a pet clinic at the Berlin Township Fire Station. As this photograph shows, the clinic is well attended.

Eight

ODDS AND ENDS

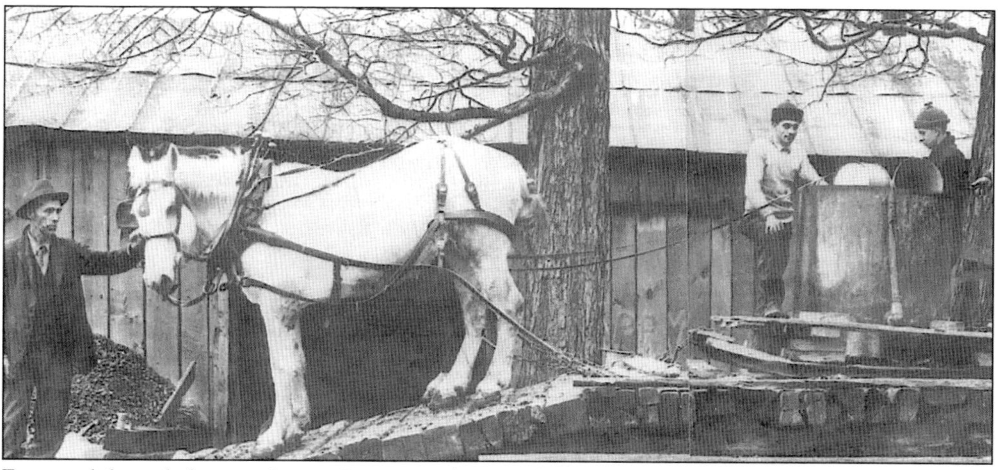

Featured from left to right are Ross Hawkins, John Hawkins, Howard Rakestraw, and Art Christler working the sugar camp on the Hawkins Farm on Berlin Station Road. The picture was featured in the "Gravure" section of the March 24, 1929 edition of the Youngstown *Vindicator*.

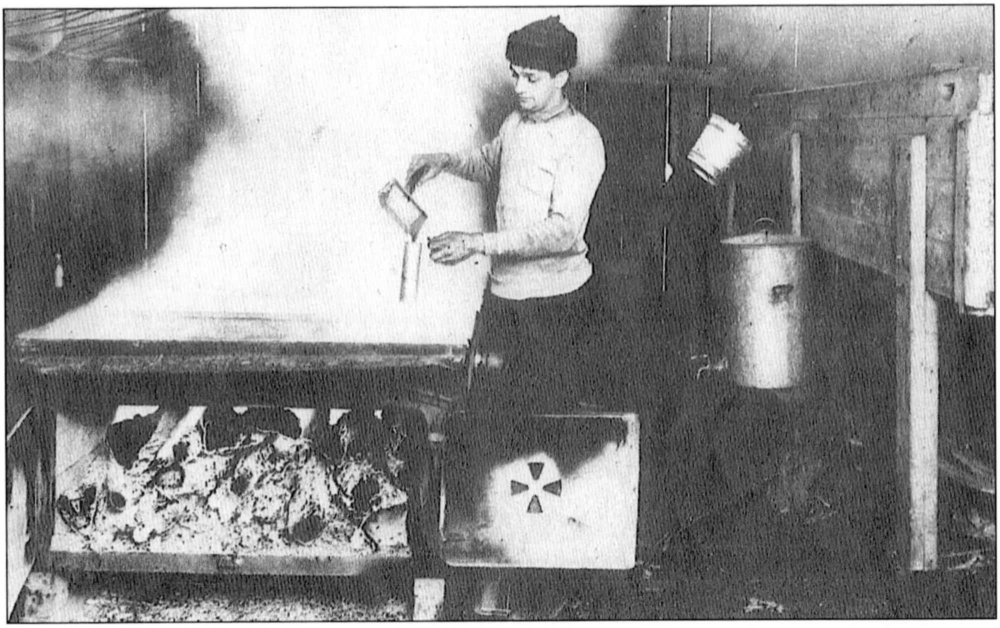

John Hawkins undertakes the sweet job of boiling down sap into maple syrup. In this picture from the 1929 Youngstown *Vindicator*, he tastes the fruits of his labors. The sugar camp was located on the farm at 15134 Berlin Station Road in Berlin Center, now the Richard Marshall farm.

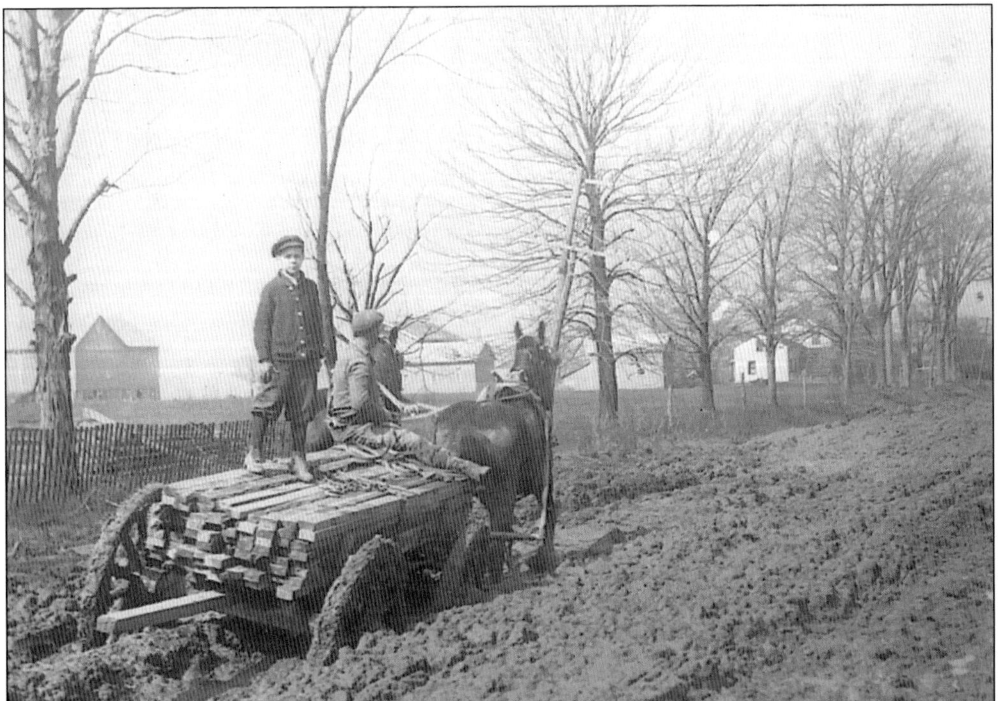

Charley McGranahan drives his horse and wagon on Route 224 near Weaver Road. Before roads were improved, travel proved quite difficult.

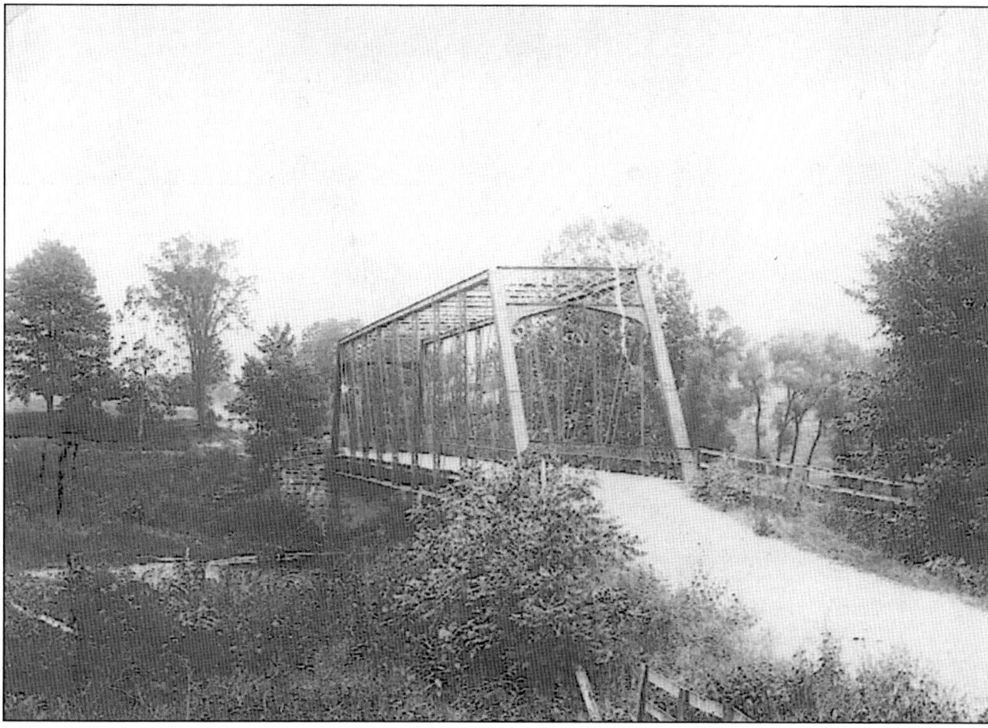

This photograph of an old steel bridge over the Mahoning River on the Akron-Canfield Road (Route 224) pre-dates the construction of the Berlin Dam.

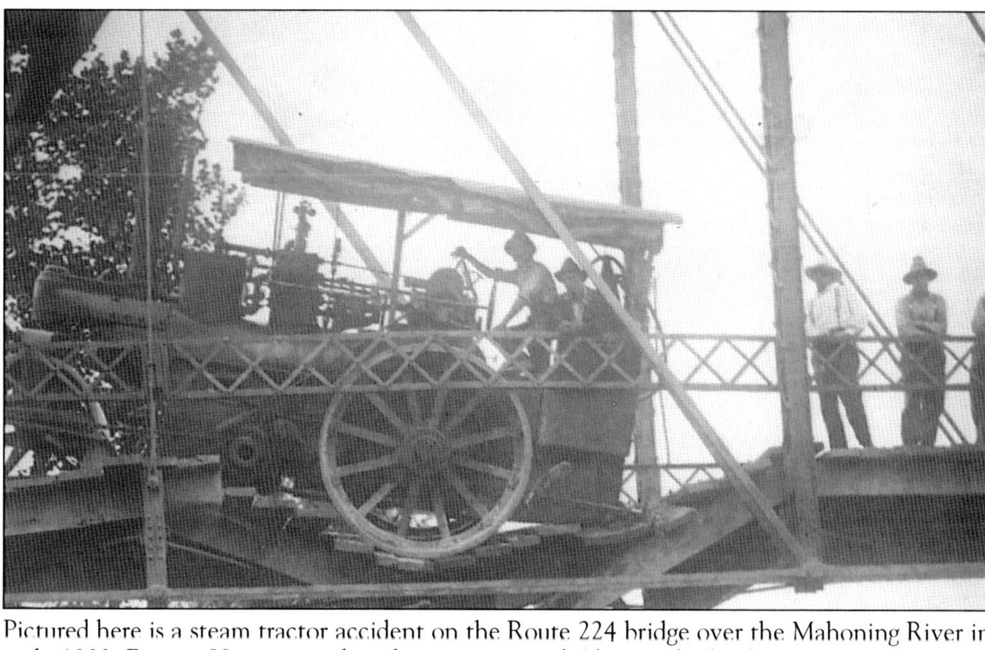

Pictured here is a steam tractor accident on the Route 224 bridge over the Mahoning River in early 1900. Dennis Hawn served as the operator, and Clayt and Claude Cover appear on the bridge. These old plank bridges were appropriate for horse and buggy, but lacked the strength for heavy equipment.

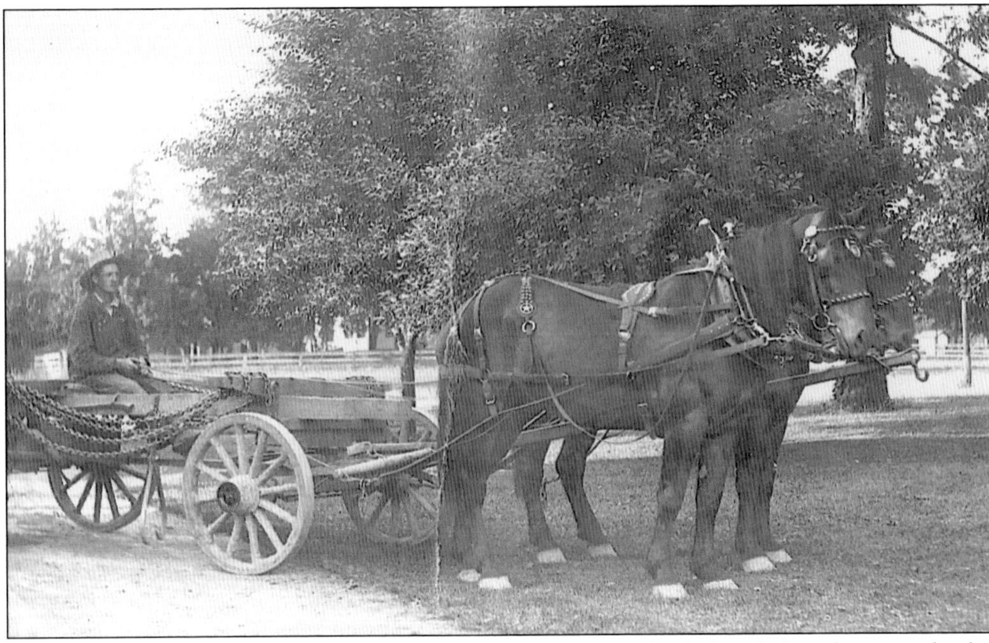

Clyde Keslar appears with his team of horses. His wagon is loaded with log chains and a log hook in preparation for hauling timber.

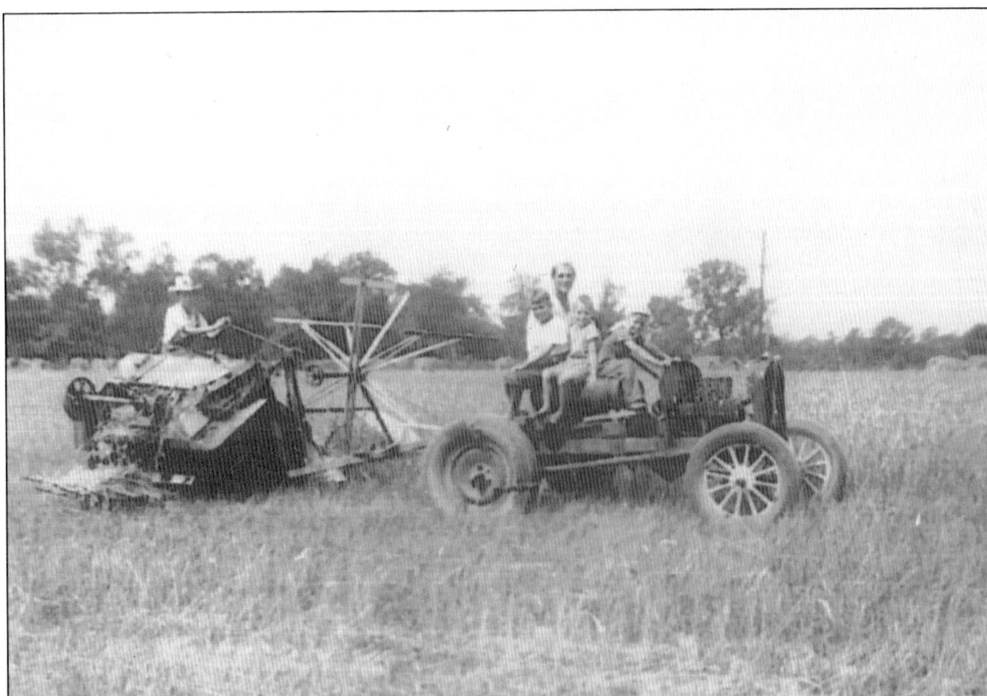

Clyde Baringer's tractor had been adapted from an old car. In this picture, the vehicle pulls a binder to make sheaves of grain.

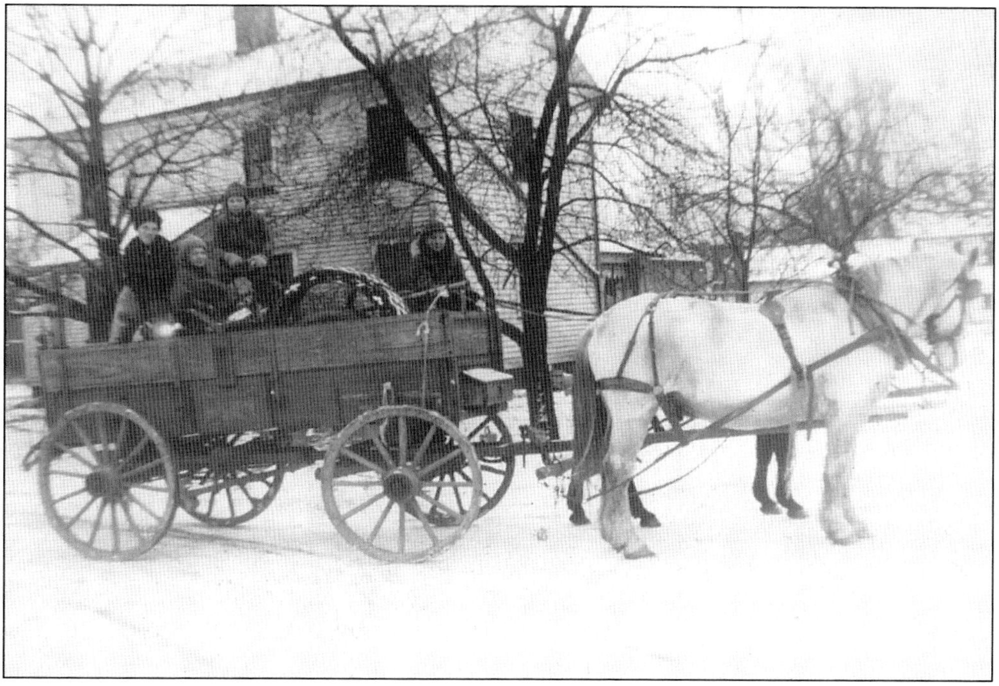

Four eleven-year-old Berlin Township schoolchildren gather scrap for World War II in this 1942 photograph. Because of gas rationing, horses were then a common sight on the roads. Shown from left to right on the wagon are Wylie Rakestraw, Ivan Hoyle, Stanley Clark, and Bob Woolman.

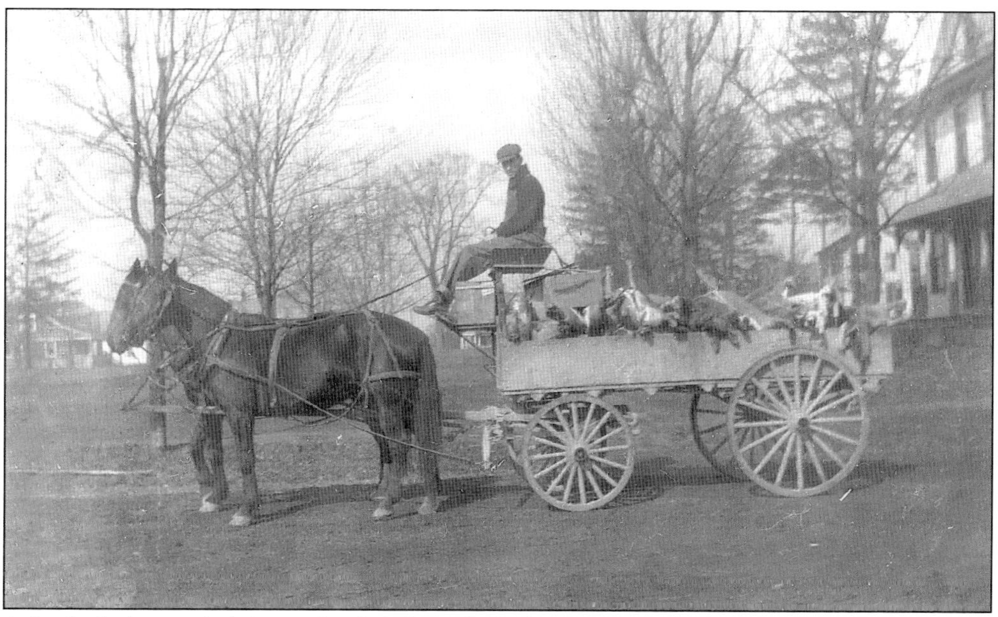

A load of white-tailed deer is hauled through Berlin Center with the Central Hotel visible in the background. When first settled, the area was rich with wild game.

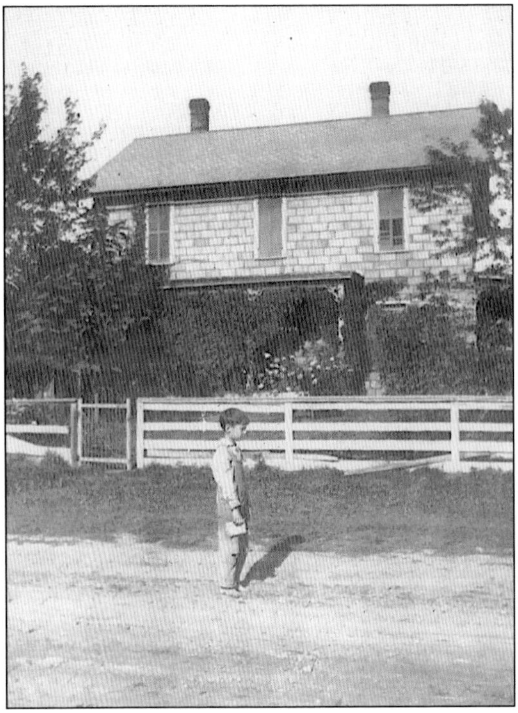

The Dustmans constructed this house of glazed building blocks made at their pottery, operated by Andy Dustman and his five bachelor sons. This Christytown house, where the Boyle family now lives, is located at 8244 Bedell Road.

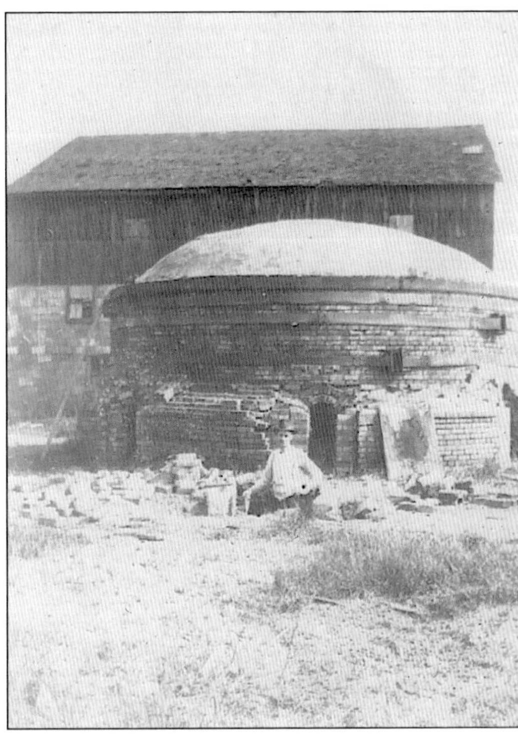

Pictured here is one of many brick kilns located at the Dustman Pottery. The bricks were often stacked as high as 70 feet to offer adequate kiln space. When fired, they would burn for 24 hours a day for five consecutive days. The business began in the late 1870s and ran until 1912, when the cost of coal became prohibitive.

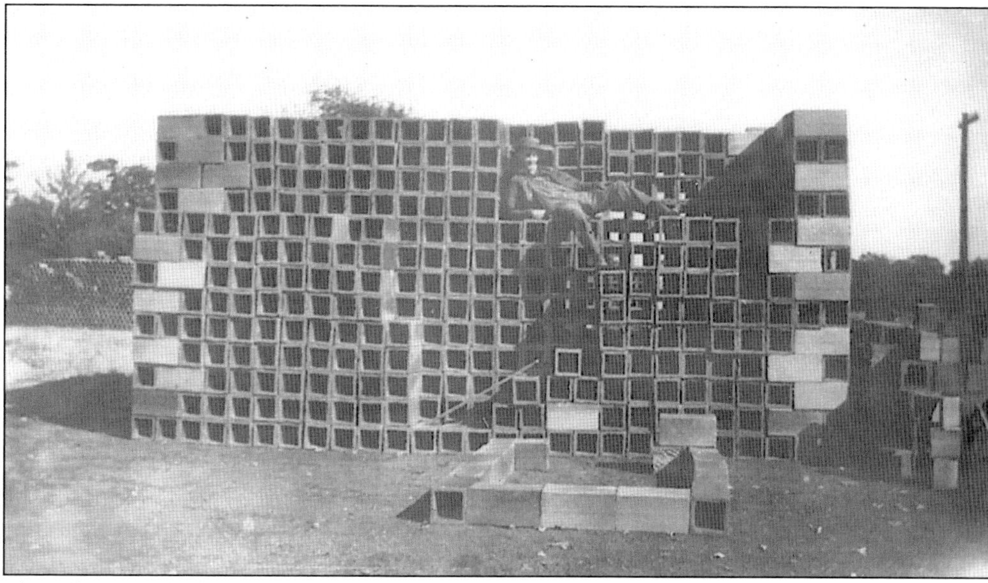

This photograph showcases some of the building tile manufactured at the Dustman Pottery, which also made drain tile, jugs, and crocks. Because money was scarce, most products were exchanged locally through bartering. People traded maple sugar, meat, and flour for the clay products.

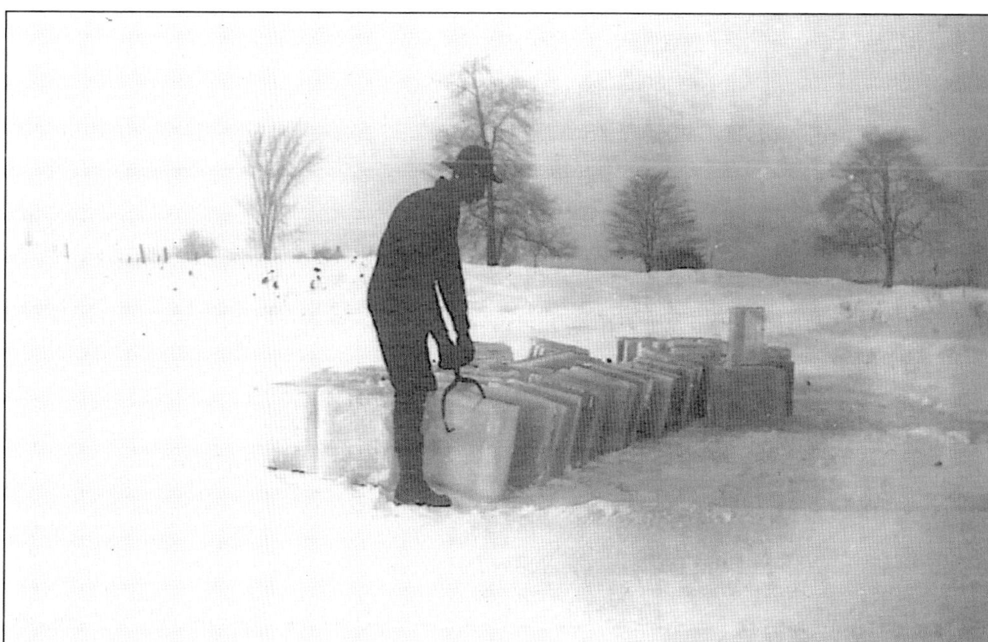

Large pits were dug to retrieve the blue clay for the pottery. In the winter, blocks of ice were cut from these pits and stored in an ice house for summer use.

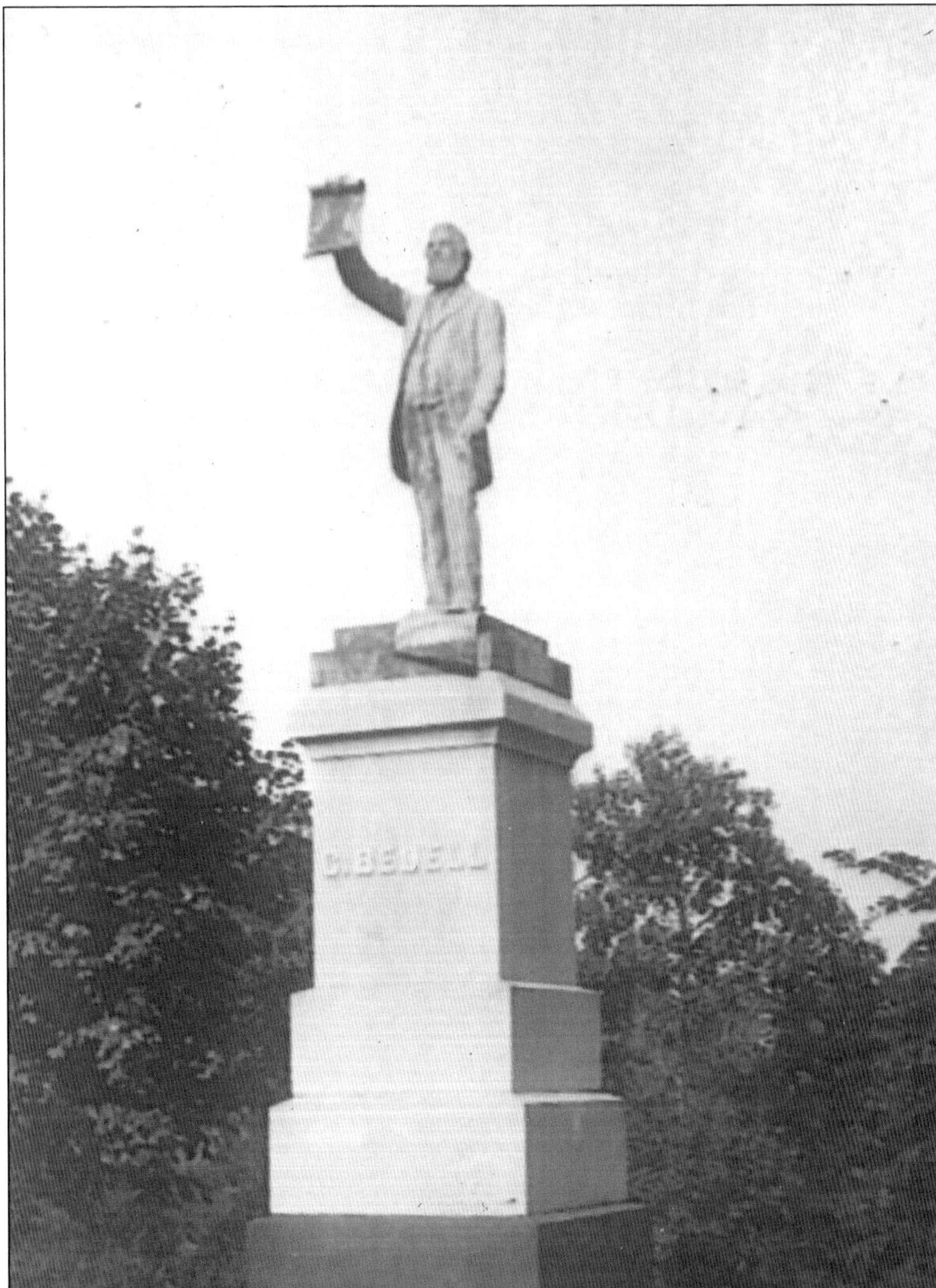

Chester Bedell, wealthy farmer and sheep man, had this bronze statue made of his likeness by the Mullins Company in Salem, Ohio. It was placed on his grave stone at the Hartzell Cemetery in North Benton. His left foot rests on a stone scroll inscribed with the word "superstition." His right hand holds a bronze scroll that reads, "universal mental freedom." Mr. Bedell's home was always open to visiting ministers or hoboes for a meal, lively discussion, or night's stay. He donated the church bell to the Berlin Methodist Church, and his statue is now on display at the Weidenmier House in Berlin Center.

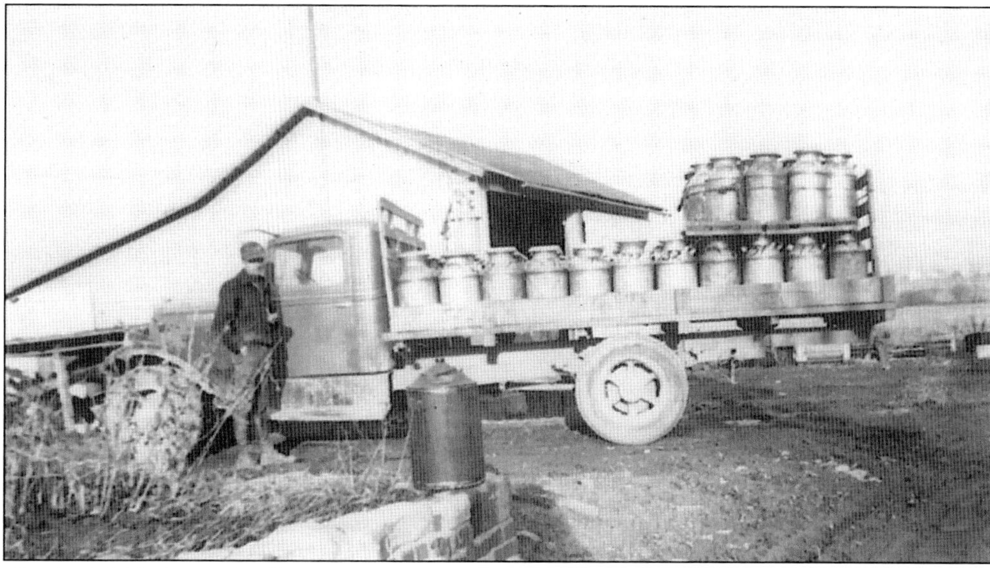

Charles Noble hauled milk cans on an open truck to the creamery in the 1920s and 1930s. He acquired an enclosed truck in 1937.

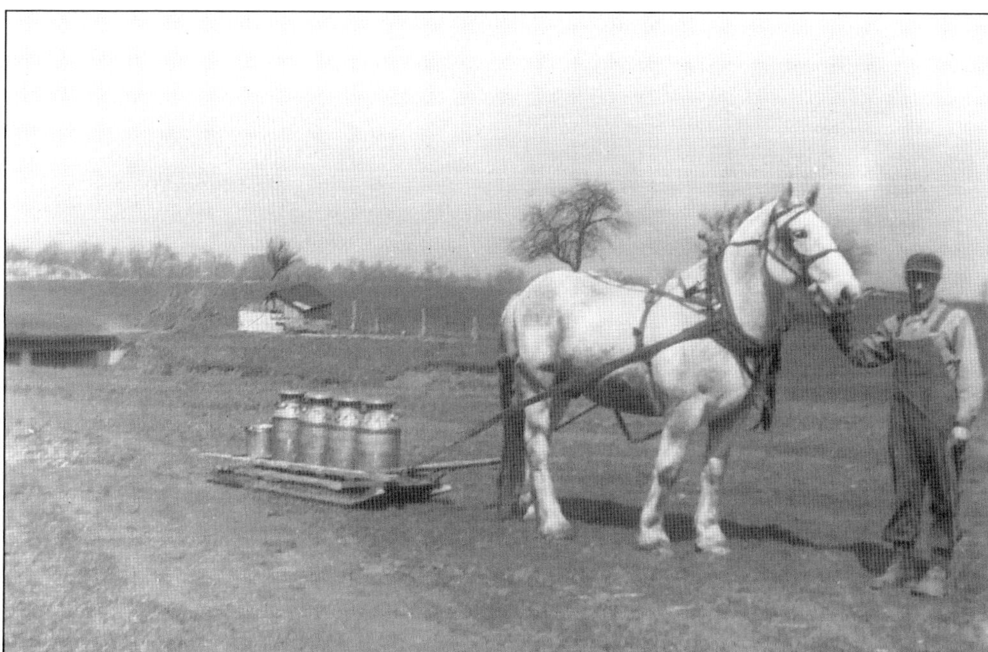

Charles Hoyle with "Bill" the horse hauls milk cans full of maple sap to be boiled down. The picture was taken near Turkey Broth Creek on the Hoyle Farm on Hoyle Road.

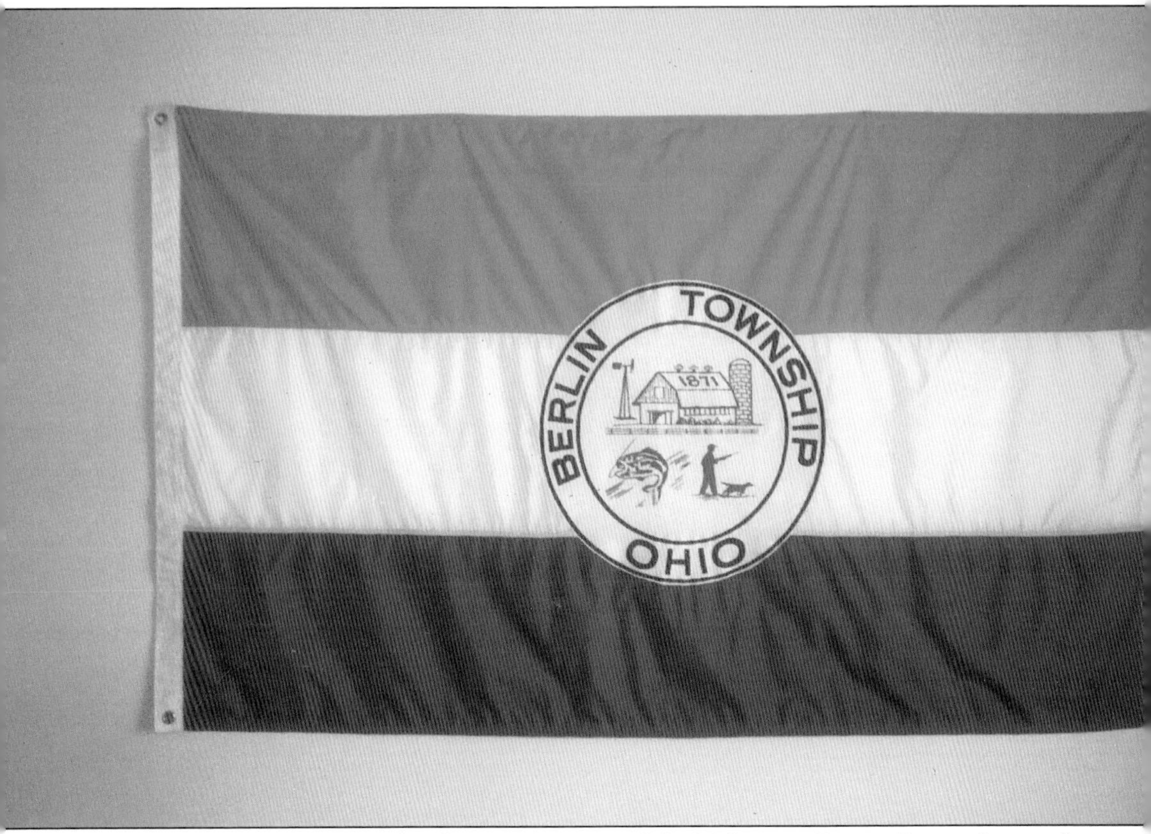

For the 125th anniversary of Mahoning County and the Mahoning County Fair, each township was asked to design a township flag. The trustees invited the 1971 Western Reserve School art class to hold a contest, the winner of which would receive a $50 savings bond. Richard E. Truitt, a senior, designed the red, white, and blue winning entry. The center design illustrates farming, fishing, and hunting, all of which are plentiful in Berlin Township.

This closes the final chapter of our photographic history book, offering a chronicle of Berlin Township's past. It is the hope of the book committee that you have enjoyed this publication, and that future generations will be inspired to continue writing the history of our past, present, and future.